AF598715

Praise for *Praying Like the Early Church*

"Dr. Papandrea has devoted his life to the retrieval of ancient disciplines, from the reading of Scripture to the offering of prayers. That alone would be service enough. But he has gone a step further and has taught us how to adapt these practices to ordinary Christian life today. His work is a model of scholarship in service to the Church."

— Scott Hahn, author of *The Creed: Professing the Faith Through the Ages* and founder of the St. Paul Center for Biblical Theology

"Our traditions of prayer and worship are deeply rooted in the Fathers of the Church. In the first few centuries after Christ's earthly ministry, the Spirit inspired the Christian community to pray together and individually in the language given to us in Israel's Scriptures, to develop forms of worship that unite us to the prayer of the angels and in Christ, and to develop traditions of self-examination and attention to God that have borne fruit ever since. Jim Papandrea offers a clear, practical guide for contemporary Christians seeking to draw from this great source, a guide that draws together themes from the early Christians and some of those who have most deeply lived the life of prayer they hold out to us."

— Lewis Ayres, professor of Catholic and historical theology, Durham University; McDonald Agape Distinguished Chair in Early Christian Theology, Pontificia Università San Tommaso d'Aquino (Angelicum); Professorial Fellow, Institute of Religion and Critical Inquiry, Australian Catholic University

"The teachings of the Fathers are permanently relevant. James Papandrea makes that clear in this profound and practical book. Drawing key insights from the ancient Church, he guides readers through Christianity's classic spirituality. This is something more than lessons to study. It's spiritual direction for life ahead."

— Mike Aquilina, author of *The Fathers of the Church* and *The Apostles and Their Times*

"Professor Papandrea is a master of opening up the Church Fathers to all believers today. In this must-read book, he shows how the early Christians communed with the living God — which is the very purpose of our lives but often seems just out of our grasp. I was especially struck by Papandrea's insights into the Sign of the Cross. This is a powerful book, in which every chapter flows from and leads into the embrace of God."

— Matthew Levering, James N. Jr. and Mary D. Perry Chair of Theology, Mundelein Seminary

"You've probably heard the saying 'when the going gets tough, the tough get going.' In these challenging times in which we're living, Catholics can toughen up for the spiritual battles by going back to the basics, beginning with prayer. As James Papandrea explains in *Praying Like the Early Church,* the good news is that we don't have to go very far. We have a great cloud of witnesses in the early Church Fathers to guide us to a stronger and much deeper relationship with God."

— Teresa Tomeo, syndicated Catholic talk show host; author of *Listening for God* and *Everything's Coming Up Rosie*

"Much has been written about the life and thought of the earliest Christians in regard to theology, biblical interpretation, and even liturgy. However, the nature of how the earliest followers of Jesus understood the concept of prayer remains a territory largely unexplored. Papandrea's research into primary sources from the early Church provides a fascinating look at what the first generations of Christians believed about what it means to engage in the practice of prayer, both corporately and individually, in harmony with the Jewish tradition but transformed by the incarnation of Jesus."

— Matt Swaim, director of outreach, The Coming Home Network; host of *The Son Rise Morning Show*

"As far as I know, this book is utterly one of a kind. Instead of asking simply what the early Christians believed, Dr. Papandrea explores how they prayed: not only the words and prayers they used but the manner in which they prayed (for instance, the role of the Sign of the Cross, the liturgy, and particular bodily postures). The book is both a fascinating insight into an under-examined aspect of early Christianity and an eminently practical help for the spiritual life for Christians today."

— Joe Heschmeyer, staff apologist, Catholic Answers

Praying Like the Early Church

James L. Papandrea

Praying Like the Early Church

Seven Insights from the Church Fathers to Help You Connect with God

SOPHIA INSTITUTE PRESS
Manchester, New Hampshire

Copyright © 2024 by James L. Papandrea

Printed in the United States of America. All rights reserved.

Cover design by LUCAS Art & Design, Jenison, MI.

Cover image from G. Wilpert, *Roma Sotterranea: Le Pitture della Catacombe Romane* (Rome: Desclée Lefebure and C., 1903), vol. 1, tav. 88, p. 94. Photo courtesy of Robin M. Jensen.

Scripture texts in this work are taken from the *New American Bible, revised edition* © 2010, 1991, 1986, 1970 Confraternity of Christian Doctrine, Washington, D.C. and are used by permission of the copyright owner. All Rights Reserved. No part of the New American Bible may be reproduced in any form without permission in writing from the copyright owner.

No part of this book may be reproduced, stored in a retrieval system, or transmitted in any form, or by any means, electronic, mechanical, photocopying, or otherwise, without the prior written permission of the publisher, except by a reviewer, who may quote brief passages in a review.

Sophia Institute Press
Box 5284, Manchester, NH 03108
1-800-888-9344

www.SophiaInstitute.com

Sophia Institute Press® is a registered trademark of Sophia Institute.

paperback ISBN 978-1-64413-816-8
ebook ISBN 978-1-64413-817-5

Library of Congress Control Number: 2023952499

First printing

Dedicated to my two dissertation advisers:

Dennis E. Groh
1939–2023

Robert L. Jewett
1933–2020

It is impossible that anyone could know
such great and holy matters,
without learning them first from
those who knew them before. . . .
These we assert to have been our teachers,
who taught us nothing from their own human conception,
but from the gift entrusted to them by God from above.

— St. Justin Martyr, Address to the Greeks

Still Quiet Voice (Vox Aurae Tenuis)
Psalm 46, I Kings 19

Be still and know that I am God
Your refuge and strength when life is hard
There is no need to fear earth-shattering change
For God is not moved and the sun will rise again

All creation proclaims the great works of the Lord
Who is present here still in the Body and Blood
He is not in the earthquake, the wind, or the noise
But in the eye of the storm, there's a still quiet voice

Be still and know that I am God
Be lifted up by the Spirit of the Word
There's a river of life that flows from on high
And it streams to your heart where the Lord hears you cry

All creation proclaims the great works of the Lord
Who is present here still in the Body and Blood
He is not in the earthquake, the wind, or the noise
But after the fire, there's a still quiet voice
He is not in the earthquake, the wind, or the noise
But deep in your soul, there's a still quiet voice

From the album *Still Quiet Voice* by Jim Papandrea

Contents

Insight 1

The Most Important Prayer . . .

is the prayer most people will never pray themselves:
the Eucharistic Prayer

For as often as you eat this bread and drink the cup,
you proclaim the death of the Lord until he comes.

— St. Paul, 1 Corinthians 11:26

As we begin our journey through the prayer lives of the earliest Christians, it's important to understand a few things. First of all, while it is true that the first Christians met in homes, and the setting for their worship was necessarily less formal than what we might experience today in our churches, that does not mean that their worship was free-form and spontaneous. It was not what some today would refer to as "low church," and it was not without a hierarchy of authorized leadership.[1] Most important, from the very beginning, the heart of Christian worship was what they called the *Thanksgiving*, which in Greek is the word *Eucharist*. In other words, the core of Christian worship was not "preaching the gospel," in the sense of a homily or sermon. They did that, of course, though in the early Church the homily was meant to be an explanation of the Scriptures and how to live according to their expectations, so it was more catechesis than evangelization. Rather, the core of Christian worship was the proclamation of the gospel of Christ's Passion in the Sacrament of the Eucharist. Notice how St. Paul said that every time the Eucharist is offered, we "proclaim the death of the Lord until he comes," a line that is repeated in our liturgy to this day.

We also know that, from the beginning, only a person who was chosen and consecrated to be in the succession of bishops and priests could

[1] Despite scholarly (and other) attempts to find clues to the form of early Christian worship in the New Testament, the reality is that there is none. It is left to the early Church Fathers to tell us everything we know about early liturgy, which, in any case, is still not nearly as much as we wish we knew. The form of liturgy, however, is outside the scope of the present book, and, for the most part, we will be concerned with what is directly relevant to the prayer lives of the laity in the early Church.

preside over the sacraments.[2] Writing in the early second century, Ignatius of Antioch made it clear that no sacrament could be valid if done outside of the authority of the bishop. So it was not the case that just anyone could preside — and we'll come back to that point a bit later. But for now, we need to be clear that, for the early Christians, prayer was something that was done when the community gathered, and it was led by someone with the authority that comes from having been taught by the leaders who came before him. The early Christians would have seen it as the ideal to gather — as the church in any given place — every day, if possible.

At the beginning, the Sacrament of the Eucharist was probably offered as a part of an evening meal, a potluck of sorts, that took place every day wherever that was possible. But it seems that by the end of the first century or so, the Sacrament had been separated from the meal, in part because of the kinds of abuses St. Paul criticizes in 1 Corinthians 11 — Gentile Christians (former pagans) were treating the *agape* meal like a pagan banquet. Also, Roman laws against the meeting of "secret societies" forced the early Christians to move the Sacrament to the morning, before dawn — that is, before everyone went to work — and soon the Church emphasized Sunday morning as the most appropriate day of the week for the liturgy, though a daily Eucharist would still have been seen as the ideal wherever possible.

The point of all this is that, at the beginning, the early Christians didn't really have a concept of "personal devotion" outside of the liturgy. Jewish Christians certainly would have brought their ideas about household spirituality and mealtime prayers into the Church with them, but for the most part, Christian prayer meant being with the Church, gathered and praying together. This is why the most important prayer is the Eucharistic Prayer, which includes the calling of the Holy Spirit and the words of Jesus: the words of institution that consecrate the sacred elements to become the Body and Blood of the Lord.

2 It is not the case that everyone who was named as the host of a house church was therefore a presider over the sacraments there. The owner of the house where Christians met would have been considered a *patron* of the congregation, but the presider would have been considered the "father" of that Christian family.

What Is Prayer, and How Does It Relate to Worship?

Before we go any further, we should define what prayer is. We may think we know, but let's make sure. It's easy to say that prayer is talking to God, but that's only a part of it. If we take a step back and think about our relationship with God, we remember that we are created in the image of God. And part of what that means is that we are spiritual beings, with rational souls, who are created to be in an ongoing relationship — that is, to be *in constant communication* — with our Creator. But this is much harder than it sounds because, while rational, our minds are also finite and very limited. We think we're so smart, but every thought we ever have is absolutely shortsighted due to the simple fact that we cannot see the future. What that means is that we often mistake short-term (apparent) goods for long-term (ultimate) goods. Or, to put it more simply, we really do not know what's best for us. On top of that, we are incapable of reaching out to God unless God reaches out to us first. Fortunately, He has done that through the Incarnation of His own rationality, or *Logos* in Greek. Or as St. John put it, *the Word became flesh and lived among us* (see John 1:14). That's a game changer because now that the Divine Word has taken on our common human nature, we can really connect with our Divine Creator in a way that was never possible before the coming of Christ. But here's the point: prayer is not our reaching out to God. Oh, sure the Psalms are full of the prayers in which the psalmist says "I'm calling out to You, God!" But in reality, prayer can only respond to a God who has already reached out to us and continues to do so. In other words, prayer is being receptive to the ways in which God is reaching out to us.

Ultimately, prayer is meant to be more passive than active. It is a receptivity to God's self-revelation. It is welcoming the ways in which God reaches out to us and inspires us. We cannot reach out to God first, and there is no need for our self-revelation to God, since He already knows us better than we know ourselves. Because the Holy Spirit of God indwells us, prayer is a Spirit-to-spirit meeting in which we grow in the experience of God's presence. So prayer is not a work that we do, *per se* — though the discipline of making time for prayer and giving it our attention is one of the duties of every Christian; prayer is (or results in) the work that God does in us, if we are open and receptive to it. God is the one who is truly active in our prayers, and He does a lot: communicating grace, inspiring, forming our consciences, convicting us of sin, and healing us. But because God is love, and love does not coerce, God waits for us to open ourselves to Him in prayer; in effect, we have to say *yes* to God — just as Mary did, when she said, "May it be done to me according to your word" (Luke 1:38). We refer to this as Mary's *fiat* because the Latin word *fiat* means "let it be done," with the implication of: *God, let Your will be done in me*. And *that* is what prayer really is, as we will see.

For all of these reasons, prayer cannot be reduced to the speaking of words, much less to concepts such as "petition" (asking for things). Since human language is both limited and limiting (our very thought processes are confined, based on various factors, such as culture, language, education, and even mental capacity), language fails to adequately express the most important things in the universe — and yet that's exactly what prayer is all about — the most important things in the universe. We will cover all of these ideas more completely in the chapters to come, but for now, just keep in mind that our job is to make the time and give God the permission to do the work of prayer, and to be open to increasing union with Him.

It is important to point out that prayer is not the same thing as praise, or the same thing as worship, though there is some overlap with these concepts. We could say that all prayer is a form of praise, since to pray is to ascribe some assumption of worthiness in the one to whom we pray.[3] But not all praise is prayer, since it is possible to praise someone without speaking directly to that person. So some praise is directed toward God — that is, spoken to God in the second grammatical person (*You* are awesome, God!). This kind of praise is a prayer because it is spoken directly to God. In fact, it is also an act of worship. But there is another kind of praise that is spoken as if to other people, in which God is referred to in the third grammatical person (*Our God* is awesome!). This kind of praise is worship, but it's not really prayer, because we are not speaking directly to God. So not all praise is prayer, and

[3] If we take the original definition of the verb "to pray," meaning "to ask," it is possible to ask something of someone we would not praise. For example, the line, "I pray thee, cease thy counsel, which falls into mine ears as profitless," from Shakespear's *Much Ado about Nothing*. But for our purposes in the present book, we will limit the definition of the verb "to pray" to religious or devotional prayer.

not all worship is prayer (and as we will see below, not all prayer is worship). Therefore, in the present book, we are focusing on prayer as that which is directed to God in the second grammatical person (calling God "You"). For the earliest Christians, though — and this is the point — for the most part, prayer was thought of as happening within the context of the liturgy.

The Priority of the Eucharist

Jesus said:

> *Remain in me, as I remain in you. Just as a branch cannot bear fruit on its own unless it remains on the vine, so neither can you unless you remain in me. I am the vine, you are the branches. Whoever remains in me and I in him will bear much fruit, because without me you can do nothing. Anyone who does not remain in me will be thrown out like a branch and wither; people will gather them and throw them into a fire and they will be burned.* (John 15:4–6)

That sounds serious. The failure to remain connected to Jesus could result in the loss of salvation. But how can we make sure we "remain in" Jesus and He "remains in" us? Fortunately, He already told us, just nine chapters earlier:

> *Amen, amen, I say to you, unless you eat the flesh of the Son of Man and drink his blood, you do not have life within you. Whoever eats my flesh and drinks my blood has eternal life, and I will raise him on the last day. For my flesh is true food, and my blood is true drink. Whoever eats my flesh and drinks my blood remains in me and I in him.* (John 6:53–56)

The point here is that when Jesus said, *Do this in remembrance of me,* He did not mean that the Sacrament would be simply a memorial ritual to commemorate a past event (Luke 22:19; 1 Cor. 11:24–25). He meant that this Sacrament would be the very way that we would remain in Him, and He in us — the means by which we remain connected to Him — and that it would be a source of God's grace every time we receive it. The Eucharist is the very "throne of grace," which we approach in confidence (not confidence in ourselves, of course, but confidence in the merit and mercy of Christ) (Heb.

4:16). In other words, Jesus Himself said that the regular reception of the Sacrament of the Eucharist is *necessary for salvation!*

As I mentioned above, the early Christians called the Mass simply the *Thanksgiving*, which brings to mind the story of the Ten Lepers in the Gospel (Luke 17:11–19). Jesus healed ten lepers, but only one returned to thank Him and give glory to God. To come to the liturgy is to be the leper who returns to offer thanks and praise, and it is primarily within that context that we pray. We bring our weaknesses, vulnerabilities, failures, and needs before the "throne of grace," and we listen for God's wisdom and words of healing. But above all, we come in an attitude of thanksgiving. For the early Christians, thanksgiving is not so much a particular kind of prayer but the foundation of every prayer, the very motivation for worship.

The *Catechism of the Catholic Church* (CCC) notes, "The Eucharist contains and expresses all forms of prayer: it is 'the pure offering' " (Mal. 1:11) of the whole body of Christ to the glory of God's name.... It is *the* 'sacrifice of praise' " (2643).

The Prayer You Don't Pray (Unless You're a Priest)

And so we can see that, for the early Church, the most important prayer in our Faith is the prayer that is necessary for our salvation — the prayer of the Eucharist. Of course, the liturgy is really a set of prayers, and there are a few different forms, or sets of prayers, some in Latin and some translated into vernacular languages. But the point is that the liturgy is mostly prayer — but most of the prayers are prayed, that is, voiced, by the clergy, not by the laity. The role of the laity is to agree to the prayers by saying *Amen*, thus participating in the prayers and making them effective for each individual. Notice that St. Paul, when he was writing to the Corinthians, addressed the presider(s) of the church at Corinth when he said, "How shall one who holds the place of the uninstructed say the 'Amen' to your *Eucharist*, [if] he does not know what you are saying?" (1 Cor. 14:16).[4] St. Paul assumes that the priest(s) whom he has appointed to preside over the Eucharist in Corinth are praying the Eucharistic Prayer, but the rest of the people say "Amen" to confirm their agreement.

As you probably know, the word "Amen" means something like "so be it" or "it is true" and is translated into Latin as *fiat*, which means "let it be

[4] This is in the context of his discussion of speaking in tongues.

done."[5] This is the moment in the Mass when you make the prayers your own. Perhaps you've noticed that there is a point in the liturgy called "the Great Amen." We say, or sing, *Amen*, and unfortunately a lot of people let that moment go by as though it's not particularly significant — but that is meant to be the moment when you take to heart all the prayers that the priest has prayed on your behalf. It is quite significant, because that is where you claim for yourself the most important prayers of the Church — the Eucharistic Prayer.

As with Scripture, prayers in the early Church were primarily read by the clergy out loud and heard by the laity. Notice that St. James, in his letter, says that if someone is sick and needs prayer, "summon the priests of the church, and they should pray over him and anoint [him] with oil in the name of the Lord" (5:14).[6] James is saying that if prayer is needed (in this case, specifically the Sacrament of Anointing), don't just presume to do it yourself; go and get the clergy to do it. We might wonder why it has to be clergy, and part of the answer may be that with regard to the Eucharist and Anointing, we are dealing specifically with sacraments. But there is also an assumption in early Christianity that praying out loud, especially extemporaneously, is reserved for the clergy. This is because the act of *leading* prayer is a kind of teaching — since, after all, it would be very easy to say something in a prayer that would be theologically incorrect — and then the person praying would be teaching bad theology and modeling a kind of prayer that would be, at best, ineffective and, at worst, heretical. And so, since the teaching office of the Church was reserved for the bishops, and those to whom the bishops might delegate, the kind of extemporaneous

[5] There are three significant *fiat*s in Scripture. Mary's *fiat* (Luke 2:36–38), the line in the Our Father, "may your will be done" (Matt. 6:10) and Jesus' own *fiat* in his prayer in the Garden of Gethsemane (Matt. 26:39, 42, Mark 14:36). In each of these cases, the point is that the person praying is submitting to the will of God, so one could include that in the definition of the word *Amen*, as if to say, "Let it be so/done, according to your will."

[6] The word I've translated "priests" is the Greek term *presbyteros*, which is often translated "elders." The point at issue is that these "elders" would be the ones appointed by the apostle as having the authority to preside over the sacraments. There is no evidence in the early Church of the Protestant practice of a "council of elders" made up of laypeople.

prayer that we might think of someone "leading" in a group — that kind of prayer was reserved for the clergy.[7]

It may be the case that earlier in the history of the Church there was more room for ad-lib embellishments by the clergy in the prayers of the Mass, but there is no evidence from the early Church that laypeople prayed out loud extemporaneously, with one exception, which is addressed in the appendix on charismatics in the early Church. In any case, the use of extemporaneous prayers in the liturgy decreased over time, and by the fourth century at the latest, it had become the norm that all the liturgical prayers were prewritten.

Of course, there are other responses of the laity built into the liturgy besides just the *Amen,* and it may surprise you to know that the form of prayers and responses in the Novus Ordo (the Ordinary form of the Mass, created in 1969 and celebrated in the vernacular) *is actually more like the liturgy of early Christianity than the Tridentine Mass* (the Latin Mass of 1570).[8] The differences are not great enough for us to outline them here; we only need to note that the responses such as the Kyrie eleison (Lord, have mercy), "and with your spirit," the Alleluia, the "mystery of faith," and a version of "Lord, hear our prayer," as well as the recitation of the Our Father go back to our earliest liturgies, and with the eventual addition of the Creed, these elements in which we as laypeople participate more actively are very ancient, and we should pray them with all the reverence and attention that we can.

Nevertheless, it is still the case that for the most part our participation in the liturgy is passive, to listen to the readings and prayers and to agree with the prayers prayed by the clergy, especially by saying *Amen.* In the ancient liturgies, it is even the case that some of the responses were recited by a deacon or a cantor on behalf of the laypeople. So even when there were more interjections from the laity, it was often done by representation,

[7] See the *Apostolic Tradition* 9, 19. See also Ignatius of Antioch, *Letter to the Magnesians* 6–7, *Letter to the Trallians* 2, 7, *Letter to the Philadelphians* 8, *Letter to the Smyrnaens* 8, and Irenaeus of Lyons, *Against Heresies* 4.26. There were lay catechists in the early Church, who were given the authority to teach by the bishops because they were vetted for their orthodoxy and their ability to correctly articulate the Faith. Presumably they would also have had the authority to lead group prayer.

[8] Roch A. Kereszty, *The Church of God in Jesus Christ: A Catholic Ecclesiology* (Washington D.C.: Catholic University of America Press, 2019), 229.

which emphasizes the passive nature of prayer on the part of the laity. But, of course, that comes with the danger of the laity becoming disengaged and failing to follow along attentively. Eventually the Latin Mass made following along attentively impossible, and with the loss of the Latin language as something most people could understand, it became necessary to bring back some of the earlier responses, not to mention translate the liturgy into a language the people could understand, in order for them to sincerely give their assent to the prayers.

Incidentally, it's worth noting that *Amen* is primarily for when someone else prays, and we agree with the prayer at its end. It is not really necessary to end all of our own prayers with an *Amen.* Simply by having prayed a prayer, God knows we agree with it. We don't need to cap it off with "so be it" at the end of our own prayers. (Notice there is no *Amen* at the end of the Our Father when we say it in liturgy.) It's not wrong to add it to our own prayers, but it's not necessary — it's really meant to be our response to the prayers vocalized by our clergy or another prayer leader.

Now, it goes without saying that individual Christians did pray their own prayers outside of the liturgy, in their own homes. We must assume that parents prayed for their children, spouses and friends prayed for each other, and in general the practices of Jewish personal prayer continued on in the early Church. The problem is that we don't know very much at all about what that looked like. The Church order document known as the *Apostolic Tradition* is written with the assumption that when people are in their own homes, is it acceptable for them to pray in their own words, and this might include heads of households leading family prayer, though we don't know for sure. So it's not the case that in their private prayer lives, people were restricted to prewritten prayers.

However, it's interesting that we do not see much evidence of private *silent* prayer. It seems to be assumed that even the private prayers of individuals were prayed out loud. Note how the Greek and Latin versions of Psalm 35:28 (which is actually Psalm 34 in the Greek and Latin) say, "My tongue will meditate on your righteousness." Meditation here is described as something the *tongue* is doing. In other words, even meditation is out loud. Perhaps it was a function of a lower literacy rate than we are used to, or maybe there was an assumption that vocal prayer was better for avoiding distracting thoughts, but in the ancient world, reading and praying was done out loud, and silent prayer (or "mental" prayer) was seen as a more advanced form of prayer practiced by the monks. Even in the late fourth century, we read that St. Augustine was surprised when he saw his mentor St. Ambrose reading silently to himself: "When he read, his eyes scanned the page and his heart explored the meaning, but his voice was silent and his tongue was still."[9] Imagine that — St. Ambrose read without moving his lips! We will return to the idea of silent prayer later, but for now it is enough to keep in mind that the early Christians would have thought of silent prayers as something outside the experience of most believers.

Have You Heard of the Didache?

The *Didache* is the earliest Church order manual, and the earliest known Christian document outside of the New Testament. In fact, it was written at the same time as some of the New Testament documents — most likely before the end of the first century, and probably even roughly contemporary with the Gospel of Matthew. A few of the Church fathers thought it should have been included in the Bible. The title *Didache* is really just the Greek word for "teaching," and it's a short version of the document's actual title, *The Teaching of the Lord … Through the Twelve Apostles,* or sometimes called simply, *The Teaching of the Twelve Apostles.* It's not clear that it was actually written by any of the apostles in particular, but there's no reason to doubt that the teaching does go back to the time of the apostles and that it does give us a window into the practices of the Church of the first century. And one of the most important things about the *Didache* is that it includes our earliest excerpts of Eucharistic prayers.[10]

The *Didache* says to "permit the prophets [most likely a reference to any remaining apostles and their disciples, the earliest bishops] to give thanks however they wish,"[11] and Justin Martyr would tell us that the prayers are

[9] Augustine of Hippo, *The Confessions* 6.3.

[10] *Didache* 9–10.

[11] *Didache* 10. There are two ways to translate this phrase. Michael Holmes translates it as above, implying that there was some room for improvisation in the prayers, and this would be consistent with what we know from other sources. However, the version in the Ante-Nicene Fathers series translates it, "allow the prophets to make [the] Thanksgiving as much as they desire," which seems to imply that it was more about how often they offered the

offered by the presider, "according to his ability."[12] This means that in earliest Christianity, there was some room for improvisation, or at least embellishment, even in the Eucharistic Prayer, but as we have noted, that's only for the clergy. The *Apostolic Tradition* also notes that the prayers do not have to be verbatim, but, of course, by the time of the later Church order manuals and the earliest preserved complete liturgies, the prayers are all written out and the expectation is that they be prayed using the same words every time.

Ideally, the Eucharist was celebrated daily wherever possible, even after the Sacrament was moved to a morning liturgy with the emphasis on Sunday as the most important (or appropriate) day for it.[13] It may be that the Eucharist offered on other days was less formal, and it is possible that in some places the very early expectation of two fasting days per week meant that on Wednesdays and Fridays the liturgy may have been something like a Service of the Word (probably without Communion) rather than a Mass.

Here is an excerpt from the *Didache*, with the earliest known examples of Eucharistic prayers:

> Now concerning the Thanksgiving [Eucharist], give thanks in this way:
>
> First, concerning the cup, "We thank you, our Father, for the holy vine of David Your servant, which You made known to us through Jesus Your Servant; to You be the glory forever."

Eucharist than about how they prayed the prayers. It would seem to make at least as much sense in the context of the passage that itinerant presiders should be given the freedom to offer the Eucharist *as often as they wish*. But if that's how it should be translated, then the passage says nothing about improvisation in prayer. With regard to the "prophets" as apostles and early bishops, see chapter 13, where the "prophets" are referred to as the "High Priests," a term we know to refer to the earliest bishops (itinerant apostles and regional or metropolitan authorities), even before the term "bishop" became the designation for this office. See below for the information on Holmes's translation of the *Didache* and the Apostolic Fathers.

[12] Justin Martyr, *I Apology* 67.

[13] St. Augustine's mother, St. Monica, attended daily Mass, which was seen as something that particularly pious people did. Augustine of Hippo, *Confessions* 9.13. Justin Martyr explained that Sunday was chosen as the primary day for the Eucharist because, among other things, this was the day of the Resurrection of Jesus. Justin Martyr, *I Apology* 67.

And concerning the broken bread, "We thank You, our Father, for the life and knowledge which You made known to us through Jesus Your Servant; to You be the glory forever. Even as this broken bread was scattered over the hills, and was gathered together and became one, so let Your Church be gathered together from the ends of the earth into Your kingdom; for Yours is the glory and the power through Jesus Christ forever."

... But after you are filled, give thanks in this way:

"We thank You, holy Father, for Your holy name which You caused to tabernacle in our hearts, and for the knowledge and faith and immortality, which You made known to us through Jesus Your Servant; to You be the glory forever. You, Master almighty, created all things for Your name's sake; You gave food and drink to people for enjoyment, that they might give thanks to You; but to us You freely gave spiritual food and drink and life eternal through Your Servant. Before all things we thank You that You are mighty; to You be the glory forever. Remember, Lord, Your Church, to deliver it from all evil and to make it perfect in Your love, and gather it from the four winds, sanctified for Your kingdom which You have prepared for it; for Yours is the power and the glory forever. Let grace come, and let this world pass away. Hosanna to the God of David! If anyone is holy, let him come; if anyone is not so, let him repent. Maranatha! Amen."

But permit the prophets to make Thanksgiving as much as they desire.[14]

So unless you are a priest, the most important and primary prayer of the Christian faith is not even one that you will pray for yourself at all. It's one that you will hear and one to which you will agree by saying *Amen*. It bears repeating, then, that the point in the liturgy at which we say or sing *Amen* is extremely important, and we should never just let it go by as though we are absentmindedly going through the motions. We must pay attention with all reverence to the Eucharistic Prayer and be ready to make them our own by enthusiastically saying the Great Amen.

[14] *Didache* 9–10, translation adapted for clarity.

Now, in case someone should find it off-putting that we laity don't actually get to pray the most important prayer, I want to say, don't be offended as though it's some kind of privilege that you are not given. Rather see it as a great service that our clergy do for us, which takes all of the pressure off us to have to establish our prayer connection with God in worship. In other words, it's not our responsibility to know the right words to say or to get the theology right. Our priests do all the heavy lifting with regard to this most important prayer, and our job is the easy one: to listen and agree and open ourselves to be joined to Christ in His Passion, so that the grace of forgiveness will be ours. One of the words for "priest" in Latin is *pontifex,* which means "bridge builder." Our priests make that bridge between God and us by representing us to God and by representing God to us — or, more accurately, by standing in the place of Christ relative to us. And in the Eucharist, they are re-presenting the Passion of Christ so that we can join ourselves to it, not individually, but as part of the Body of Christ. Or, to use another metaphor, the priest stands in for the Bridegroom, Christ Himself, so that we can become the Bride of Christ, as members of the Church. And by participating in the Eucharistic Prayer with our responses and our "Amen" and by receiving the consecrated elements of the Body and Blood of Jesus, we remain in Him, and He remains in us, and we grow in sanctification and in union with our Creator.

Two Sacraments in One

There have always been seven sacraments, though some of them took a little longer than others to be formalized and standardized. But what most people don't realize is that, in earliest Christianity, the Sacraments of Baptism and Eucharist were each actually two sacraments in one. In the early Church, Baptism always included Confirmation (as it still does in the Eastern communions), and the Sacrament of the Eucharist always included Confession. One would never have dreamed of coming to receive the Eucharist without first confessing one's sins.[15] But in the earliest centuries of the Church, we didn't yet have the formalized Sacrament of Confession and Reconciliation, and so Confession was always part of the Mass — and prayers of confession

[15] See Gregory of Nyssa, *Sermons on the Lord's Prayer,* Sermon 2.

made up part of the liturgy.[16] One of our earliest complete liturgies, the Liturgy of St. James, includes the prayer (recited by the people): *Forgive, remit, pardon, O God, our transgressions, voluntary and involuntary, in deed and in word, in knowledge and in ignorance, by night and by day, in thought and intent; in Your goodness and love, forgive us them all.*

We still do this, of course, when we pray the *Kyrie* (Lord, have mercy) or the Confiteor, often prefaced with the words "Let us acknowledge our sins." Even the very act of kneeling is an act of confession, especially when accompanied by the words "I am not worthy that You should enter under my roof, but only say the word and my soul shall be healed" (Matt. 8:8; Luke 7:6–7). And this is so that our venial (minor, everyday) sins may be forgiven by our participating in the Mass and receiving the Eucharist. Of course, for mortal sins, we have the separate Sacrament of Confession to the priest, but the point is that one of the reasons the prayers of the Mass together make up the most important prayer of our Faith is that it is through them that we receive grace — grace that brings forgiveness for our daily sins and spiritual empowerment for ongoing faithfulness.

In the *Didache*, we read:

> Every Lord's day gather yourselves together, and break bread, and give thanksgiving *after having confessed your transgressions*, that your sacrifice may be pure. But let no one that is at variance with his fellow come together with you, until they be reconciled, that your sacrifice may not be profaned.[17]

Another (later) Church order document, known as the *Didascalia*, advises, "When you stand in the church to pray, let the deacon say with

[16] There are, of course, specific prayers of confession that are meant to be prayed as part of the liturgy. But these prayers were not originally meant to be prayed as part of private devotion. The Church Fathers did not think of contrition and confession as a type of prayer that people might pray at home, since venial sins are covered by the Mass, which includes confession, and mortal sins require the separate sacrament of Confession. For the history of the development of a standardized sacrament of Confession, see James L. Papandrea, *Reading the Church Fathers: A History of the Early Church and the Development of Doctrine* (Manchester, NH: Sophia Institute Press, 2022), chap. 9.

[17] *Didache* 14, emphasis added. Cf. Matt. 5:23–26.

a loud voice, 'Is there anyone who holds anything against his fellow?' So that if there are found any who have a lawsuit or quarrel with one another, you may urge them to make peace between them."[18] The third-century theologian Tertullian wrote that prayer proceeds out of our conscience, and so it requires a clear conscience. He said that since it is the Holy Spirit who brings our prayers from our conscience to God, we cannot afford to keep the Holy Spirit too busy, constantly having to convict our conscience of sin.[19] And St. Cyprian of Carthage said that humble confession should come before we ask anything of God in prayer.[20] All of this sounds rather daunting, and we should not take it lightly, but the good news is that simply by going to Mass, we *are* confessing our sins, as we are preparing ourselves to receive the grace of the Eucharist — assuming we are paying attention, that is.

So we should never miss an opportunity to receive forgiveness for our venial (everyday) sins. We go to Mass because we are grateful for all that God has done for us in Jesus Christ — and that's why it's called the *Thanksgiving* — but we also go because we need God's grace. St. Faustina had a vision of Jesus in which He told her:

> My daughter, do not omit Holy Communion unless you know well that your fall was serious. Apart from this, no doubt must stop you from uniting yourself with me in the mystery of my love. Your minor faults will disappear in my love like a piece of straw thrown into a great furnace. Know that you grieve me much when you fail to receive me in Holy Communion.[21]

St. Faustina would later write in her diary, "However, in all these sufferings and struggles, I was not omitting Holy Communion. When it seemed to me that I should not communicate . . . I went." The great eighteenth-century spiritual director Jean-Pierre de Caussade wrote, "It is a temptation

[18] *Didascalia* 2.54. The *Apostolic Constitutions* expands on this by adding, "Let no one come in hypocrisy." *Apostolic Constitutions* 2.54, 57.

[19] Tertullian, *On Exhortation to Chastity* 10.

[20] Cyprian of Carthage, *Treatise IV: On the Lord's Prayer* 26.

[21] Maria Faustina Kowalska, *Divine Mercy in My Soul: The Diary of Saint Maria Faustina Kowalska*, 3rd ed. (Stockbridge, MA: Marian Press, 2019), 87.

and a false humility to keep away from the sacraments."[22] Note, however, that he said "sacraments" (plural), so whenever we are convicted of mortal (serious) sin, we do need to prepare ourselves for reception of the Eucharist by first confessing our sins to a priest and receiving the Sacrament of Reconciliation.[23]

It is not for nothing that St. James wrote, "Confess your sins *to one another*" (5:16, emphasis added). It's true he didn't say, "Confess your sins to your priest," but the point is that he also didn't say, "Confess your sins directly to God in your heart." We often hear people say they don't think they need the Sacrament of Confession because they can confess directly to God. However, even if it's true that they *can*, that doesn't mean that they *do*, and in any case, the point of James's statement is that confession to someone else includes an element of accountability beyond yourself. We confess our sins as part of the Body of Christ, in liturgy, and in the confessional, always having to admit our sin in some concrete way that goes beyond simply a vague acknowledgment that we are sinners. We have to bring to mind our specific sins, as much as we are conscious of them; and by doing that, we confront them, name them *as sin* (and thereby we do not give ourselves permission to justify them or minimize them), and, by naming them — whether in our minds during the liturgy, or with our voice in the confessional — we place them before our God for forgiveness. And both of these ways of confronting of our sin are forms of confession because simply by asking God for forgiveness, we are admitting our guilt.[24]

And so, as the author of the letter to the Hebrews tells us, in every Mass, we "confidently approach the throne of grace to receive mercy and to find grace for timely help" (4:16). The same apostolic author goes on to say:

> Therefore, brothers, since through the blood of Jesus we have confidence of entrance into the sanctuary by the new and living way he opened for us through the veil, that is, his flesh, and since we have "a great priest over the house of God," let us approach with a sincere

[22] De Caussade, *Letters on the Practice of Abandonment* 6.26 (1733).

[23] In the early Church, before the formal list of the "seven deadly sins," mortal sins were thought of as anything that broke one of the Ten Commandments.

[24] Tertullian, *On Prayer* 7.

> heart and in absolute trust, with our hearts sprinkled clean from an evil conscience and our bodies washed in pure water. (10:19–22)

Have You Met Egeria?

Egeria (or sometimes called Etheria) is one of our Mothers of the Church. Probably from northwest Spain, she was most likely a wealthy widow or possibly a member of an early community of consecrated female monastics. We don't know very much about her, but what we do know comes from a document she wrote — which makes her a rare example of an early Christian woman whom we meet through her own writing. In the late fourth century, Egeria went on a pilgrimage to the Holy Land. She was in Jerusalem between 381 and 384, during the time that Cyril of Jerusalem was the bishop there. In what is often called a diary but seems to be a letter to her "sisters" (whether biological or monastic is unclear), she described the liturgies of Holy Week in Jerusalem. Unfortunately, the document is incomplete, but what remains is a kind of liturgical itinerary of worship in Jerusalem.

The practice of pilgrimage developed from the very early practice of the feasts of the saints. Already in the first century, Christians were continuing the Roman practice of the memorial meal (the *refrigerium*) — not only for their loved ones but also for the martyrs. On the anniversaries of the martyrs' deaths, early Christians celebrated their lives, asked for their intercession, and remembered them with a meal (often including the Eucharist). As a part of these memorial feasts, the early Christians would read Scripture (usually the Psalms originally, but later including the Gospels), would pray, and would tell the stories of the lives and deaths of these saints, for their martyrdoms were nothing less than a victory over death itself. But this memorial feast could not be done just anywhere. It was done at the site of the martyr's tomb. This was considered holy ground, because it was there that the martyrs' relics were venerated.[25] The doctrine of the resurrection

[25] *Martyrdom of Polycarp* 18. Bishop Polycarp of Smyrna was martyred in about AD 156. The martyr document describes how the Christians of Smyrna collected his bones and placed them where they could be venerated and where his martyrdom could be celebrated every year on the anniversary of his death.

of the body, described by St. Paul in 1 Corinthians 15 and further clarified by apologists such as Justin Martyr, assumes that there is an unbreakable connection between a person's body and soul.[26] Therefore, since it is safe to assume that a saint's soul is in Paradise with the Lord, being close to the remains of the saint's body is like being closer to God. Thus, the tomb of a martyr or another saint is holy ground. The point being that if you didn't live near the tomb of a particular saint whose feast day you wanted to celebrate, you had to travel to there.

And so this is the origin of Christian pilgrimage: to travel to visit a holy site. But this was not meant to be some kind of personal, introspective retreat. The early Christians went to the holy sites on the specific dates when others would be traveling there as well, to gather with fellow Christians and worship together on holy ground. The purpose of a pilgrimage was to have a communal experience of being the church on holy ground, primarily to commune with God through prayer in these places where the veil between this life and the next was somehow thinner because of the presence of the sacred relics of a saint. Only secondarily (in the case of the Holy Land) was a pilgrimage taken for the purpose of learning about the holy places to aid in the understanding of Scripture.

So when we read of Egeria's pilgrimage, we can see that it was not about personal prayer and devotion, but it had everything to do with going to participate in the liturgies that were taking place at the holy sites. The prayers are led by the clergy, and everything built up to the celebration of the Eucharist at specific times in specific places. Thus, we can see from Egeria's writing what liturgy was like at that time in Jerusalem, and the practices in Jerusalem, or any pilgrimage site, would have been very influential on Christian liturgy around the world, as people brought back stories of their experiences and descriptions of the celebrations from their pilgrimages. And we can also see the development of the lectionary, as well as the Stations of the Cross, coming from the practice of reading appropriate Scripture passages at each "station" of the Passion story. Egeria wrote:

[26] For more on the doctrine of the resurrection in the early Church, see James L. Papandrea, *What Really Happens After We Die?: There WILL Be Hugs in Heaven* (Manchester, NH: Sophia Institute Press, 2019).

> For this was always very much our custom, that, whenever we should come to places that I had desired to visit, the proper passage from Scripture should be read.[27]

> Whenever we were empowered to reach our destination, it was always our custom first to say a prayer, then to read a passage from the Bible, sing a psalm fitting the occasion, and finally say a second prayer.[28]

In general, we can see from Egeria's descriptions of her experiences that not only was the liturgy the priority, but every possible occasion for liturgy was taken advantage of, and the visit to every significant site was turned into a prayer service, with the Sacrament of the Eucharist whenever possible. To pray was to *gather* for prayer, with someone in authority leading the prayers, choosing the Scripture readings, and presiding over the Eucharist.

Learning by Imitation

When we consider how important prayer is for the life of the Church, it is very surprising just how little the Church fathers and mothers wrote about prayer. They talk about it, of course, but they almost never engage in teaching their people *how* to pray. If you want to write a book on how the early Christians read Scripture, it's not that difficult because the Church fathers come right out and tell you how they read Scripture. But they don't do that with prayer. It's as though they thought it unnecessary to teach people how to pray, since Jesus Himself already did that, when He taught His disciples the Our Father. There are a few commentaries on the Our Father that were written by the Church fathers, and we will look at those in a chapter to come when we discuss the Lord's Prayer, but for the most part, the Church fathers simply don't tell us how they prayed, or how we should pray.

This only emphasizes the importance of the Mass for prayer, since the Church fathers would have maintained that any lessons on prayer that we need beyond the Our Father would come to us from paying attention in the Mass. And so it's fair to assume that the earliest Christians learned how to

[27] Egeria, *Itinerary* 4, in *Egeria: Diary of a Pilgrimage* [hereafter *Diary*], trans. George Gingras (New York: Newman Press, 1970), 54.

[28] Egeria, *Itinerary* 10, in *Diary*, 66. It is clear from what she says that she and her group are being guided by monks, who are the ones leading the prayers.

pray their own prayers by imitating the prayers they heard the clergy pray in liturgy (and, of course, the prayers in Scripture that they heard read as part of the Liturgy of the Word).[29] Thus, we can look at the earliest liturgies to make some guesses about how the early Christians prayed, and what they prayed for, when they prayed at home. For the most part, the private prayers of individuals would have mirrored the intercessions.

St. Cyprian said that he kept a list of names of people to include in the prayers at Mass.[30] Egeria noted that in Jerusalem, a deacon would call out the names of those preparing for Baptism, and the children had been instructed to stand at that point and respond with "Lord, have mercy!"[31] Sts. John Chrysostom and Cyril of Jerusalem prayed regularly for the clergy and the local churches, for the government leaders, and for the welfare of the world; they prayed for the troops, and for their allies, and for the sick and the suffering.[32] However, they don't specify exactly what to ask for (we'll return to this observation in a moment). They also prayed for the dead. St. Augustine wrote that prayers for the dead are appropriate because such prayers help the souls in Purgatory (another concept we will come back to later).[33]

In the Liturgy of St. Mark, the priest prays the intercessions. These include prayers for the clergy (which would have comprised all ranks, offices, and orders, including monastic men and women); prayers for the local church as well as the churches at Rome and Jerusalem, the Church throughout the world, and protection for the orthodox against heresy and persecution; prayers for souls in trouble or fallen away or in captivity and for the blessing and the perseverance of the faithful. Finally, prayers for mercy and peace for the dead, that they would be welcomed into the Kingdom, are added.

[29] In some of the early liturgies, such as the Liturgy of St. Mark, there are specific instructions for when the priest is meant to be praying "in secret," that is, in such a way that the congregation cannot hear him. However, the intercessions are not so designated, so it's clear that the people can hear these prayers.

[30] Cyprian of Carthage, *Treatise VII: On the Mortality* [Plague] 10.

[31] Egeria, *Itinerary* 24, in *Diary*, 90.

[32] John Chrysostom, *Homilies on Second Corinthians* 2; Cyril of Jerusalem, *Catechetical Lectures* 23.8–9.

[33] Augustine of Hippo, *On Care to Be Had for the Dead* 6.

In the Liturgy of St. James, the deacon prays the intercessions. These include prayers for the forgiveness of sins, for help in resisting temptation, for perseverance, and for the salvation of all present. Also included are prayers for the clergy, for all those who remember the poor and needy (interestingly, not prayers for the poor and needy but for those who care about them), for the old, the sick, the demon-possessed, and the imprisoned (presumably not meaning people who are incarcerated for committing crimes but, rather, those who have been enslaved or who are imprisoned as a result of persecution), for those who are traveling, those who have gone astray, for good weather and healthy crops, for the presider and the sacraments, and for all those who have asked "us to mention them in our prayers."

Finally, there are times when a catechist may lead prayer (including possibly lay catechists) and, by doing so, teach the people how to pray by example. St. Augustine advises all teachers to pray before teaching, for themselves and for their students, since one cannot give what one has not received, and on the assumption that God knows the hearts of the audience and what they need to hear and can inspire the teacher to say what is most needed.[34] Having said that, though, we return now to the observation that although we can find some clues as to what (or whom) the early Christians prayed for, it is apparent that these intercessions do not go much beyond simply mentioning the people or situations — they do not got very far at all into suggesting to God what should be done. Prayers ask for mercy, or for grace, or for forgiveness or peace, but that's about it. As Egeria described it, the deacon simply mentions the names of people, or a group of people, and the congregation responds with the *Kyrie* — Lord, have mercy. That's all that was necessary, the mention of a name, to remember someone in prayer.[35]

We see this even today in the intercession in our Masses, and we might be tempted to think that it's because of a limitation of time, or perhaps a

[34] Augustine of Hippo, *On Christian Doctrine* 4.15, 29. Admittedly, this may be a piece of advice given on the assumption that the prayer is made before the class gathers, so the students may not have heard these prayers.

[35] By way of comparison, note how St. Paul talks about remembering people in his prayers, and what he says he is praying for them: Ephesians 1:15–19; Philippians 1:3–11; 1 Thessalonians 1:2–4; 2 Timothy 1:3–4; Philemon 1:4–7.

sensitivity to privacy, that the intercessions are not more specific, and do not go into more detail about the situations or what exactly is being requested. However, when we consider that this is the same as it was in the early Church, we can see that it's not because of time or privacy that the intercessions are kept mostly to a mere mention. It is because God does not need us to give the backstory for any prayer request, nor does He need us to tell him how to fix a problem. We will have more to say about this later, but the point to keep in mind is that when it comes to prayer, it is not necessary to explain anything to God.

Not that we should discourage people from praying privately in their own words, but extemporaneous prayer, or indeed, even personal (individual) prayer, was not the primary way of prayer in the early Church. The primary way that Christians prayed in the early Church was by attending liturgy. And outside of liturgy, in the privacy of their own homes and their personal devotional lives, the clergy had modeled for them that they did not need to go on and on about the people they were praying for, or the situations they were praying about. We do not see evidence of early Christians telling God how to fix their problems, since they trusted that God knows what they need better than they do.

Put Your Whole Self In

Sometimes you hear people say, "I don't go to Mass anymore [or I prefer some other kind of service] because *I don't get anything out of it*." I always want to respond by saying, "Who told you that you were supposed to *get* something out of it?" That's a pretty selfish approach to worship. Worship is supposed to be when we *give* something back to God out of gratitude, like that one leper who went back to thank Jesus. Do you remember what Jesus said when the one leper came back? "Where are the other nine?" (Luke 17:17). Well, I suppose they didn't come back because they didn't think they would get anything out of it. The problem is, they forgot how much they got from Jesus already. Christian worship, which, from the beginning, had at its heart the Eucharist — the *Thanksgiving* — is not about what you get out of it. It's about what you put into it.

Having said that, it's like a lot of things — you get more out of it if you put more into it, and so if you "put your whole self in," you *will* get something out of it. If you are invested and engaged and pay attention to the prayers and really *mean* the responses, then you will get so much out it. So, before we close this chapter, I want to mention something that has always been important in Christian prayer and worship, but that we have somewhat lost, especially in some of the more recent expressions of Christianity. That is, we worship, and we pray, with our whole bodies.

That raises the question: With what bodily positions or postures did the early Christians pray? For the most part, early Christian prayer assumes that the person praying is standing, with head raised and hands lifted and open, and facing east.[36] In fact, this posture is referred to simply as the *orans* (Latin for "praying") position. The earliest Christian art — paintings on the walls of the catacombs in Rome — depict the Church at prayer, standing in the *orans* position. Sometimes early Christians went so far as to stretch their arms out and pray in a cruciform position, in imitation of Jesus on the Cross.[37] But that seems to have been a departure from the norm. St. Basil said that we pray standing because the Greek word for *resurrection* means "standing again." We have risen with Christ in Baptism and hope to rise with Him in the resurrection, and until then, we stand because we seek the things that are above.[38]

The person who prays is looking up to God and in a posture of receptivity — that is, acknowledging need and in expectation of receiving. Notice how in Psalm 141:2, the parallelism implies that "uplifted hands" is a synonym for prayer.[39] In 1 Timothy 2:8, St. Paul describes prayer as "lifting up holy hands." The person praying faces east because the sun rises in the east, and the rising of the sun is a symbol of our hope of resurrection. St. Basil and

[36] See, for example, Clement of Alexandria, *Miscellanies* (*Stromateis*) 7.7; Cyprian of Carthage, *Treatise IV: On the Lord's Prayer* 31; Augustine of Hippo, *On Our Lord's Sermon on the Mount* 2.5; and *On Care to Be Had for the Dead* 7. There is at least one reference to moving one's feet back and forth, and there is a Jewish prayer in which the people step forward and back, so these might have a single origin in pre-Christian Judaism. But the point is that prayer is normally meant to be done standing. Jesus Himself seems to assume this in Mark 11:25.

[37] See, for example, the *Odes of Solomon* 27, 29.7, 42.1–2.

[38] Basil of Caesarea, *On the Spirit* 27.

[39] See also Psalm 63:4–5; 134:2. This implies that the *orans* prayer position was inherited from Judaism.

St. Gregory of Nyssa both said that Christians face east for prayer because the Garden of Eden was in the east, and our hope is to return to Paradise.[40] So to pray was to stand up, and even when the Church was legalized in the fourth century and got around to building churches, there were no pews. Eventually, by the end of the early Christian period, we begin to read about people sitting for some parts of the liturgy, but when it came time to pray, the people stood, as we do to this day.

Kneeling was understood as a posture of penitence, with undertones of mourning. In other words, one was humbled by sorrow for one's sins, and one kneels before God in shame. There are biblical examples of people kneeling to pray: Solomon prayed kneeling; Daniel had a habit of kneeling for prayer three times each day; the apostles knelt to pray at least on occasion; and St. Paul mentions that he knelt to pray (1 Kings 8:54; Dan. 6:11–14; Acts 20:36; Eph. 3:14). But it seems that the early Christians, at least at first, considered kneeling to be the proper position only for the most desperate prayers or for situations when the person praying was most aware of his or her unworthiness to receive an answer. In the most extreme situations, the person praying might prostrate himself on the ground, the point being that the greater the humility, or the greater the desperation, the lower one places oneself before God.[41]

Originally the only people who knelt during the liturgy were those who were doing penance — in other words, they had confessed some mortal sin, and their penance prevented them from receiving the Eucharist for a

[40] Basil of Caesarea, *On the Spirit* 27; Gregory of Nyssa, *Sermons on the Lord's Prayer*, Sermon 5. Notice that the Church fathers do not say that we face east because Jerusalem is in the east. For one thing, depending on where you live, Jerusalem might be to the west, but more important, we must not make the mistake of assuming that the early Christian motivation for facing east is the same as or similar to the Islamic motivation for facing Mecca.

[41] Notice that in the accounts of Jesus' prayer in the Garden of Gethsemane, Luke tells us that Jesus knelt, but Mark and Matthew say that he "fell prostrate on the ground" (Matt. 26:39; Mark 14:35; Luke 22:41). Of course, this had nothing to do with penitence in Jesus' case, but it was due to the urgency of the situation. Cf. 2 Maccabees 3 — in verse 20, prayer is with hands raised toward Heaven, but in verses 15 and 21, those praying prostrate themselves. In 2 Maccabees 14:15, as in several other places in the Old Testament, people also put dirt or ashes on their heads as a sign of debasement motivated by sorrow.

certain amount of time, and so they spent the liturgy in a separate section of the worship space, kneeling, either for the whole time or while the rest of the congregation went forward to receive the Eucharist. At some point, the practice of kneeling was extended to the whole congregation for certain times in the vigil Masses, appropriate for the confession of sins. Eventually, kneeling came into regular Masses, again specifically for certain moments that emphasize confession of sins, but even then, it was a gradual process. At first, kneeling was forbidden at Sunday Masses, because every Sunday Mass is a celebration of the Resurrection, and our joy over that should prevent us from kneeling, since it is a position of mourning. Later, kneeling came into Sunday Masses but was prohibited on Easter Sunday and Pentecost. Yet even with this development, we still have a liturgy that is very intentional about when we stand and when we kneel. We stand because we are praying, and standing is the original posture for prayer. We kneel because we are penitent, humble before God out of sorrow for our sins.

In the early Church, the bowing of the head was something that was only for children and catechumens (those preparing for Baptism). It was understood as a sign that the person wished a blessing from God.[42] As far as I know, there is no evidence from the early Church that anyone folded or pressed his hands together in the ways we might traditionally think of for prayer, nor was there any expressed expectation that people closed their eyes.

It is also clear from the early sources that the original Christians considered prayer to involve the whole body and all five senses.[43] St. Francis de Sales would later write, "The soul will not be content to pray if the whole [person] does not. The soul, indeed, makes the eyes, the hands, and the knees pray along with it. . . . To pray in spirit and in truth is to pray with the heart and affections, without pretense or hypocrisy, and moreover to involve the whole [person] in it, soul and body."[44] And so, in our tradition, we involve our eyes

[42] John Chrysostom, *Homilies on Second Corinthians* 2.

[43] To go deeper into this concept, see my book, *What Really Happens After We Die?: There WILL Be Hugs in Heaven* (Manchester, NH: Sophia Institute Press, 2019).

[44] St. Francis de Sales, *The Sign of the Cross: The Fifteen Most Powerful Words in the English Language*, trans. Christopher O. Blum (Manchester, NH: Sophia Institute Press, 2013), 23, 27.

when we see the Eucharistic elements uplifted, and the light of the candles, and the church's art, icons, and eventually the architecture and vestments. We involve our ears when we hear the words of Scripture and the prayers, as well as the music and exhortations. We smell the incense, and we touch the holy water, the pages of our Bibles, missals, and hymn books, as well as rosary beads, and even the Blessed Sacrament itself — and yes, the early Christians did receive the Sacrament in the hand.[45] And finally, we taste the material accidents (the tangible aspects) of bread and wine as we receive the real substance of the Body and Blood of Christ.[46]

On the other hand, we are not to make bodily position into a legalistic requirement, as though our prayers will not be heard if we are not in the right position. This would be absurd. As St. Augustine said, bodily positions such as standing with hands out, kneeling, or even praying prostrate — these intensify prayer, but they are not requirements for prayer to be "correct." This is especially true when it comes to private prayer, since he says that may be done (and we can assume it was done when people were at home) in virtually any position, for God sees into our hearts.[47]

I will close this chapter with another quote from St. Faustina, who said, "When I receive holy communion, I entreat and beg the Savior to heal my tongue, that I may never fail in love of neighbor."[48] Just as the hot coals from

[45] St. Cyril of Jerusalem advised making a cross with the hands. He said, "Make your left hand a throne for the right, as for that which is to receive a king, and having hollowed your palm, receive the Body of Christ, saying over it, Amen." Cyril of Jerusalem, *Catechetical Lectures* 23.21. As additional evidence, we have apocryphal acts documents from the fringes of the early Church that assume reception is in the hand when they warn against touching the Sacrament with hands that have recently touched another person "lustfully."

[46] In the transubstantiation, in which the substance (or essence) of the elements of bread and wine become the substance (or essence) of the Body and Blood of Jesus, the accidents (physical aspects) of the bread and wine do not change, so that we should not expect them to taste or smell like anything other than bread and wine, even though we know that under the veil of the accidents is the Real Presence of the substance of the Lord's Body, Blood, Soul, and Divinity.

[47] Augustine of Hippo, *On Care to Be Had for the Dead* 7.

[48] Kowalska, *Divine Mercy in My Soul*, 248.

the altar purified the lips of Isaiah, the Eucharist purifies our tongues — indeed, our whole bodies and souls, from our venial sins, and gives us grace to produce the fruit of the Spirit in our daily lives (Isa. 6:1–7). And just as the Seraphim sang the "Holy, holy, holy," we, too, sing the "Holy, Holy, Holy" in every Mass; with threefold praise we confess our faith in the Triune God. And this "thrice-holy" praise, or *Trisagion,* in Greek, soon became one of very earliest recorded Christian prayers.[49] The *Trisagion* may be translated into English in this way:

Holy God
Holy Mighty One
Holy Immortal One
Have mercy on us

Therefore, to pray like the earliest Christians:

1. **Go to Mass.** If you receive the Sacrament of the Eucharist in the Catholic Church or one of the Orthodox communions, your liturgy will be remarkably consistent with the Eucharist of the early Christians. If you find yourself in one of the more recent expressions of Christianity, you would have to come over to a more ancient tradition in order to participate in a liturgy that is like that of the early Christians. In any case, while you're in the liturgy, really pay attention to what the priest is saying. Listen to the prayers as if you're signing a contract, because when the time comes, you need to sincerely say *Amen.* Agree with the prayers in your mind, and say (or sing) the *Amen* with enthusiasm. And by the way, if you find it hard to keep your concentration, that in itself is not a sin; it just makes you human. But if it seems like hard work to pay attention and not be distracted during the prayers that you don't get to vocalize, well, sometimes that *is* the work of prayer. But the good news

[49] Cf. Rev. 4:8. To be clear, the *Trisagion* is not a benediction or another refence to naming of the three Persons of the Trinity. It is Trinitarian, in its threefold affirmation of God's holiness, but it is not meant to imply that each line refers to one particular Person of the Trinity, as though, "Holy God" is the Father only and specifically, and "Holy Mighty One" is the Son only and specifically, and so on. In the case of this prayer, all three of the lines that begin with "Holy" are addressing all three Persons of the Trinity together.

is that by getting the whole body involved, as the early Christians did, it helps you fight off boredom and distraction. So use the movement of the liturgy to your advantage. Don't begrudge the fact that you have to stop sitting and stand up — that just tells you how important prayer is! Let the movement drive you to pay attention even more, so that you're hanging on every word. And if all this seems just too hard — the solution is to go to Mass *more often*, not less. And perhaps you might want to seek out a refresher course on the meaning and purpose of each part of the Mass. Trust me, I know this from experience. If you put your whole self in, you will get so much out of it, and the good news is that just by going to Mass, that takes care of the lion's share of your prayer life.

2. **Be conscious of the fact that in the Mass, you are confessing your sins to prepare for reception of the Sacrament.** Take that seriously, and name your sins in your mind to really take responsibility for them, and then ask God for forgiveness. Remember that if you become aware of any serious sins, such as breaking any of the Ten Commandments, or harboring any of the motivations in the traditional list of the seven deadly sins, then you may want to consider not receiving the Sacrament of the Eucharist until you can take advantage of the Sacrament of Confession and Reconciliation. But don't procrastinate that, or let scrupulosity keep you from the "throne of grace" (Heb. 4:16). Never say to yourself, "I'm not holy enough to go to Mass." Instead, you should say, "I'm not holy enough to skip Mass." Remember the words of St. Faustina: "When it seemed to me that I should not communicate ... I went." We go to Mass because we need God's grace, not because we have it. We go not because we're worthy but because we're not. Our trust is in the mercy of Christ and the merit of His Passion, not in any merit of our own.

3. **Keep a mental (or literal) list of people who need prayer.** During the time of the intercessions, or really at any time during the Mass, think of them. Remember them in the context of prayer and mention their names in your mind to God. You don't need to say anything else. God knows the backstory, He knows the situation, and He knows better than you do what they need. Just remember them, think of them. If anything, just add a word about your hope for them: *blessing, healing, protection, salvation*. That's enough. And don't forget the people who have died. Ask God to have mercy on their souls.

4. **Learn to say** Amen **to the will of God, even outside of liturgy.** I like the Latin version, *fiat*. If you're tempted to complain when things don't go your way, use the word *Amen*, or *Fiat*, as a prayer of trust in the will of God — shorthand for saying, "May Your will be done, Lord." I'll have a lot more to say below about praying according to the will of God, but if you struggle with that, make a beginning toward praying "without ceasing" (1 Thess. 5:17–18) by carrying the *Amen* from liturgy into daily life. Maybe you need to make *Fiat* your new F-word, replacing harsh, angry language with the language of saying yes to God (see Sir. 22:27; 23:7–15). You can imitate the examples of Jesus and Mary by letting go of the need to have everything your way and being open to the will of God.

To Go Deeper

If you want to read the relevant *primary sources* (the documents from the time of the early Church), here are the main ones for this chapter:

The Didache (written in the second half of the first century), in the Ante-Nicene Fathers Series, vol. 7, https://www.newadvent.org/fathers/0714.htm.

A more modern translation is included in:
Michael W. Holmes, ed., *The Apostolic Fathers: Greek Texts and English Translations*, 3rd ed. (Grand Rapids: Baker Academic, 2007), beginning on p. 344.

The First Apology of Justin Martyr (written in the middle of the second century), in the Ante-Nicene Fathers Series, vol. 1, https://www.newadvent.org/fathers/0126.htm.

The Pilgrimage "Diary" of Egeria (written in the AD 380s), in the Ancient Christian Writers Series, vol. 38, *Egeria: Diary of a Pilgrimage* (New York: Newman Press, 1970), https://www.ccel.org/m/mcclure/etheria/etheria.htm.

For a more modern translation:
Anne McGowan and Paul F. Bradshaw, *The Pilgrimage of Egeria: A New Translation of the* Itinrarium Egeriae (Collegeville, MN: Liturgical Press, 2018).

Other, modern, books — we call them *secondary sources* — to supplement some of the concepts in this chapter:

Scott Hahn, *The Lamb's Supper: The Mass as Heaven on Earth* (New York: Doubleday, 1999).

Roch A. Kereszty, *The Church of God in Jesus Christ: A Catholic Ecclesiology* (Washington D.C.: Catholic University of America Press, 2019).

James L. Papandrea, *Reading the Church Fathers: A History of the Early Church and the Development of Doctrine* (Manchester, NH: Sophia Institute Press, 2022).

James L. Papandrea, *What Really Happens After We Die?: There WILL Be Hugs in Heaven* (Manchester, NH: Sophia Institute Press, 2019).

Insight 2

The Most Powerful Prayer . . .

is also one of the shortest
and can even be prayed without words at all:
the Sign of the Cross

The first word I say
in the morning when I rise:
May Christ's Cross
be my armor about me.

— Early Welsh Poem

We finished the last chapter by noting how the whole body is involved in prayer. In fact, we saw how some people even prayed standing in a cruciform position.[1] And while this doesn't mean that we are always expected to stand with our arms up and open, or even kneel, for our private prayers, it does remind us that prayer is not something that happens only in our heads. And there is one prayer that Christians have always prayed that intentionally involves the body, marking our whole selves for Christ. That is, the making of the Sign of the Cross.

The Cross as a Symbol in Early Christianity

Many people believe that the cross did not become a symbol of the Church until after Christianity was legalized by the emperor Constantine and the use of crucifixion as a method of execution was discontinued. In fact, there was a time when I believed this too — that is, until I started exploring the catacombs of Rome. Some scholars continue to teach this fallacy, in spite of the fact that one can see in the early Christian catacombs, and on other funerary inscriptions, that there are examples of crosses worked into other

1 Note this passage from the Odes of Solomon (an early Christian collection of poems, possibly hymns): "The expansion of my hands is his sign . . . the cross." *Odes of Solomon* 27. The Church fathers remembered how Moses held up his hands as a "prayer" for success in battle (Exod. 17:8–13) and said that by doing so he was putting himself in the position of Jesus on the cross. And just as Moses in the cruciform position supported the soldiers during their battle, so the cross supports us as the Church "doing battle" (that is, spiritual warfare) in the world. See Ignatius of Antioch, *Letter to the Ephesians* 9 and the *Epistle of Barnabas* 12.

symbols (such as anchors and monograms of Christ) from long before the time of Constantine. So this is one of those die-hard myths about the early Church that could not be further from the truth. The emperor Constantine was not responsible for the symbol of the cross, not even indirectly. In reality, the cross is one of the Church's first symbols, and as a sign of the Christian faith, it has endured throughout the whole history of the Church.

In the book of Numbers, God instructed Moses to make an image, or icon, of a serpent.[2] It was made of bronze and attached to a banner pole so that it could be seen from a distance. And this icon had healing power, so that anyone who was bitten by a snake would be saved from the poison just by looking at the image. In the early Church, the Church fathers (following Jesus' interpretation from His prediction of His Crucifixion in John 3:14–15) unanimously interpreted this serpent on a pole as a symbol of the cross. So for the Church fathers, there was a saving sign of the cross even *before* Christ.[3] And just as the icon of the serpent had healing power, the Church fathers believed and taught that the Sign of the Cross had a kind of power — not in a superstitious sense, since the power is not really in the symbol itself, but in the *meaning* of the symbol and in the faith that people place in its meaning.[4]

In fact, the Church fathers went out of their way to find other examples of the Sign of the Cross in the Old Testament. Several of them saw the cross in the written text itself — for example, in Genesis, where we are told that Abram had 318 men in his army (14:14).[5] The Church fathers interpreted this number as a reference to the Sign of the Cross because the Hebrews and Greeks didn't have separate written marks for numerals; letters were used to represent numbers. And in the Greek translation that the Church

[2] Num. 21:4–9. Cf. Deut. 8:15.

[3] Justin Martyr, *Dialogue with Trypho* 60, 90.

[4] See, for example, the *Epistle of Barnabas* 12.

[5] See, for example, the *Epistle of Barnabas* 9 and Ambrose of Milan, *Exposition of the Christian Faith* 1.3. See also Irenaeus of Lyons, who saw in the Tree of Life in the Garden of Eden a foreshadowing of the cross. Other Church fathers followed him in this, to the point where some early depictions of the cross combine it with a Tree of Life motif, as if the cross is growing out the tree. For a beautiful example of this, see the apse mosaic in the basilica of San Clemente in Rome.

fathers used, the number 318 could be derived from the letter *Tau* (*T*) plus Iota (*I*) and Eta (*H*). *Tau* by itself could represent 300, and *Iota* and *Eta* together represented 18. So for the Church fathers, 318 was itself a symbol of the Crucifixion, because *Tau* looks like a cross and *Iota* and *Eta* are the first two letters of *Jesus*. The point is that for the Church fathers, the Greek letter *Tau* was itself a symbol of the cross.[6] And although it would be easy to say that these early Christian references to the cross are only about the actual cross, and not the *Sign* of the Cross, that would miss the point that *Tau* was considered by the early Christians as not only a symbol but a *sign* of God's grace.

This is even more evident when we see that some of the earliest existing manuscripts of Christian documents include a kind of pictogram, in which a stylized crucifix replaces the Greek letter *Tau* in words that have to do with the cross or the Crucifixion.[7] The pictogram is made from the two Greek letters *Tau* and *Rho*, functioning as an abbreviation for the Greek word *stauros* (cross). It was drawn by the scribes with the loop of the *Rho* (the part of the letter that makes it look like the English letter *P*) extending above the "crossbeam" of the *Tau*, so that it looks like the head of a man on a cross. We refer to this pictogram as a Tau-Rho, or staurogram, but there is no mistaking its meaning, and for all intents and purposes, it is a crucifix — written into some of the earliest Christian manuscripts that we have.

By the third century, the cross could even be found imprinted on jewelry, including rings — a sign of Christian identity even while Christianity was still illegal.

Have You Met Sts. Helena and Macrina?

Another one of our mothers of the Church, St. Helena was the mother of the famous emperor Constantine. Constantine had become emperor of the western half of the Roman Empire after defeating the usurper Maxentius at the Battle of the Milvian Bridge, outside Rome, on October 28 in the year AD 312.

6 For examples, see the *Epistle of Barnabas* 9, 12, and Clement of Alexandria, *Miscellanies* 6.11.

7 This is documented in detail in Larry W. Hurtado, *The Earliest Christian Artifacts: Manuscripts and Christian Origins* (Grand Rapids: Eerdmans, 2006).

And within a year, Constantine had issued the Edict of Milan, which legalized Christianity and granted freedom of religion to everyone in the empire. In the year 324, he defeated his eastern rival to become the sole emperor of the Roman Empire, and when that was done, it made some things possible that were never possible before. The one thing that concerns us for the moment is that it opened the way for pilgrimages to the Holy Land — and one of the first pilgrims to take that trip (even before Egeria) was Constantine's mother, Helena, now known to the Church as St. Helena (or St. Helen).[8]

In Bethlehem and Jerusalem, Helena talked with Christians whose families had lived in the Holy Land since the time of Jesus Himself, and from them she was able to determine the locations of the important events in Jesus' life, including — and especially — the tomb where He was laid after His death and where He rose from the dead.[9] In fact, the location of the tomb was known even to the pagans, and a previous emperor had tried to obscure it and prevent Christians from visiting it by building a pagan temple over the site. Once Helena identified the location, the pagan temple was destroyed, the site was excavated, and the tomb of Jesus was found and opened. And there, in the tomb, was the crossbeam of the Cross of Jesus. We call this the *True Cross*, and it was found on September 14, in the year AD 326 (though some scholars date this a bit later in the 320s, or even into the early 330s). In any case, although there may be some question about the exact year of the discovery of the True Cross, September 14 is still celebrated as the feast of the Exaltation of the Holy Cross.[10]

Versions of the story differ as to whether Helena was a Christian first, and influenced her son, or whether Constantine converted to Christianity

[8] The main primary sources for this information are the early Christian historians Eusebius, *Life of Constantine*, book 3, and Socrates, *Ecclesiastical History* 1.17.

[9] Cf. Justin Martyr, *Dialogue with Trypho* 70, 78, and Origen, *Against Celsus* 1.51.

[10] Technically, the feast is the celebration of three historical events: the discovery of the True Cross by St. Helena, the dedication of the Basilica of the Holy Sepulchre (which Constantine built on the site), and the return of the Cross to Jerusalem by the emperor Heraclius in 629, after it had been stolen by the Persians in 614, when they sacked Jerusalem. The feast has been celebrated at least from the end of the seventh century.

and then influenced his mother. Either way, the two of them became a force for the promotion of the Church at the top of the social hierarchy. As you can imagine, in that position, the people of the empire — especially newly converted Christians — would look to Constantine and his mother for how they practiced the Faith. But the emperor himself was not much of an example (though he is considered a saint in the Eastern churches). Helena, on the other hand, became one of the first "famous" Christians, and as such, she had the position to influence the faith of many people, including through her prayers, because she was given the authority to lead prayer with groups of women. Among other things, Helena promoted devotion to the wood of the True Cross. The major portions of the True Cross became the primary relics in the new Church of the Holy Sepulchre in Jerusalem, the Cathedral of Holy Wisdom (Hagia Sophia) in Constantinople, and the Church of the Holy Cross (Santa Croce in Gerusalemme) in Rome. Smaller pieces of it were given as gifts to important people.

Fast-forward a few years, and one of these important people was St. Macrina the Younger. She was the older sister of two of the most important Eastern Church fathers, Sts. Basil of Caesarea and Gregory of Nyssa. She was, in fact, their first catechist, having been brought up on the Scriptures (and taught to memorize the Psalms) by their mother. It was Macrina who influenced her brothers — and through them, many in the Eastern Church — to embrace a life of prayer and simplicity, uncluttered by the accumulation of possessions. Unfortunately, unlike Egeria, we don't have any documents written by Macrina herself, but her brother Gregory preserved much of her teaching in some of his writings, and he presents her as an inspired teacher — though it is sometimes hard to tell when he is preserving what she actually taught him, and when he is using her voice to present his own teachings. In any case, after she died (in 379), he wrote a tribute to her called the *Life of Macrina*, and it is in this document that we learn that Macrina had a ring with a compartment in it that held a sliver of the True Cross. She also wore an iron cross around her neck, which she referred to as a phylactery, bringing to mind the Hebrew practice of strapping the words of Scripture to their bodies, often on their foreheads. This may have been a relatively new thing in the fourth century, but by the seventh century, Christians were wearing crosses and crucifixes, some of which contained relics.

Making the Sign of the Cross

In the Old Testament book of Ezekiel, the prophet is instructed by God to place a mark on the foreheads of those who remained faithful (Ezek. 9:3–6).[11] Anyone without the mark was to face destruction, but the mark was meant to be a kind of brand, marking the persons as belonging to God and placing them under His protection. The Hebrew word for *mark* is the same word as the name of the Hebrew letter *Tov*, so naturally, the Jewish people assumed that the mark itself was the letter *Tov*. This mark of protection was even used in Jewish funerary inscriptions. When translated into Greek, *Tov* becomes the letter *Tau*, and in Latin, it's *T*. So when the Church fathers read Ezekiel, they understood it to mean that the faithful person of God was marked on the forehead with the letter *T*, the Sign of the Cross.[12] Some combined this passage from Ezekiel with the account of the Passover, noting that just as the mark of the blood of a lamb on the lintel of the doors was a mark of protection for the people of Israel, so the mark of the Cross, on which Jesus, the Lamb of God, had shed His blood, was a mark of protection on the "lintel" of the body, which is the forehead.[13] Early Christians also put the cross on their literal lintels, or doorposts, as well as on their walls and in their windows after Chrisitanity was legalized.

This biblical concept of marking the forehead as a way to "brand" a person as belonging to God, and as a sign of protection, came into Christianity in the practice of making the Sign of the Cross on the forehead of a person being baptized.[14] Along with the anointing with oil, this was considered the

[11] This is part of a vision that God gave the prophet, not something that really happened, but the fact that it was part of a prophetic vision would be even more of a motivation for the Church fathers to see it as something that could be applied to the Church.

[12] For example, see Tertullian, *Against Marcion* 3.22.

[13] For example, see Cyprian of Carthage, *Treatise 1: On the Unity of the Church* 18, *Treatise 12: Testimonies ...* 2.21–22. See also *Apostolic Tradition* 42.

[14] The "mark" of Baptism would have been universally understood as including the Sign of the Cross. For example, see Cyprian of Carthage, *Treatise V: Address to Demetrianus* 22, and the *Apostolic Constitutions* 3.16. For Cyprian, to be a baptized Christian is to be someone who is "new-born and signed with the cross." See also Augustine of Hippo, *Confessions* 1.11, where Augustine includes not only Baptism but the assumption that babies and children are

"seal" of Baptism, and it constitutes the "mark" of God on a person — like a soldier's brand, as St. Augustine said,[15] and in direct opposition to the "mark of the beast," which would mark one as belonging to Satan (Rev. 7:2–3; 9:3–4; cf. chap. 13).[16] In fact, the Sign of the Cross was often made over several places on the body of the person being baptized, including the eyes. It seems that the Sign of the Cross was made on the person's body by the bishop or priest, using his thumb. And from the very beginning, people regularly imitated this action, either on themselves or their loved ones. And so in the early Church, making the Sign of the Cross meant tracing the cross on the forehead with the thumb, much as we still do in Mass at the reading of the Gospel.

To be clear: there is no evidence that there was ever a time when Christians did not make the Sign of the Cross, on themselves and on others; there was never any controversy over the practice and no evidence that anyone in the early Church objected to it.[17] It seems to be assumed as common practice for all

---

repeatedly and regularly blessed by having the Sign of the Cross made over them. The Sign of the Cross was also used in the Sacrament of Holy Orders (ordination); see Hippolytus, *Apostolic Tradition* 21.

[15] Augustine of Hippo, *On the Creed* 16.

[16] Lactantius, *Epistome of the Divine Institutes* 71. Note also that Irenaeus of Lyons referred to the three Persons of the Trinity as "the three principals of our seal," meaning that when we are sealed in Baptism, we are sealed in the name of the Father, Son, and Holy Spirit; cf. Matt. 28:19. Irenaeus of Lyons, *Demonstration of the Apostolic Teaching* 99–100.

[17] Both Tertullian and St. Basil did explain that Christians should not be concerned if a practice like this was not explicitly taught in Scripture. Just like facing east for prayers, or the content of the Eucharistic prayers themselves, it is enough that it is handed down by tradition. Tertullian, *On the Crown* 3–4, Basil of Caesarea, *On the Holy Spirit* 27. Minucius Felix may have had to defend Christians against the charge of worshipping crosses, but that was in opposition to outside criticism, not internal conflict. Minucius Felix, *Octavius* 29. In the seventeenth century, when St. Francis de Sales wrote his defense of the practice against Protestant objections, he said, "Having no written commandment to make the Sign of the Cross, he [the Protestant] will not make it. Having no written prohibition of it, I will not cease to make it." St. Francis de Sales, *The Sign of the Cross: The Fifteen Most Powerful Words in the English Language*, trans. Christopher O. Blum (Manchester, NH: Sophia Institute Press, 2013), 51. It is clear from

Christians, and it seems to be another practice that was learned by imitation, without anyone having to write a whole treatise on it. The Sign of the Cross was the "mark of salvation."[18] It was a mark of identity — and a public one at that. It was, as it still is, a proclamation of the gospel, imprinted on our bodies.

Have You Met Tertullian?

Tertullian was a North African theologian, writing around the turn of the third century. His writings were extremely influential at the time, especially as the Church clarified the doctrine of the Trinity. In fact, Tertullian is the one who gave us the Latin technical terms for the doctrine: that God is a *Trinity* of three *Persons* in one *substance*. For that reason (and because he was the first theologian to write in Latin), he's often called the father of Latin theology. But he's a very interesting character because he was also what we call a *rigorist*; that is, he was on the extreme strict side of the Church on disciplinary matters, which sometimes put him at odds with the popes. Eventually, he associated with, and defended, a group known as the Montanists. They were not heretics exactly, but they were seen as suspect by some (see the appendix on charismatics in the early Church).

While many of the Church fathers write about making the Sign of the Cross, Tertullian refers to it in a way that is worth quoting here:

> At every forward step and movement, at every going in and out, when we put on our clothes and our shoes, when we bathe, when we sit at table [i.e., to eat a meal], when we light the lamps, when we recline on a couch, sit down on a seat, and in all the ordinary actions of daily life, we trace upon the forehead the sign.[19]

---

even a surface reading of the Church fathers that they read Scripture like de Sales (that Scripture was not meant to be considered exhaustive) and not like his opponents. See James L. Papandrea, *Reading Scripture Like the Early Church: Seven Insights from the Church Fathers to Help You Understand Scripture* (Manchester, NH: Sophia Institute Press, 2022).

[18] Note that in the book of Wisdom, the bronze serpent on the pole is referred to as the "sign of salvation" (16:6–7, 12).

[19] Tertullian, *On the Crown* 3. Translation slightly adapted for clarity. See also the even earlier document *Epistula Apostolorum* 16, and Cyril of Jerusalem, *Catechetical Lectures* 4.14.

"In all the ordinary actions of daily life," Christians make the Sign of the Cross. Of course, we have to admit that this statement of Tertullian may give us something closer to his own idea of what Christians *should* do than what every Christian actually practiced. But there does seem to be an assumption among the Church fathers that it is appropriate to make the Sign of the Cross regularly and often, especially at significant moments, and certainly when getting up in the morning, at mealtime, and when going to bed at night.

We don't know for sure when the Sign of the Cross developed from a small cross traced on the forehead to a larger cross traced over the whole upper body. It may have been due to the fact that, in giving benedictions, bishops and priests traced a larger cross in the air, in the direction of the gathered faithful, who, in turn, imitated that larger form of the cross on themselves.[20]

The Sign of the Cross as a Prayer

The Sign of the Cross is an identity marker, "branding" one as belonging to Christ and even publicly proclaiming the gospel of the Cross.[21] But it is so

[20] This probably happened by the end of the early Church era. There are stories of Muslims in Iran who make the Sign of the Cross, simply because their ancestors did, and the practice was handed down through the generations as a tradition, in spite of the fact that they are not Christian. This implies that they are descended from Persian Christians who were forced to convert to Islam or who converted under pressure to assimilate. In any case, the fact that they make the Sign of the Cross on their whole upper body shows that their ancestors — before the Islamic conquest in the seventh century — must also have done so. There was a controversy in the Middle Ages over how many fingers one should use to make the Sign of the Cross, and some speculate that this controversy was the cause of the shift from forehead to upper body, as if making the Sign of the Cross larger was required to show or to see how many fingers were being used. However, I believe it is much more likely that the controversy came after the shift to upper body, when the Sign of the Cross was no longer being made by the thumb, and that raised the question of hand position and number of fingers. In other words, the shift to a larger Sign of the Cross made on the upper body is what caused the controversy over how it should be made.

[21] Clement of Alexandria interpreted Jesus' statement "Whoever does not carry his own cross and come after me cannot be my disciple" (Luke 14:27)

much more than that: it is a powerful prayer — specifically, a prayer for blessing, healing, and protection, including protection against evil and temptation. As a blessing, the Church fathers pointed out how Jacob crossed his hands when blessing his sons in Genesis 48:14 and how that was a foreshadowing of the Sign of the Cross.[22] Early liturgies instruct the presider to make the Sign of the Cross over the Eucharist and over the people. In fact, St. Augustine said that the Sign of the Cross was required for the Sacrament of the Eucharist, and, in fact, no sacrament could be valid without the Sign of the Cross.[23] Tertullian mentioned that people make the Sign of the Cross over not only their bodies but also their beds, and other sources mention making the Sign of the Cross over one's home.[24] And we can also see that early Christians made the Sign of the Cross over those who needed healing and for exorcisms.[25] St. Macrina herself was once healed of a tumor when her mother made the Sign of the Cross over that part of her body.[26]

The early Christian witnesses to the use of the Sign of the Cross as a prayer of protection are many. The *Apostolic Tradition* advises that Christians should constantly make the Sign of the Cross on their foreheads as a protection against the devil.[27] One version of the *Apostolic Tradition* calls the Sign of the Cross a shield that makes the devil flee, by the power of the

---

as a reference to the *Sign* of the Cross — implying that "bearing one's cross" includes not being ashamed to make the Sign of the Cross. Clement of Alexandria, *Miscellanies* 7.12. See also Augustine of Hippo, *On Christian Doctrine* 2.41, and Ambrose of Milan, *On Belief in the Resurrection* 2.46. Ambrose says that the Sign of the Cross is a proclamation of the gospel, as he says, "We are signed with the sign of his death," and yet it is a sign of victory over death. For the early Church, to make the Sign of the Cross is to proclaim and affirm one's acceptance of Christ as Savior (John 1:12).

22 See for example, the *Epistle of Barnabas* 13.

23 Augustine of Hippo, *Tractates on the Gospel of John* 118.5.

24 Tertullian, *To His Wife* 5; Athanasius of Alexandria, *Life of Antony* 35.

25 The second-century apocryphal document *The Acts of John* shows the popular practice of using the Sign of the Cross as a healing prayer. Athanasius of Alexandria, *Life of Antony* 80, mentions the use of the Sign of the Cross in exorcisms.

26 Gregory of Nyssa, *Life of Macrina*.

27 *Apostolic Tradition* 41–42. One version of the text advises making the Sign on the Cross on the eyes as well as on the forehead.

Holy Spirit.[28] It goes on to say that the Sign of the Cross sanctifies the body and protects a person from evil and from temptation.[29]

In the third century, the bishop Methodius preached, "By this figure [of the cross], in truth, the passions are blunted — the passion of the passions having taken place by the Passion."[30] In other words, by making the Sign of the Cross, we are given help to avoid temptation, and we are reminded of the Passion of Christ on His Cross, which overtakes in our minds the passions that tempt us.

St. Cyril of Jerusalem wrote that we make the Sign of the Cross "so that the demons may behold the royal sign and flee, trembling, far away."[31] This is another reason we must not be ashamed of the Sign of the Cross, says St. Cyril. We have to make the Sign of the Cross openly and publicly, so the demons can see it and run from us. St. Cyril goes on to quote the passage from Tertullian above, saying that we should make Sign of the Cross, "at every act" — meaning in everything we do.

St. Athanasius speaks for the consensus of the Church fathers when he says:

> Who is so silly, or who is so incredulous, or who so maimed in his mind, as not to see and infer that Christ, to whom the people witness, himself supplies and gives to each the victory over death, depriving death of all its power, in each one of them that hold his faith and bear the Sign of the Cross. . . .
>
> For by the Sign of the Cross, if a person only use it, [Christ] drives out the demons' deceits . . . by its use demons flee, oracles cease, all magic and witchcraft is brought to nothing. . . .
>
> Those who are called gods among [the pagans] are routed by the Sign of the Cross. . . . Demons are put to shame by the Sign of the Cross. . . .

[28] Note the "shield of faith" in 1 Thessalonians 5:8 and Ephesians 6:16; cf. Isaiah 59:17 and Wisdom 5:17–20.

[29] *Apostolic Tradition* 41.

[30] Methodius, *Homily on the Cross and Passion of Christ*, Fragment 2.

[31] Cyril of Jerusalem, *Catechetical Lectures* 4.14. See also Lactantius, *Divine Institutes* 4.27.

> [St. Antony] said, "The demons make their apparent attacks against those who are cowardly. Therefore, sign yourself with the Cross."
>
> Sign yourselves, and your houses, and pray, and you will see [the demons] vanish. For they are cowards, and greatly fear the Sign of the Lord's Cross.[32]

As we can see, it's not for nothing that in all those movies vampires and demons are afraid of the cross. But of course, this is not superstition, because the power is not in the physical cross or the crucifix, but in *the One who is named* when we make the Sign of the Cross. In Athanasius's *Life of Antony,* the great hermit St. Antony of Egypt explains it this way: "Why do you marvel at this? We are not the doers of these things, but it is Christ who works them by means of those who believe in him."[33] The *Apostolic Tradition* clarifies that the power is in the faith of the person making the Sign of the Cross, and so it must be done with sincerity, and not to draw attention to oneself or for show.[34] In other words, it is not a magic spell, since only a Christian indwelt by the Holy Spirit can make the Sign of the Cross and expect the prayer to have its power.

Having said that, the Church fathers were not afraid to admit that the Sign of the Cross made a good replacement for the superstitions of the pagans, including the amulets that pagans wore and which would have to be given up when one converted to Christianity. In fact, St. John Chrysostom wrote that this should be emphasized at a person's Baptism: that the Sign of the Cross replaces the amulets, that adults should be taught to make the Sign of the Cross at their Baptism, and that even in the case of infant Baptism,

[32] Athanasius of Alexandria, *On the Incarnation* 29, 47–48, 53–55, *Life of Antony* 13, 35. Translation adapted for clarity. On the subject of the Sign of the Cross obstructing pagan oracles and augury, see Lactantius, *Divine Institutes* 4.27, and note that there are several accounts from the time of the Great Persecution when Christians were executed for making the Sign of the Cross during ceremonies of pagan soothsaying. This shows that the Romans believed there was power in the sign, though they obviously did not understand the source of the power.

[33] Athanasius of Alexandria, *Life of Antony* 80.

[34] *Apostolic Tradition* 42.

the priest or bishop makes the Sign of the Cross on the little forehead in the hope that later the child will develop the habit of making the Sign of the Cross regularly.[35] It is the Sign of the Cross that will protect the child (not to mention adults) from evil, not an amulet or another superstition.

In Gregory of Nyssa's *Life of Macrina*, St. Macrina prayed as she lay dying, saying to her Lord, "You have given a sign to those who fear you, in the symbol of the Holy Cross, to destroy the adversary and save our life." At the end of her prayer, her brother writes, "As she said these words she sealed her eyes and mouth and heart with the cross."[36] Although her lips continued moving, indicating that she died in continual prayer, we get the sense from this account — and it is consistent with what we see in the rest of the document and what we know from other sources — that there is an expectation that Christian prayer is meant to be concluded with the Sign of the Cross. This is, of course, still practiced to this day, and this explains the current practice. When we finish a prayer, we make the Sign of the Cross and pronounce the name of the Trinity, "In the name of the Father, and of the Son, and of the Holy Spirit."

The truth is that the *figure or form* of the cross in the Sign of the Cross is inseparable from the *name* of the One who hung on the Cross, and from the Trinity of which He is one Person.[37] To put it another way, you can't separate the *symbol* of the cross from the *Person* who was crucified, and you can't separate Jesus Christ from the Trinity. We can truthfully say that the power of the Sign of the Cross is not in the hand gesture that we make but in what it symbolizes: the actual Cross of Christ's Passion — but it is equally true that the power is not really in the wood of the historical Cross, but in the Person who hung there, His divine and human natures, and His sacrifice. So even though it is not technically required to say the words out loud every time we make the Sign of the Cross, the real power of the prayer

[35] John Chrysostom, *Homily on I Corinthians 12:13–14.*

[36] Gregory of Nyssa, *Life of Macrina.*

[37] Note Revelation 14:1, where what is on the foreheads of the faithful is the *name* of God. Note also that when St. Paul talks about "the *word* of the Cross" (sometimes translated "the message of the Cross") in 1 Corinthians 1:18, the Greek word for *word* or *message* is *logos,* a term that can refer to Jesus Himself (as in John 1:1). Thus, the power of the Cross is in the *word* of the Cross, which is also the *name* of the One who hung on the Cross.

is in what the sign signifies: the God who is Trinity and who is incarnate in Jesus Christ. St. Francis de Sales wrote that the Sign of the Cross is like a banner on a castle wall. The power of the castle is not in the banner *per se,* and it is not the banner itself that frightens enemies. The real power is in what the banner represents — in the fact that a powerful army stands behind the wall and threatens any who would attack.[38] For Christians, the power of the Sign of the Cross is in the omnipotence of the triune God and in the legions of angels who are ready to protect us.

Admittedly, it may be a bit of an exaggeration to say that the Sign of the Cross is "the most powerful prayer." After all, the Eucharistic Prayer results in the miracle of the Real Presence. In the Eucharistic Prayer, the presider prays the words of Jesus from His institution of the Sacrament. But in the Sign of the Cross, we as laypeople get to pray not only the words of Jesus from Matthew 28:19 but also the *name* of God — not just Jesus but the Trinity — and there is power in that name.[39] And at least on the basis of word count, the Sign of the Cross is as powerful as it is concise. And the reason it is so powerful is that we can pray (out loud or mentally as we make the gesture) the name of the Trinity and identify ourselves as belonging to the God who will protect us as His own, marking ourselves with the sign of his ultimate victory over evil. Beyond that, it is a prayer of trust in God, because we leave it to God to determine what to do about our situation — we are not asking for anything specific, only calling on the name of God. And when we do this with holy water, we are also reaffirming our Baptism and our commitment to Jesus Christ as our Savior.[40] Thus, the most powerful prayer — that laypeople can pray anyway — is the prayer you pray on your body, again bringing into prayer your whole self, not just your mind.

Finally, it's interesting to note that, although the Church fathers talk about making the Sign of the Cross, they don't say much about the specific words that are to be said when making the Sign. This is why we wouldn't say

[38] St. Francis de Sales, *The Sign of the Cross,* 83.

[39] Compare the Hebrew practice of referring to God as "The Name" (*Hashem*), for example, in Sirach 47:10, with the importance of the "name that is above every name" in the New Testament (John 1:12; 3:18; Acts 5:41, Phil. 2:9–10).

[40] *Apostolic Tradition* 41.

that you must say the words out loud for it to "work"; again, we never want to turn it into something that makes it seem like an incantation. Nevertheless, it is assumed that the Trinity is named, at least by implication, each time we make the Sign of the Cross. We can be confident that the name of the Trinity was associated with the Sign of the Cross from the beginning, since Jesus Himself instructed His apostles to baptize in the name of the Trinity, and the Sign of the Cross originated in the Sacrament of Baptism. So when we pray the Sign of the Cross, we are praying the words of Jesus: "In the name of the Father, and of the Son, and of the Holy Spirit" (Matt. 28:19). Incidentally, one of the Church's other earliest prayers is a variation on the naming of the Trinity in the Sign of the Cross. That is the Gloria Patri, or in English, the Glory Be:

Glory be to the Father
And to the Son
And to the Holy Spirit.
As it was in the beginning,
Is now, and ever shall be,
World without end.

Therefore, to pray like the earliest Christians:

1. **Make the Sign of the Cross often**. Be conscious of the fact that when you do, you are not engaging in a superstitious act, like throwing a pinch of salt over your shoulder, but you are praying a powerful prayer. As often as possible, say the words out loud: *In the name of the Father, and of the Son, and of the Holy Spirit.* Whenever you can, use holy water to remember your Baptism and renew its commitment.

Make the Sign of the Cross whenever you need help — when you are afraid, or tempted, or need healing. Make the Sign of the Cross on yourself but also on others, especially your loved ones. If you are a parent, make the Sign of the Cross on your children. Make the Sign of the Cross when anyone needs prayer, even (or especially) if you don't know what they need (you may be familiar with the habit some people have of making the Sign of the Cross whenever they see an accident or an ambulance or pass a hospital). Make the Sign of the Cross any time you want to bring God into a situation, when there is danger, tragedy, or celebration and thanksgiving. Make the Sign of the Cross when you receive bad news but also when you receive good news. Make the Sign of the Cross to express thanksgiving, especially at mealtime. In fact, even if you're not used to praying before meals, at least making the Sign of the Cross is an adequate grace. Make the Sign of the Cross for blessing as you begin any new project. Use the Sign of the Cross to bless your home as well.

Take note of what St. Francis de Sales wrote to explain how to make the Sign of the Cross:

> As a rule, the Sign of the Cross is made in the following way. It is made with the right hand, which as Justin Martyr says, is esteemed the more worthy of the two. It is made either with three fingers, in order to signify the Blessed Trinity, or five, in order to signify the Savior's five wounds; although it does not much matter whether one makes the Sign of the Cross with more or fewer fingers, still one may wish to conform to the common practice of Catholics in order not to seem to agree with certain heretics such as the Jacobites and the Armenians, who each make it with one finger alone, the former in denial of the Trinity, the latter in denial of the two natures of Christ.
>
> The Christian first lifts his hand toward his head while saying, "In the name of the Father," in order to show that the Father is the First Person of the Blessed Trinity and the principle and origin of the others. Then, he moves his hand downward toward the stomach while saying, "and of the Son," in order to show that the Son proceeds from the Father, who sent him here below into the Virgin's womb. Finally, he pulls his hand across from the left shoulder to the right while saying, "and of the Holy Spirit," in order to show that the Holy Spirit, being the Third Person of the Blessed Trinity, proceeds from the Father and from the Son and is their bond of love and charity, and that it is by his grace that we enjoy the effects of the Passion. When we make the Sign of the Cross, therefore, we confess three great mysteries: the Trinity, the Passion, and the remission of sins, by which we are moved from the left, the hand of the curse, to the right, the hand of blessing.[41]

[41] St. Francis de Sales, *The Sign of the Cross*, 8–10. Cf. Ps. 103:12.

2. **Many people begin their prayers with the Sign of the Cross, but at least end every prayer with the Sign of the Cross.** You may be used to ending your prayers by saying something like "in the name of Jesus. Amen," but that is not how the early Christians ended their prayers, which is to say that it isn't bad, exactly, but it is incomplete. The more ancient, and more complete, conclusion to prayer is to end with the Sign of the Cross, in which we name the Trinity. In fact, it may be that the practice of ending prayers with "in the name of Jesus" developed out of a Protestant desire to do away with the Sign of the Cross. But using the name of Jesus, while a good thing, is still really just a shortcut for naming the Trinity. Even when the New Testament says that people were baptized "in the name of Jesus," that is just a shorthand for Baptism in the name of the Trinity, since it would be unlikely that the apostles would have failed to follow Jesus' own instructions to baptize in the name of the Father, Son, and Holy Spirit (Matt. 28:19).

Also, remember that you don't need to say *Amen* at the end of your own prayers. Again, there's nothing wrong with it, but it's not necessary to agree with your own prayers. We usually do say *Amen* after pronouncing the names of the three Persons of the Trinity in the Sign of the Cross, but that is only because we are used to saying *Amen* when a bishop or priest pronounces the triune name and makes the Sign of the Cross over us. When a bishop or priest blesses us with the Sign of the Cross, we say *Amen* at the end to agree with the prayer. When we make the Sign of the Cross ourselves, it's not strictly necessary to say *Amen* at the end, though it's fine if you do. The point, though, is that in our prayers, it is more important to end with the Sign of the Cross and say the words "In the name of the Father, and of the Son, and of the Holy Spirit" than it is to say "Amen."

3. **Do not let the Sign of the Cross become a mindless habit or, worse, a superstition.** Making the Sign of the Cross is not meant to be something we do obsessively, out of fear that if we forget to do it, something bad will happen. Failing to make the Sign of the Cross is not a jinx. Do not treat it like magic, but also do not underestimate its power and your need for this prayer for divine protection, given the very real spiritual warfare that goes on unseen. Make the Sign of the Cross intentionally, and often, but not for show or to call attention to yourself; and do not be ashamed to make it in public, as a statement of faith and a proclamation of the gospel.

4. **In general, the Sign of the Cross is a prayer to the Trinity**, naming God as the three Persons of Father, Son, and Holy Spirit. But for what it's worth, you don't need to worry about whether you are praying to one particular Person of the Trinity more than the others. God is one God, not three, so whether you pray to the Father, to the Son, or to the Holy Spirit, you will not offend the Person(s) you name or talk to less frequently. Praying to any one of the three Persons is as good as praying to all three, since the three are inseparable. Having said that, praying the Sign of the Cross regularly is a good way to keep from letting our conception of God get skewed in one direction or another. There are some Protestant groups that have focused so much on one particular Person of the Trinity or another that they have strayed into heresy and have ended up implicitly rejecting the doctrine of the Trinity. So while you can pray to any one of the three Persons of the Trinity when you talk to God, ending all of your prayers with the Sign of the Cross, and in the name of the Trinity, is a good way to keep your prayers, and your conception of God, on the right track.

To Go Deeper

Primary Sources

Tertullian, *On the Crown* (or *Chaplet*) (written around the turn of the third century), in the Ante-Nicene Fathers Series, vol. 3, https://www.newadvent.org/fathers/0304.htm.

Gregory of Nyssa, *Life of Macrina* by Gregory (written in the late fourth century), https://www.ccel.org/ccel/pearse/morefathers/files/gregory_macrina_1_life.htm#8.

Secondary Sources

Larry W. Hurtado, *The Earliest Christian Artifacts: Manuscripts and Christian Origins* (Grand Rapids: Eerdmans, 2006).

Bruce Longenecker, *The Cross before Constantine : The Early Life of a Christian Symbol* (Minneapolis: Fortress Press, 2015).

James L. Papandrea, *Reading Scripture Like the Early Church* (Manchester, NH: Sophia Institute Press, 2022).

Insight 3

The Most Perfect Prayer …

is the one that Jesus taught us:
the Our Father

He was praying in a certain place,
and when he had finished,
one of his disciples said to him,
"Lord, teach us to pray
just as John taught his disciples."
He said to them, "When you pray, say …"

—Luke 11:1–2

In the first chapter, I remarked that the Church fathers didn't explicitly teach the early Christians *how* to pray. At least, not in any document that still exists. This is because they believed that Jesus had already done all that was needed, when He taught His disciples how to pray, and that prayer was recorded in the Gospels. The Church fathers apparently reasoned that as long as Christians had the Our Father, they knew how to pray (the rest could be learned by imitation from attending the Mass and participating in the sacraments).

Christians were expected to pray the Our Father from memory, verbatim — because in praying this prayer, we are praying the words of Jesus — and so it was never thought of as simply a suggestion, or just an example of a good prayer, or an outline or template for prayer (I'll have more to say about that in the next chapter).[1] It was always understood to be *the* prayer that the faithful pray. The Church fathers called it "the most excellent prayer" or "the most perfect prayer." St. Augustine said that after the Eucharistic Prayer, the primary Christian prayer is the Our Father.[2]

1 Augustine of Hippo, *On the Lord's Prayer* 9.1. Augustine said that Jesus didn't just "teach" the Our Father; he *dictated* it. The consensus of the Church fathers is that the Our Father is meant to be prayed verbatim. See, for example, Cyprian of Carthage, *Treatise IV: On the Lord's Prayer* 3, 29, and *Treatise VII: On the Mortality* 18. We should note that any distinction between the titles Our Father and the Lord's Prayer was not in the minds of the Church fathers. In general, ancient documents were titled by their first line, so the original title for the prayer would have been the Our Father. However, the English translations of many of the writings of the Church fathers were made by Protestant scholars, who seem to prefer the title Lord's Prayer.

2 Augustine of Hippo, *Handbook on Faith, Hope, and Love (Enchiridion)* 7.

Have You Met St. Cyprian?

St. Cyprian was the bishop of Carthage, in North Africa, in the third century, during one of the worst times of persecution in the history of the Church.[3] In December of the year AD 249, the Roman emperor Decius issued an edict requiring all inhabitants of the empire to demonstrate their patriotism by participating in pagan sacrifices.[4] Within a month, the bishop of Rome, Pope Flavian, had been executed for refusing the order, and Cyprian went into hiding to avoid the authorities. During the time of the persecution, he did his best to shepherd the Christians of North Africa from his place in seclusion, and he corresponded with the church at Rome in an attempt to manage the situation.

In AD 251, the emperor was killed in battle and the persecution subsided for a while. Bishop Cyprian came back to a divided church and was involved in several controversies that resulted from the confusion over Christians' having denied the Faith to save their lives (or their livelihoods). He weighed in on the formalization of the Sacrament of Confession and Reconciliation and even opposed Pope St. Stephen (unsuccessfully) on matters related to Baptism. Cyprian wrote many letters and several important treatises, including one called *On the Unity of the Catholic Church*, but the one most relevant for our purpose is a commentary on the Our Father. In the year 257, persecution was renewed and in 258, Cyprian was arrested and executed.

Cyprian wrote that, as a prayer, the Our Father is complete.[5] There is nothing that can be added to it, because it is a prayer composed by Jesus Himself and in His own words. The point of calling it "the most perfect prayer" is that there is nothing we could add to it to improve it. "It is a loving and friendly prayer to beseech God with his own word," says Cyprian.[6] Therefore, it is meant to be prayed verbatim, since God could hardly ignore the words of His own Son: "Let the Father acknowledge the words of his

[3] For details on this time in the Church's history, see Papandrea, *Reading the Church Fathers*, 290–291.

[4] Timeline taken from James L. Papandrea, *Novatian of Rome and the Culmination of Pre-Nicene Orthodoxy*, Princeton Theological Monograph Series, vol. 175 (Eugene, OR: Pickwick, 2011), 63–68.

[5] Cyprian of Carthage, *Treatise IV: On the Lord's Prayer* 9.

[6] Cyprian of Carthage, *Treatise IV: On the Lord's Prayer* 3.

Son when we make our prayer, and let him who dwells within our breast himself dwell in our voice."[7] In fact, for the Church fathers, this is what Jesus meant when he said we should pray in His name — the best way to pray in the name of Jesus is to pray in the words of Jesus.[8]

Cyprian went on to say that it is a sin to pray in any way other than the way that Jesus taught, "for what could be a more spiritual prayer than that which was given to us by Christ?"[9] St. Augustine would later follow the lead of his fellow North African, saying, "The words which our Lord Jesus Christ taught us in this prayer are the rule and standard of our desires. You may not ask for anything but what is written there."[10] Of course, this is a bit of hyperbole, because elsewhere Augustine says that it never hurts to ask for anything, as long as we are ready to accept that the answer might be no.[11] But there is a sense in which it would seem arrogant on our part to presume that we could add anything to Jesus' perfect prayer with our own words. Cyprian, too, is not implying that this is the only prayer any Christian can pray, but the point is that they both want to emphasize that the Our Father is complete as it is, that nothing needs to be added to it, and that it is meant to be prayed verbatim and repeated.[12]

Cyprian wrote that by praying the Our Father every day, we are praying to continue in the life of faith that was begun in Baptism and to receive grace for daily sanctification, and because we are asking for the forgiveness of daily sins, we receive that forgiveness.[13] The prayer itself is a means of grace, and Cyprian said that it contains, "deep mysteries," using the Latin word *sacramenta*.[14] Thus, Cyprian considered the Our Father to be what we would call a *sacramental*.[15]

[7] Cyprian of Carthage, *Treatise IV: On the Lord's Prayer* 3.

[8] John 16:23. Cyprian of Carthage, *Treatise IV: On the Lord's Prayer* 3.

[9] Cyprian of Carthage, *Treatise IV: On the Lord's Prayer* 2.

[10] Augustine of Hippo, *On the Lord's Prayer* 6.4.

[11] Augustine of Hippo, *Sermons on New Testament Lessons: Sermon 30 on Matthew 17:19* 2.

[12] Augustine of Hippo, *On the Lord's Prayer* 9.1.

[13] Cyprian of Carthage, *Treatise IV: On the Lord's Prayer* 12, 22.

[14] Cyprian of Carthage, *Treatise IV: On the Lord's Prayer* 9.

[15] The *Catechism of the Catholic Church* defines sacramentals in paragraphs 1667–1679. It does not mention the Our Father specifically, but the prayer

There Is No *My* in the Our Father

Prayer in the early Church is always corporate, never individual. It is always assumed that the person praying is doing so as a part of a people who serve God *as a people* (see 1 Pet. 2:9). In other words, we pray as members of the Body of Christ, not as isolated individuals. In fact, apart from perhaps a few examples in Celtic Christianity (like the so-called Breastplate of St. Patrick), it is not until the Middle Ages that we ever see prayers with the words *I* or *me* in them.[16] And so it is with the Our Father, which is prayed from the perspective of the first person plural: *our* and *us*, not *my* and *me*. St. Cyprian wrote:

> First of all, the Teacher of peace and the Master of unity would not have prayer to be made singly and individually, as one who prays for himself alone. For we do not say, "My Father who is in heaven," nor "give me this day my daily bread," nor does each person ask that only his own debt should be forgiven him, nor does he request for himself alone that he may not be led into temptations and delivered from evil. Our prayer is public and common, and when we pray, we pray not for one but for the whole people, because we the whole people are one. The God of peace and the Teacher of concord, who taught unity, willed that one should thus pray for all, even as he himself bore us all in one.[17]

Cyprian would go on to say that we can hope to receive salvation only if we pray with the Church because it is only within the Church that the valid sacraments may be found.[18] Therefore, all Christian prayer is to be conducted with the whole body of Christ in mind — we pray on behalf of others, never only on our own behalf. Even St. Augustine's very introspective *Confessions* begins with the prayer, "*Our* hearts are restless until they rest in you."[19]

---

would, at the very least, fall under the category of sacramentals of popular piety.

[16] Apart from the Breastplate of St. Patrick, the thirteenth-century Anima Christi may be the first true Christian "I/me" prayer. However, as we will discuss below, the Psalms do include "I/me" prayers.

[17] Cyprian of Carthage, *Treatise IV: On the Lord's Prayer* 8.

[18] Cyprian of Carthage, *Treatise IV: On the Lord's Prayer* 2, 8, 24.

[19] Augustine of Hippo, *Confessions* 1.1, emphasis added.

All of this is consistent with what we saw with regard to the primacy of the Mass in the first chapter. However, this does not mean that the Our Father was not prayed in private. The Church fathers assume that faithful Christians are praying the Our Father every day, as part of their personal prayers. In fact, it seems clear that praying the Our Father at home, apart from Mass, is the earliest form of Christian private devotion. Cyprian recommends that his people make their private prayers in their bedrooms, presumably because this was the one room in the house most set apart from the distractions of the world, and Jesus Himself said to pray in secret (Matt. 6:6; cf. Isa. 26:20).[20] St. Cyprian also gives us another one of the earliest indications of silent prayer, or what the later fathers called "mental" prayer. Cyprian says our private prayers should be modest — that is, quiet — because God hears what is in our hearts, citing the Old Testament example of Hannah, who prayed silently, speaking a "hidden prayer," moving her lips but not making a sound.[21]

What this means is that when a person prays the Our Father as a part of the liturgy, he or she is praying not just with but also *for* all the people gathered — indeed, all Christians everywhere. When a person prays the Our Father privately, as a part of his or her personal devotional life, that person is still praying with and for others, especially anyone for whom he or she is responsible. Parents who pray the Our Father are praying for their whole households, especially their children, for their salvation and for their consciences to be formed correctly, and for the forgiveness of their sins.[22] And just as we can remember loved ones in prayer in the intercessions at Mass, we can also pray the Our Father for others simply by calling them to mind and naming them as we begin to pray.

We should keep in mind that the early Christians accepted the reality of what we call *vicarious faith*. "Vicarious" means that one thing stands in for another, and in the early Church, it was always assumed that one person's faith could benefit another person in certain ways — for example, when an infant or child is baptized on the basis of the faith of the parents and sponsors. So when you pray, as a person who is a member of *a people*, you bring

[20] Cyprian of Carthage, *Treatise IV: On the Lord's Prayer* 4.

[21] Cyprian of Carthage, *Treatise IV: On the Lord's Prayer* 4. See 1 Sam. 1:9–13.

[22] Cyprian of Carthage, *Treatise VIII: On Works and Alms* 18.

your people into the prayer with you. This is more than simply saying that you are praying for someone in the sense of praying for their benefit. You are also praying for them in the sense of praying on their behalf.

What Are We Praying For?

The disciple who came up to Jesus and asked him to teach them how to pray was a faithful Jew — so it's not that he didn't know how to pray. But with the Incarnation and mission of Jesus came a new way to pray — and this New Covenant prayer is encapsulated in the Our Father.[23]

As I have noted, the Church fathers assume that the Our Father is being prayed verbatim, as Jesus taught it. But as you may know, there are two versions of the Lord's Prayer in the Gospels. Mark doesn't include it at all, Luke gives us a shorter version (11:1–4), and Matthew gives a longer version (6:9–13). So which one did the Church fathers have in mind when they talk about memorizing and reciting the prayer verbatim? For the Church fathers, Luke's version leaves out lines that Jesus did include, probably because Luke considered them redundant.[24]

Personally, I am convinced that Luke gives an abbreviated version of the prayer that Jesus taught, and Matthew, writing later, corrects the prayer from his own memory to the verbatim prayer that Jesus dictated. We must keep in mind that as one of Jesus' disciples, Matthew didn't hear this just once; he would have recited this prayer many times. He and the other apostles would have had it memorized. Why wouldn't they? Why should we assume that they didn't start praying it regularly as soon as Jesus taught it to them? And so we don't have to wonder how Matthew remembered it when it came time to write his Gospel. Luke, on the other hand, was not one of the twelve disciples and would not yet have had the benefit of so many years of reciting the prayer from memory when he wrote his Gospel. In any case, even

[23] Christian prayer is not a complete departure from Jewish prayer. Jesus Himself was brought up with the prayers of the Hebrew people, and these became the foundation for His institution of specifically Christian forms of prayer.

[24] For example, Augustine says that Luke conflates the line "deliver us from evil" into the line "lead us not into temptation" because it means basically the same thing.

if I'm wrong about all that, the Church fathers assume that the prayer to be prayed is Matthew's version, and they use that version in their commentaries on the Our Father.

For the sake of comparison, and to get the text in front of us, here are the two versions of the prayer that we receive from the evangelists:[25]

Luke 11:1–4	**Matthew 6:9–13**
Father	**Our** Father **in Heaven**
May Your name be revered	May Your name be revered
May Your Kingdom come	May Your Kingdom come
	May Your will be done
	On earth just as it is in Heaven
Give us each day our daily bread	Give us **today** our daily bread
And forgive our sins	And forgive us our **debts**
For we forgive everyone indebted to us	As we have forgiven our debtors
And do not bring us into temptation	And do not bring us into temptation
	But rescue us from the evil one

The first thing one might notice is that the familiar ending "for the kingdom and the power and the glory are yours, now and forever," is not included in either version. This *doxology* is not in the text of the Gospels at all but is found for the first time in the version of the Our Father in the Didache with no explanation or justification — which means that it was already being recited as part of the prayer by the end of the first century.[26] John Chrysostom assumed that it was part of the prayer, but in general, the

[25] The translations are my own, from the Greek text; however, this is only to illustrate the differences between the two versions of the prayer in Matthew and Luke and to begin to think about what each line is actually asking for. These translations are not intended to be a substitution for or alternate versions of the traditional version we recite in the Mass. Since this is a prayer that the whole Body of Christ prays together, we must all pray the same version from memory.

[26] *Didache* 8. The version in the *Didache* says simply, "For the power and the glory are yours forever." No doubt "the kingdom" was an even later addition. There are Bibles that include this doxology in the text of Matthew;

Church fathers do not include it in their commentaries. It is clear that it was not part of what Jesus originally taught His disciples but was added later. This is why it is separated from the rest of the prayer in the Mass and is not included at other times when the prayer is recited. Apart from the doxology at the end, the version of the prayer in the *Didache* and in the commentaries is the one in Matthew.[27]

Looking at the direct translations from the Greek text of the Gospels helps us begin to think about what each line of the prayer really means. But this brings us to the question of what the Church fathers believed we are meant to be praying for when we pray the Our Father. This is especially important since the Church fathers saw this prayer as *perfect,* in the sense of *complete* — in other words, there's nothing else we should need to ask for. In any case, sometimes we pray it so much by rote that we don't really think about what we are saying, and perhaps we shouldn't assume that we know how the Church fathers would interpret it. So let's take a look at the prayer that Jesus taught us, line by line, and dig into its meaning, with the hope of discovering something more about Jesus' intent for our prayers. What follows comes from the Church fathers' commentaries on the Our Father, especially those of Tertullian, Cyprian, Gregory of Nyssa, Cyril of Jerusalem, and Augustine.

Our Father who art in Heaven

The Church fathers treat this first line as the address, and not part of the prayer proper, in the sense that we are not yet praying *for* anything. But the address sets the tone for the entire prayer, by acknowledging our position before God. We are children, which means that we are dependent on God, and it is in that spirit of dependence that we come to God in prayer.

God is our Father. And it is significant that when Jesus says, "Our Father," He includes Himself, so that we should know that His Father is our Father (cf. John 20:17). And yet God is our Father by adoption, which is not the

---

however, that is based on later manuscripts that were influenced to add it after the *Didache* was written.

[27] The version in the *Didache* has the singular "debt," as opposed to the plural "debts" and renders the past tense, "as we have forgiven," in the present, "as we also forgive."

same as the relationship of the Father with the Son. As we know from the Creed, the Son is *consubstantial* with the Father, which means that He is the same divinity as the Father (and the Spirit — this is because God is one and there is only one God), and it also means that the Son is eternal, as the Father is. In other words, Jesus Christ is not a mere human; He is the Divine Word who took on humanity for our sake. So Jesus is the Son of God by nature, and we are sons and daughters of God by adoption (John 1:12–14). Still, that makes Jesus Christ our Brother in the common Father that we share.

God's fatherhood is all about providence. God, in His eternal will, created us and cares for us.[28] There are, of course, attributes of God that we might associate with motherhood, and there are a few motherly metaphors for God in Scripture and in early Christian literature.[29] But Jesus Himself gave us the way to refer to the first Person of the Trinity, and this is included in the Lord's Prayer. In the tradition of the Hebrew religion, one maintained proper respect for the name of God (for example, *YHVH*) by refusing to say it out loud. When reading the Scriptures, Jews substitute the word *Lord* (*Adonai*) for the name of God. But with the coming of Christ in the Incarnation, the word *Lord* now also describes the Son and the Holy Spirit as well, and so a new substitution for the divine name of the first Person of the Trinity was needed. Jesus gave us that when He called the first Person of the Trinity His Father and our Father.[30]

Thus, we begin the prayer with an acknowledgment that everything good comes from God, including our very existence. Providence — God's loving care for us based on His perfect and eternal will for us — is one of

[28] Gregory of Nyssa, *Sermons on the Lord's Prayer*, Sermon 2.

[29] See, for example, the *Odes of Solomon* 8.4, 19.1–4, and Clement of Alexandria, *The Instructor* 1.6.

[30] John 17:26. It is often unclear whether we should interpret the divine name in the Old Testament as a reference to the first Person of the Trinity only or to the "whole" Trinity, all three Persons together. The Church fathers have no consensus on this point. But since the Church fathers understood references to the "Angel of the Lord" to be the second Person of the Trinity, the pre-incarnate Word, it seems reasonable to assume that in general, if the "Angel" is the second Person, then "the Lord" refers to the first Person specifically. On the other hand, the divine name *Elohim*, which is grammatically plural, could be said to refer to the Trinity.

His attributes. It's not that God *has* this tendency to provide for us and protect us, or even that He *exercises* providential care. It's that God *is* love, and because of that, God *is* provision and protection. So we should never give credit to nonpersonal entities such as "the universe" or even luck. All credit for everything good goes to the Creator. It's better to speak of God as providence personified, and our traditional Christian shorthand for that is to call God our Father.

The concept that God is "in Heaven" is, of course, not meant to negate God's omnipresence. God is always everywhere. Gregory of Nyssa explains that we refer to God as "in Heaven" or "heavenly" to remind ourselves that Heaven is our "fatherland," our true home. When we sin, we are like the prodigal son, who admitted to having sinned "against Heaven," and we leave our heavenly home behind and become exiled from it. But when we come to God in prayer, asking for forgiveness, He welcomes us home like the father in the parable.[31]

After the address, we get into the prayer proper, and the Church fathers saw this as seven prayers in one: three prayers for eternal blessings and four for temporal blessings.

The Three Eternal Blessings:

Hallowed be Thy name

We have begun by calling on the name of God, since "everyone who calls on the name of the Lord will be saved" (see Joel 3:5). St. Augustine notes that catechumen need to be taught the Creed so that they will know *who* this God is (the Trinity), in order to know whom they are calling upon.[32]

As it was in the Hebrew religion, the name of God is held as sacred. And because the name of God is holy, if we hold it up as holy and give it the proper respect, it will make us holy. So there is a sense in which we are praying for our own sanctification here — in other words, that we might continue to revere and respect the name of God and that our doing so may contribute to our sanctification.[33] It's as though we are praying for God's grace that we

[31] Gregory of Nyssa, *Sermons on the Lord's Prayer,* Sermon 2. Cf. Luke 15:11–32.

[32] Augustine of Hippo, *On the Lord's Prayer* 6.1.

[33] Augustine of Hippo, *On the Lord's Prayer* 7.4.

might always keep the second commandment: *You shall not take the name of the Lord your God in vain* (Exod. 20:7; Deut. 5:11; cf. Sir. 27:13–15).

For some of the Church fathers, *hallowed* meant "glorified," and so this line was also a prayer for God's name to be glorified — that is, revered throughout the world by all people, in the spirit of Matthew 5:16: "that they may see your good deeds and glorify your heavenly Father." Cyril of Jerusalem noted that this prayer was especially important given the fact that God's name is often disrespected among the people of the world (cf. Isa. 52:5; Ezek. 36:20; Rom. 2:24).[34] So this is a prayer for God's name to be glorified by our lives, and by our witness in the world. Finally, when we pray this line, we are praying for the spread of the gospel throughout the world, which leads us into the next line, since it is only when the gospel has reached the whole world that the Kingdom will be revealed in its fullness.[35]

Thy Kingdom come

The prayer for the coming of the Kingdom has two levels of meaning, related to the two aspects of the Kingdom of God. In its present, or concealed, aspect, the Kingdom is already among us and within us (Luke 17:21). So as we pray this line, we are praying that the Kingdom would come *in us* — that is, grow in us, like that mustard seed, so that it would govern us in this life and, as Gregory of Nyssa wrote, free us from the tyranny of sin and death, liberating us to live in virtue.[36] We are praying for help in resisting temptation and sin and for discipline over our passions. We are calling for backup in the spiritual battles we face — in essence, we are praying for God to call in the cavalry, so to speak. We are praying to be filled with the Holy Spirit. We are praying that we should not lose sight of the big picture of eternity, keeping in mind to seek the Kingdom first above all, so that we don't get too attached to this life and then find ourselves unprepared for the coming of the Kingdom in its fully revealed aspect.

[34] Cyril of Jerusalem, *Catechetical Lectures* 23.11–18. See also Gregory of Nyssa, *Sermons on the Lord's Prayer,* Sermon 3.

[35] Augustine of Hippo, *On the Lord's Prayer* 6.5, *Our Lord's Sermon on the Mount* 2.5.

[36] Gregory of Nyssa, *Sermons on the Lord's Prayer,* Sermon 3.

In terms of the future revelation of the Kingdom of God, we are praying for the Second Coming of Christ, as the early Christians also prayed in the Aramaic, *Marana tha*, "our Lord, come" (1 Cor. 16:22; Rev. 22:20).[37] So the prayer is for the return of Christ to be soon, at which time He will bring in the Kingdom in its fully revealed aspect, there will be a final judgment and the general resurrection, and we will enter into the eternity of the New Jerusalem.[38] So this is a prayer for the end of all things to come soon, for the ultimate goal of God's will to be accomplished, and for peace to finally come to God's people, for the Church fathers seem to assume that there will be no peace on earth — no end to wars — until Jesus returns.[39]

Thy will be done, on earth as it is in Heaven

Omitted by Luke, this is obviously a prayer that God's will should be done in the world, but the Church fathers explain the Heaven and earth comparison on several levels:

1. May humanity in general do as the angels do and obey God, and especially may non-Christians be converted to the Faith. St. Cyprian reminds his readers that God wills that everyone should come to salvation, so praying for the will of God means praying for the salvation of all people.[40]
2. May the enemies of the Faith do as Christians do, with the hope that enemies may become friends. This is one way to pray for our enemies, as Jesus instructed us to do.
3. May the Church do as Jesus, her Bridegroom, does. May Jesus truly be the head of His Body, the Church, and may the Church not only follow His example but also do His will.
4. Within the Church, may those of us who are living do as the saints who went before us have done. They are in Heaven, but the prayer is for their lives to be an example that the living will follow. There

[37] Augustine of Hippo, *Our Lord's Sermon on the Mount* 2.6.

[38] Augustine of Hippo, *Our Lord's Sermon on the Mount* 6.6.

[39] Cf. Matt. 24:6–8, 14; Mark 13:7–8; Luke 21:9–11.

[40] Cyprian of Carthage, *Treatise IV: On the Lord's Prayer* 17. Cyprian did not believe that all people would be saved, but he believed that we should pray for that nevertheless (cf. 1 Tim 2:1-6)

are also holy ones who are still alive but are living as though they are already in Heaven, and the prayer is that the rest of us may follow their example as well and live virtuously.

5. Within individual Christians, may our flesh do as our spirit directs. Since God's will is that everyone should be saved, that means us as individuals as well, and so we are also praying for our own salvation.[41] Keep in mind, though, that the Church fathers all assumed that a person can lose salvation, and so the prayer is for perseverance in the Faith.[42] And since there is no evil in Heaven, doing God's will as it is in Heaven would mean ridding our lives of all evil.

The Four Temporal Blessings:

Give us this day our daily bread

As in the two previous lines, there are layers of meaning here as well. The Church fathers believed that there is a double meaning to the concept of "daily bread" and that when we pray this line, we are praying for both material and spiritual bread. On the material level, this is a prayer for God to provide for our daily needs. It includes bread (food), of course, but it can be understood in a more general sense to include other necessities as well.

However, whenever the Church fathers interpret "daily bread" as material needs, the emphasis is on the word *daily*. St. Cyprian referred to the Old Testament account of God's providing the manna in the desert and said that we should ask only for *today's* bread, not tomorrow's bread. He said that since we have already prayed for Jesus to return soon and the Kingdom to come quickly, we should take Jesus at His word when He said, "Do not worry about tomorrow," and we should not be praying for necessities in the future.[43] Cyprian goes on to cite Psalm 37:25, which promises, "Neither in my youth, nor now in old age, have I seen the righteous one abandoned,

[41] Gregory of Nyssa, *Sermons on the Lord's Prayer*, Sermon 4.

[42] It is clear from the teachings of Jesus that He did not think perseverance was guaranteed (Matt. 10:22; 24:13; Mark 13:13; Luke 21:19; cf. Rev. 2:26). The Church fathers did not believe in a "once saved, always saved" doctrine.

[43] Cyprian of Carthage, *Treatise IV: On the Lord's Prayer* 19, 21. Cf. Matt. 6:31–34.

or his offspring begging for bread." So we should trust in the providence of God for tomorrow and demonstrate that trust by praying only for today, and there is a sense in which worry about the future is a lack of trust in the providence of God (we will explore this concept more in a later chapter). Gregory of Nyssa, too, emphasized that we should be content with bread for today. We should not pray for our needs in the future, and we should never pray for luxuries, only necessities. The "daily" aspect of this prayer should lead us to grow in contentment with what we have and in moderation.[44]

Gregory of Nyssa also connects this prayer to the lines above, saying that it would never be God's will for our "bread" to come to us unjustly. In other words, our food should never come by making another person go hungry, and our gain should never come by another person's loss. This is why we ask only for today, since storing up our own bread for tomorrow might mean that another person will starve today. He says you have already prayed for the future when you prayed for God's Kingdom to come, and that's all the prayer for the future that you need; "therefore look to your own conscience before you ask God for bread."[45]

On the spiritual level, our daily bread is the Eucharist, and the assumption is that the ideal is to receive it daily.[46] Cyril of Jerusalem noted that the Greek word for *daily* in Matthew can be translated to mean "supersubstantial." So we can read the text as referring to *supersubstantial bread* — that is, bread in which the very substance has been superseded by another substance; in other words, transubstantiation.[47] This *supersubstantial bread* is bread in which the substance (or essence) has become the Body and Blood

[44] Gregory of Nyssa, *Sermons on the Lord's Prayer*, Sermon 4.

[45] Gregory of Nyssa, *Sermons on the Lord's Prayer*, Sermon 4.

[46] St. Augustine acknowledged that not all Christians were receiving the Sacrament daily in his time, but he noted that it was still the norm in the East, and he held this as an example to follow. Augustine of Hippo, *On the Lord's Prayer* 7.7.

[47] The word *transubstantiation* had not been coined yet in the time of the Church fathers, but it does accurately describe what the early Christians believed about the Eucharist. For a detailed treatment of the Eucharist in the early Church and into the Middle Ages, see James L. Papandrea, *Handed Down: The Catholic Faith of the Early Christians* (El Cajon, CA: Catholic Answers Press, 2015), chap. 4, "The Eucharist."

of our Lord Jesus, and so the bread *is* Christ Himself; and the Church fathers are unanimous in the early (and medieval) Christian conviction of the Real Presence of Christ in the Sacrament. In praying for this bread daily, we are praying that we might receive Christ daily (or at least regularly) in the Sacrament and, thus, that it might contribute to our sanctification. We are praying that we might not fall into mortal sin and end up having to miss out on receiving the Eucharist, and ultimately that we will "remain in" Christ (John 15:1–10), as members of His Body, the Church, and that we will persevere in Him to the end and receive salvation (Matt. 24:13; Mark 13:13; James 1:25).[48] Finally, by extension, this can also be seen as a prayer for the continued ability to participate in the liturgy in general, which can be important in those times and places where it is not always guaranteed that the Mass will be available.

And forgive us our trespasses

It is significant that sins are described in the Greek (and in the Latin) as debts. This comes from Jesus Himself, in His parable of the unmerciful servant (Matt. 18:23–35).[49] A debt owed to someone is a metaphor for having sinned against a person (or against God). The situation of being in debt puts one in a very specific position relative to the one who is owed; that is, there is an imbalance in the relationship, and the person who owes the debt needs to pay it in order to restore equilibrium. In the Middle Ages, St. Anselm of Canterbury clarified that since God is our Creator, we owe Him our obedience, but when we fail to obey God, we fall into debt with Him — a debt that must be paid. But this is a debt we cannot pay, because our sin only puts us deeper in dept.

Of course we know what God's solution to the problem is: the divine Son of God took on a human nature so that He could pay the debt owed by humanity. He became one of us so that He could pay the debt for us. And His "credit" was applied to each of us as individuals when we were baptized. Any sins we had committed before our Baptism were forgiven in the grace of that sacrament. However, we didn't stop sinning after our Baptism, and the grace of the Baptism only results in the forgiveness of sins up until the

[48] See Cyprian of Carthage, *Treatise IV: On the Lord's Prayer* 18, and Augustine of Hippo, *On the Lord's Prayer* 7.7.

[49] Cyprian of Carthage, *Treatise IV: On the Lord's Prayer* 22.

moment of Baptism.[50] Baptism does not erase future sins. So how do we deal with post-baptismal sin? This was a real question in the early Church, and it took a bit of time for it to be sorted out. When it was sorted out, the Sacrament of Confession and Reconciliation was standardized to deal with mortal sin. But as far as the venial (everyday) sins, these are forgiven through the grace of receiving the Eucharist and, as some of the Church fathers pointed out, simply by asking for forgiveness. So here in the Our Father, we have a prayer for the forgiveness of our sins.

One of the metaphors the Church fathers used is that of a boat. Imagine that your life is a boat, and sins are like little leaks in the hull. If you let even the smallest sins go unconfessed, your boat will fill up with water and eventually sink. So what do you do? You must constantly bail out the water. And this prayer, the Our Father, is your bucket. Every time you pray this prayer, you remove some of the water from your boat. And that's good, but you can't pray it just once. You need to pray it all the time, constantly. But there's one other thing. If you don't also forgive others for their sins against you, that's like having holes in your bucket. You can bail all day long, but it won't work.

As we forgive those who trespass against us

Notice that in the Greek of both Luke and Matthew, the grammar of this line assumes that we *already have* forgiven the people who have sinned against us. Our traditional English translation of this line, "as we forgive those," is actually closer to the grammar in the *Didache*, but it is a bit more open as to when this forgiving is taking place. So if we don't think about it too much, we could give ourselves permission to put off forgiving others — "I'll get around to forgiving when I feel ready" — and we can go on praying the Our Father without doing the one thing in the prayer that *we* are promising God we will do. As Gregory of Nyssa said, we can pray the Our Father "with the confidence of children of God," but *only* if we are willing to forgive others.[51]

We will turn back to this concept of forgiving others, but for now, it's enough to note that the Church fathers talked about forgiving others in two ways. One is praying for our enemies. For the Church fathers, the best way we can forgive others is to pray for them. And, of course, Jesus said we

[50] Augustine of Hippo, *On the Lord's Prayer* 7.8; *On the Psalms* 143.3.

[51] Gregory of Nyssa, *Sermons on the Lord's Prayer,* Sermon 5. Cf. Sir. 28:2–3.

should pray for our enemies and not hold grudges (Matt. 5:43–44; Luke 6:27–31). It should go without saying that praying for your enemies means praying for their well-being, not simply praying for them to change, to be nicer to you, or to get what's coming to them. Resist the temptation to pray *against* your enemies, since by doing so, you pray against God's will: God wills their sanctification and their salvation, and whatever they have done to you, or whatever is going on between you, is putting their souls in danger as much as your own, so don't pray for your enemies' downfall, or you play right into the evil one's hands.

St. Augustine acknowledged that it's virtually impossible to live in the world without enemies, but we need not fear our enemies because there is no way they can hurt us more than we would hurt ourselves by holding a grudge against them.[52] And in case you don't think you have any enemies, the Church fathers defined an enemy as anyone you need to forgive or anyone who "has anything against you" (Matt. 5:23–24), to whom you need to apologize or who may need to forgive you. Sometimes we forget about people with whom we need to reconcile, and we keep a low-grade anger simmering under the surface of our psyche without even realizing it. Other times, the hurt is such that we feel we could not possibly bring ourselves to forgive someone.

The advice of the Church fathers is that if you don't feel ready to forgive someone, start by praying for that person. If you're not ready to pray for his well-being, pray that God will give you the grace you need to get there. Start by praying for the strength to pray for your enemy. Then pray for your enemy. Praying for that person will lead to peace with him because it will help you have empathy for him. And if you have just prayed for the forgiveness of your own sins (and really brought those sins to mind to ask God to forgive them), it would be hard to pretend that you are perfect. Remembering your own sins should also help give you empathy for those who have sinned against you. In fact, the Church fathers would say that even if you never get around to praying for your own forgiveness, you are much more likely to receive it if you've prayed for your enemies and forgiven them.

[52] Augustine of Hippo, *On the Lord's Prayer* 6.6. See also *Confessions* 1.18. Augustine says it is perverse "to imagine that our enemies can do us more harm than we do ourselves by hating them."

Eventually you will be able to forgive your enemy, and then pray for reconciliation, and then you will get to the place where you can truly love your enemy. But we should not wait until we feel ready to forgive before we pray for our enemies. When Jesus said that we must forgive "from the heart" (see Matt. 18:35), remember that in the ancient world's concept of the human body, the heart is the place of the will, the place where *decisions* come from, not where emotions come from (that would be the guts). So Jesus is not saying that you have to *feel* like forgiving someone, he's saying that you have to *decide* to forgive that person. And St. Augustine would say that if you can't at least pray for God to help you forgive someone, then don't bother praying the Our Father, because you would just be heaping hypocrisy on yourself, praying as though you are willing to forgive when you're not.[53]

The other way that the Church fathers talked about forgiveness is as spiritual almsgiving. We're going to cover almsgiving in a later chapter, but in this case, forgiving another person is like almsgiving because it's an act of generosity; it's the canceling of a kind of debt. If the forgiveness includes the actual canceling of a monetary debt, then it's also a case of literal almsgiving, but in any case, when the Church fathers talk about almsgiving, they often include what they considered to be spiritual (or nonmonetary) forms of almsgiving, including forgiving others. As Jesus' parable of the unmerciful servant implies, when we forgive others, we are imitating God and doing what God does.[54]

And lead us not into temptation

The meaning of this line is complicated because the Church fathers tend to make distinctions between three concepts, but these distinctions are not clear in the biblical text, since the same Greek word(s) can be used for all of them. In general, in the Greek, the same word can be translated "tempt" or "test," yet the Church fathers do not see these as synonyms. In fact, there are three categories of tempting/testing that the Church fathers recognize:

1. *Temptation.* To actively tempt someone is something God would never do because it involves deception (James 1:13). Active

[53] See also Gregory of Nyssa, *Sermons on the Lord's Prayer,* Sermon 5.

[54] See also Gregory of Nyssa, *Sermons on the Lord's Prayer,* Sermon 5.

temptation is what comes to us from the demonic or from our own desires. Demons lie to us, or our own "passions" lie to us when we are presented with what seems to be an immediate good but is not a long-term good.

2. *Trial, or abandonment to temptation.*[55] This simply means allowing us to be tempted, and it is obviously something that God does; otherwise, no temptation could ever take place if God did not permit it. After all, the Father allowed the Son to be tempted in the desert. This means God *permits* temptation to come to us, though the temptation itself does not come from God. Since temptation involves deception, this also means that sometimes God does permit us to be deceived.
3. *Testing.* The Church fathers all believed that God does sometimes test us. Testing may be active (God directly putting us in a situation that tests us) or passive (allowing us to be tested by some other entity or situation). Apparently, there is no clear line between passive testing and trial; the only difference may be that passive testing doesn't have the element of deception. A test is a situation in which we know right from wrong, we don't have to discern the right thing to do, but it will require courage and strength to do it. However, a test might include temptations within it. For example, Job was tested, but within his testing was the temptation to give in to despair.

   But the Church fathers point out that the purpose of testing is not for God to learn anything about us or to see what we will do. God already knows how we will respond and whether we will pass or fail the test. The point of testing is for us to discover the truth about ourselves and possibly to be confronted with our weaknesses, perhaps for the sake of humility. This would hopefully result in some kind of improvement in ourselves, such as an increase in faith, or courage, or strength, or a detachment from pride.

55 The clear demarcation of three terms that all begin with *T* is not really there in the Church fathers (nor is the alliteration). This is my way of sorting out what they are saying. To a certain extent, the distinctions between them are more implied than explicit.

To that end, the Church fathers also believed that God might test us as a form of discipline, to chastise us, but ultimately to correct us.[56] Even though God may know that we will fail a test, He may allow us to fall in order to humble us or to drive us back to Him if we have strayed, or both.[57] Like a good parent, God sometimes engages in tough love in order to sanctify us.

With all of this in mind, the Church fathers weigh in on the meaning of this line in the prayer. They all seem to agree that it cannot mean, "Do not allow us to be tempted," since we are constantly tempted, and temptation is a part of the human condition, so that would be a prayer that would never be answered for any significant length of time. Cyril of Jerusalem said that it's not a prayer to avoid temptation but, rather, a prayer that we would not be overwhelmed by temptation — in other words, that we would not be tempted beyond what we can handle (1 Cor. 10:13) and that we would be given the strength to get through the temptation without having given in to it. Like the Red Sea, you can't go around it; you can only go through it, and only with God's help.

Cyprian said that we are praying that God will not test us or discipline us. He makes a distinction between testing and disciplining, but in both cases, he says it's ultimately a case of God's giving us over to the devil or giving the devil power over us.[58] So this is a prayer that God will not give up on us or hand us over to evil (Rom. 1:24). But in the end, he says it's not necessary to understand the ways in which God may test us; it's enough to understand that we are praying for protection from testing.[59]

Other Church fathers, perhaps in an attempt to justify Luke's omission of the last line, conflate this line with the last, as though they mean the same thing.[60]

[56] Augustine of Hippo, *Confessions* 2.2. Heb. 12:7–11. See also Wisd. 1:5; 6:17–18; 7:14.

[57] John Chrysostom, *Homilies on the Gospel of Matthew* 10. Cf. Ps. 119:71; Rom. 1:24; and 2 Cor. 12:7–10 (St. Paul's "thorn in the flesh").

[58] Note that Jeremiah 20:12 says that God tests the just, so testing is not necessarily discipline for sin.

[59] Cyprian of Carthage, *Treatise IV: On the Lord's Prayer* 26–27.

[60] It seems that they are trying too hard to justify Luke's omission, since to say that the two lines mean the same thing would seem to imply that God might be responsible for evil, which every Church father would maintain could not be the case. Cf. Augustine of Hippo, *Confessions* 7.12.

Tertullian said that it means, "Do not allow us to be led into the temptation of the evil one," meaning, "Do not hand us over to the devil." So for Tertullian, this is a prayer for protection from the tempter, the devil.[61] Tertullian specifically mentions the temptation to deny the Faith during times of persecution, and so, for him, this is also a prayer for protection during persecution.[62]

But deliver us from evil

Like Tertullian, Augustine said that this last line means the same thing as the one before it, so the two could be combined as if to say, "Protect us from evil," or "Do not hand us over to the evil one." Gregory of Nyssa said that "temptation" is another name for the devil, and so temptation and "the evil one" are the same thing.[63]

Although some translations will render this in the impersonal, simply "evil" rather than "the evil one," the consensus among the Church fathers is that it should be "the evil one" — that is, the devil (and his demons).[64] Cyril of Jerusalem commented that it doesn't much matter how it's translated, since evil *is* the evil one.

The Our Father Includes a Promise We Are Making

Immediately after teaching His disciples the Our Father, Jesus made a startling statement, highlighting one particular line of the prayer. He said, "If you forgive others their transgressions, your heavenly Father will forgive you. But if you do not forgive others, neither will your Father forgive your transgressions" (Matt. 6:14–15).[65] In other words, our forgiveness — our very salvation — depends on our willingness to forgive others. God will not answer the part of the prayer about forgiving our sins unless we have already forgiven those who have sinned against us. Remember that the line where we make this statement is, grammatically speaking, a done deal. We are saying, in effect, *since I have* forgiven those who sinned against me, *I now ask You, God,* to forgive my sins. The whole thing depends on our not holding a grudge, and if we do hold a

[61] Tertullian, *On Prayer* 8.

[62] Tertullian, *On Fleeing in Persecution* 2.

[63] See also Gregory of Nyssa, *Sermons on the Lord's Prayer,* Sermon 5.

[64] Cf. John 17:15.

[65] Cf. also Mark 11:24–25.

grudge, as Augustine said, we might as well not bother to pray the prayer at all. It is as if we only have the right to ask for the forgiveness of our sins *to the extent that* we have forgiven others or are willing to forgive others.

In this context, the Church fathers bring in not only the parable of the unmerciful servant but also Jesus' words in Matthew 5:23–24, "Therefore, if you bring your gift to the altar, and there recall that your brother has anything against you, leave your gift there at the altar, go first and be reconciled with your brother, and then come and offer your gift," as well as Mark 11:25, "When you stand to pray, forgive anyone against whom you have a grievance, so that your heavenly Father may in turn forgive you your transgressions."[66] The implication is clear: the failure to forgive others is an obstacle to our own prayer and worship and blocks grace — even the grace of the Eucharist.[67] John Chrysostom said that if we do not forgive others, we are "unworthy" of God's forgiveness, calling to mind St. Paul's warning in 1 Corinthians 11, that one might receive the Eucharist "unworthily."[68] Not only that, but if we refuse to forgive others, not only will God refuse to hear our prayers, but He will also refuse other people's prayers for us![69]

To nurse a grudge and refuse to forgive another person is not only the mortal sin of anger; it is also to engage in sinful pride.[70] It is to be the unmerciful servant who forgot just how much was forgiven of him, and by failing to be humble and have empathy for the one who owes him, he insults and offends the judge who forgave him a much greater debt. Cyril of Jerusalem wrote:

> Considering then what we receive, and in return for what, let us not put off nor delay to forgive one another. The offenses committed against us are slight and trivial, and easily settled, but those which we have committed against God are great, and need such mercy as his only is. Take heed, therefore, lest for the slight and trivial sins against you, you shut out for yourself forgiveness from God for your very grievous sins.[71]

[66] See Cyprian of Carthage, *Treatise IV: On the Lord's Prayer* 23.

[67] John Chrysostom, *Homilies on Second Corinthians* 4.

[68] John Chrysostom, *Homilies on Second Corinthians* 2.

[69] John Chrysostom, *Homilies on the Gospel of Matthew* 60.

[70] John Chrysostom, *Homilies on the Gospel of Matthew* 19.

[71] Cyril of Jerusalem, *Catechetical Lectures* 23.16.

And if someone should complain that they have been very greatly wronged, John Chrysostom advises that person to meditate on the ways in which he has greatly wronged God and the mercy God has shown him. In fact, nothing makes us more like God than to be merciful. To be holy is to be forgiving, and to grow in sanctification is to grow in mercy. This is why the Our Father is not the "My Father," so that we are constantly reminded that we are united in prayer to our fellow members in the Body of Christ (even when we pray alone) and so that we will be prevented from harboring anger against anyone, while praying.

Therefore, the Our Father includes a serious responsibility. We make a promise when we pray it, a promise to be grateful enough for God's mercy to be willing to pay it forward to those who have wronged us. If we are not willing to do this, St. Augustine warns, then the whole prayer is a lie and is fruitless.[72] Our prayer is pure only if we can pray it without holding a grudge against anyone.[73]

As we close this chapter, let's compare the traditional translation of the Our Father with the Church fathers' understanding of what each line means:

Traditional Version	**Church Fathers' Interpretation**
Our Father who art in Heaven	Our Father, eternal Creator, Provider, and Protector
Hallowed be Thy name	May Your name always be respected by us and throughout the world
Thy Kingdom come	Fill us with Your Holy Spirit Jesus, return soon, reveal Your Kingdom
Thy will be done On earth as it is in Heaven	May Your will be done, in our lives, in the Church, and in the world
Give us this day our daily bread	Meet our material and spiritual needs
And forgive us our trespasses	Have mercy on us and forgive our sins
As we forgive those who trespass against us	As we show mercy and forgive others
And lead us not into temptation	Do not discipline us, or test us, Give us strength in trial and temptation,
But deliver us from evil	And protect us from the evil one

72 Augustine of Hippo, *Our Lord's Sermon on the Mount* 2.11.

73 Augustine of Hippo, *On Man's Perfection in Righteousness* 9. Cf. Eph. 4:26.

Therefore, to pray like the earliest Christians:

1. **Ask yourself: Who are my enemies?** Think about whether you are holding on to any anger toward anyone. Or is there anyone who has anything against you? If there is anyone with whom a conversation would be awkward for you, consider whether you need to forgive that person. The eighteenth-century spiritual director Jean-Pierre de Caussade wrote, "When you find yourself contradicted or humiliated, [that] is the time to prove to your God the sincerity of your love. Put your trust in his goodness and the power of his grace."[74] Make a decision to forgive, whether you feel like it or not, and begin by praying for the grace to truly forgive. If it's hard to do, think of it as spiritual almsgiving — an act of generosity. De Caussade said, "Pray for the person who is the cause of your trouble."[75] Don't gossip or vent about such people to others; in fact, speak well of them to others. Don't fantasize about conversations with them in which you get the upper hand; instead, think about how you might reconcile with them. As John Chrysostom advised, take the energy you are tempted to use complaining about them, and put that into praying for them, and for yourself, in recognition of your own need to avoid pride and anger. Finally, get to the point where you can pray for your enemies to become your friends, and pray for that. Confront evil with prayer, and with the Sign of the Cross, but confront people with generosity and spiritual almsgiving (Rom. 12:14–21). Repay hurts and wrongs with love and good works (1 Pet. 2:15). Even in those extreme cases in which it might be appropriate to avoid a person, remember that victory over enemies is not in conquering them but in not letting them turn you into an angry person, not letting them steal your joy.

2. **Pray the Our Father; and pray it every day** (as we will see, the early Christians prayed it three times each day). Make it the primary prayer of your private devotions. As you pray this prayer, remember that there is no *my* in the Our Father, and be mindful that you are a part of something greater than yourself — the Body of Christ — and that, even when you are alone, you pray it as a part of a people, and you pray it with and for others. Think about

[74] De Caussade, *Letters on the Practice of Abandonment* 6.2.

[75] De Caussade, *Letters on the Practice of Abandonment* 6.20.

your loved ones when you say the first-person plural pronouns, *our* and *us*. Especially if you are the head of a household or a parent, carry in your mind your household and your children as you pray this prayer. Pray it for them too. Bring everyone in your circle into this prayer, and if there are any who especially need your intercession, remember them in prayer as you pray the Our Father.

3. **Try to limit yourself to praying for today's bread**, not tomorrow's bread. We will go deeper into this concept, but for now, think about this: If it seems awkward to you to pray for Jesus to return soon, consider that you may be a little too attached to the things of this world and this life (another concept we will return to). Consider that you may be a little too focused on the wrong things and not seeking first the Kingdom of God, and work harder to make that your priority. Increasingly, try to live, and pray, one day at a time.

To Go Deeper

Primary Sources[76]

Tertullian, *On Prayer* (written in the early third century), in the Ante-Nicene Fathers Series, vol. 3, https://www.newadvent.org/fathers/0322.htm.

Cyprian of Carthage, *Treatise IV: On the Lord's Prayer* (written in the third century), in the Ante-Nicene Fathers Series, vol. 5, https://www.newadvent.org/fathers/050704.htm.

Gregory of Nyssa, *Sermons on the Lord's Prayer* (written in the late fourth century), in the Ancient Christian Writers Series, vol. 18, trans. Hilda C. Graef (Mahwah, NJ: Paulist Press, 1954).

[76] Origen has been omitted from this study due to the heterodox nature of his writings. In particular, he was reluctant to pray to Jesus Christ, probably out of a subordinationist bias. In any case, he does not represent the mainstream of early Christian practice. St. Maximus the Confessor also has a commentary on the Our Father, which is not included here, only because he is rather late in the early Christian period.

Cyril of Jerusalem, *Catechetical Lecture* 23 (written in the late fourth century), in the Nicene and Post-Nicene Fathers, Series 2, vol. 7, https://www.newadvent.org/fathers/310123.htm.

John Chrysostom, *Homilies on the Gospel of Matthew* (written in the late fourth century), ed. Philip Schaff, trans. George Prevost, rev. M. B. Riddle, in the Nicene and Post-Nicene Fathers, First Series, vol. 10 (Buffalo, NY: Christian Literature, 1888), https://www.newadvent.org/fathers/2001.htm.

Augustine of Hippo, *On the Lord's Prayer* (written in the fifth century), trans. R. G. MacMullen, in Nicene and Post-Nicene Fathers, First Series, vol. 6 (Buffalo, NY: Christian Literature, 1888), https://www.newadvent.org/fathers/160307.htm.

Secondary Sources

James L. Papandrea, *Handed Down: The Catholic Faith of the Early Christians* (El Cajon, CA: Catholic Answers Press, 2015).

James L. Papandrea, *Reading the Church Fathers: A History of the Early Church and the Development of Doctrine* (Manchester, NH: Sophia Institute Press, 2022).

Insight 4

Don't Worry about What Kind of Prayer It Is

(and not all prayer is worship)

First of all, then, I ask that
supplications, prayers, petitions,
and thanksgivings
be offered for everyone.

— St. Paul, 1 Timothy 2:1

Are there different types of prayer? In the passage from 1 Timothy above, is Paul talking about four kinds of prayer, called "supplications," "prayers," "petitions," and "thanksgivings"?[1] If you check the Greek, the words translated "prayer," "petition," and "supplication" are all basically synonyms. Each word has a range of meaning that overlaps so much that every one of those words can be used — and is used in other biblical passages — to describe both prayer for oneself and prayer for others. These are not distinct technical terms for different kinds of prayer. It seems St. Paul is just throwing out a lot of synonyms to cover all possible scenarios (as I think he does with musical terms in Ephesians 5:19 and Colossians 3:16). And this is why the Church fathers don't care about types of prayer.

I noted in the last chapter that the Our Father was always meant to be prayed verbatim. It is not an outline for prayer. Even when the Church fathers say that it's seven prayers in one, they are not talking about different kinds of prayers, as if we could substitute our own prayers of a similar type, turning the Our Father into a kind of template for private devotion. I'm embarrassed to admit that once upon a time I thought of it this way, and early in my career, I even wrote some things about prayer that use the Our Father as a template. But after studying the Church fathers, I now know that the earliest Christians did not see it this way. They did not use acronyms such

[1] Cf. Romans 15:30, Ephesians 6:18, and Philippians 4:6, where the same Greek words are used. Other English words such as *entreaty, request, appeal,* and *intercession,* etc. can be used to translate these terms but there is no one-to-one correspondence between the Greek words and any particular English words. It is also possible that the term *thanksgivings* is a reference to the Eucharistic Prayer.

as "ACTS" (adoration, contrition/confession, thanksgiving, supplication) to create a bullet-point list of types of prayer to pray. Not that there is anything inherently wrong with this approach — it's fine for beginners — but I suspect that if you are reading this book, it's important to you to know how the earliest Christians prayed (those who were closest in time to Jesus and the apostles), and so you want to go deeper and take your prayer to the next level. And the good news is, taking it to the next level does not mean making it more complicated — quite the opposite.

We have also already seen that, for the Church fathers, thanksgiving is not a particular kind of prayer; rather, it is the attitude that we should bring to every prayer.[2] Of course there are some written prayers from the early Church that emphasize thanksgiving (I'll include one from St. John Chrysostom in the sample prayers at the end of the book), and the Eucharistic prayers are considered *the* prayers of thanksgiving, but the Church fathers never thought of thanksgiving as exclusive to certain prayers. In general, all of our prayers should be motivated by gratitude. In fact, I would go so far as to say that all prayer to God is a form of adoration and thanksgiving. Simply by going to God in prayer, we are engaging in an act of worship and thanksgiving. Maybe that's what St. Paul was getting at in Philippians 4:6: "Have no anxiety at all, but in everything, by prayer and petition, *with thanksgiving*, make your requests known to God" (emphasis added). In other words, all your prayers should be prayed, *with thanksgiving*.

When it comes to contrition and confession, the early Christians didn't see these as types of prayer either. Like thanksgiving, contrition was an attitude in which we should approach God with all prayers, and apart from the relevant lines in the Our Father, confession was something that was done in the context of the community (James 5:16) — either as a liturgical act in the Mass, where we are confessing to our fellow Christians (cf. the Confiteor: "I confess to you, my brothers and sisters …"), or directly to a bishop or priest who has the authority to absolve sin (Matt. 16:19; 18:18; John 20:23).

A few of the Church fathers did try to associate particular Greek words with prayer for ourselves versus prayer for others, but they are generally

2 See Justin Martyr, *I Apology* 65, and *Dialogue with Trypho* 117, and John Cassian, *Conferences* 9.14.

unsuccessful at creating a consistent terminology, so no technical terms develop in the early Church, and there is no consensus on which Greek word would indicate prayer for ourselves versus prayer for others. The bottom line is that you don't need to worry about what kind of prayer you are praying. There are, in fact, really only two kinds of prayer — prayer you pray for yourself and prayer you pray for someone else, but even these are not thought of as strictly separate. For our purposes, we will call prayer for others *intercession*. Beyond that, the early Christians did not parse out different kinds of prayer, and you don't need to either.

When people think of different kinds of prayer today, it often has to do with determining different categories of prayer based on what we are asking for. But again, the early Christians didn't think of prayer this way; in fact, they understood that prayer is so much more than asking for things. The Church fathers described prayer as the duty of every Christian, not based on whether you need something specific *from God* at the time but based on the fact that you need to be in prayer *with God* all the time. So it's not so much that prayer exists so that you can ask for something else that you need. Prayer exists because what you need is to pray. Still, it might be informative to see what kinds of things the Church fathers prayed for. We have already gotten a sample of the kinds of things that come up in the intercessions of early Christian liturgy. Beyond that, we can survey a couple of the Church fathers to see how they modeled prayer, and what they thought it was important to pray for.

Have You Met the Clements?

There are two important early Church fathers named Clement. The first is *Clement of Rome*. Clement was a disciple of St. Peter, and the third to succeed him in the office of bishop of Rome. We don't know Clement's given name. He had been a slave in the household of a Christian senator named Flavius Clemens; in fact, he was still a slave when he was chosen to be the bishop, in the year AD 88 — and when Senator Clemens was martyred, the slave became a freedman and took his former patron's name.[3] Clement was bishop of Rome until AD 97, when he, too, was arrested for preaching the Christian faith and

[3] St. Paul mentions a Clement in Philippians 4:3, though it's not clear whether he means the senator or the future bishop. Since the letter was written before

was sent to hard labor in the mines, where he eventually died.[4] Clement of Rome wrote one of the earliest of all Christian documents (that we still have) that is not in the New Testament. Of all existing early Christian documents outside the New Testament, only the *Didache* is earlier. Clement's letter to the church at Corinth, known as *I Clement,* was written at about the same time as the book of Revelation, in about the year 95. And in that letter, we get to see some examples of how Clement prayed. Here's an excerpt:

> [Lord] all of our hope is in your name, for you are the source of all creation. Open the eyes of our hearts so that we may know you, for you alone are the highest of the high, the holiest of the holy. You humble the proud, you confound the plans of the nations, you raise up the humble, and you humble those who try to raise themselves up....
>
> You alone are the Creator and guardian of the spirit and the God of the flesh, looking into the depths of our hearts and scrutinizing the works of our hands. You help those in danger, and save those in despair....
>
> We ask you, Master, to be our helper and protector. Save those among us who are in distress, have mercy on the humiliated, raise up the fallen, show yourself to those in need, heal the sick, turn back those of your people who wander, feed the hungry, ransom our prisoners, raise up the weak, comfort the discouraged. Let all the nations know that you are the only God, that Jesus Christ is your Son, and that we are your people and the sheep of your pasture....
>
> For you, Lord, are faithful to those who trust in you, merciful and compassionate. Forgive our sins and our injustices, our transgressions and our shortcomings. Do not take into account every sin of your servants, but cleanse us with the purification of your truth, and direct our steps to walk in holiness and justice and purity of heart, and to do what is good and pleasing in your sight....
>
> Yes, Lord, let your face shine on us in peace for our good, so that we may be protected by your powerful hand and delivered from

the future bishop's manumission, it is probably the senator who is being referred to.

[4] For more detail, see Papandrea, *Reading the Church Fathers,* 42–49.

> every sin by your outstretched arm. Deliver us also from those who hate us unjustly. Give harmony and peace to us and to all who live on the earth....
>
> You are the only one who can do these things, and even greater good things for us. We praise you through the high priest and benefactor of our souls, Jesus Christ, through whom be the glory and the majesty to you both now and for all generations and for ever and ever.[5]

The other important Clement in the early Church lived about a century later, writing at the end of the second century. This is *Clement of Alexandria.* As far as we know, Clement of Alexandria was a priest, and from AD 190, he was the lead catechist in the city of Alexandria, but he was never the bishop. We call him Clement "of Alexandria" to distinguish him from Clement of Rome. He was originally a philosopher, and, in fact, he had studied every school of philosophy available at the time, surveyed all of his options, and in the end, he decided that the best philosophy was Christianity. He wrote several lengthy documents and gives us a very detailed window into the life of the early Church — or at least he tells us how it *should* be. Often Clement of Alexandria represents the stricter side of Christianity, to the point where he writes as though anything enjoyable must be a sin. Nevertheless, we can glean from his writings some clues as to the kinds of things he thought Christians were supposed to pray for. When persecution came to Alexandria, in about AD 202, Clement fled to Jerusalem and beyond and eventually died in exile.

By looking at the two Clements, along with some of the other Church fathers, we can come up with a list of things the Church fathers prayed for, at least as evidenced in their writings.[6] But keep in mind that, most of the time, these Church fathers were not intending to teach people how to pray, and they do not give their people any new verbatim prayers to be repeated — the expectation is that people are praying the Our Father.[7]

[5] Clement of Rome, *I Clement* 59–61, paraphrased. This paraphrase was first published in James L. Papandrea, *Rome: A Pilgrim's Guide to the Eternal City* (Eugene, OR: Cascade, 2012), 90–91.

[6] See for example, Tertullian, *On Prayer* 29.

[7] By the end of the early Christian period, the Church order documents, such as the *Apostolic Constitutions,* do include some formalized prayers,

Beyond that, the lists below are simply some examples of what the Church fathers prayed for, which we can assume would have been imitated by the early Christians. You'll see that everything is grounded in biblical precedent, and much of what we see is repeated in the Our Father itself. I've divided the list according to whether the prayer is for oneself or for someone else.

Praying for Oneself

It seems the early Christians were encouraged (by example) to pray for the forgiveness of their sins, for direction in discerning God's will, for sanctification, for protection from evil and danger (including persecution), for the strength to resist temptation, and for the grace to continue to be thankful even in adversity.[8]

Beyond that, John Chrysostom notes that we should not pray for anything worldly but only for spiritual things, and in this way we "seek first the kingdom" (Matt. 6:33). He reasons that if we trust God for the things of the Kingdom, then, as Jesus promised, God will also give us the earthly things we need.[9]

We get the sense from the Church fathers that prayer for ourselves should be kept to a minimum and should not be for things or comforts but for graces and guidance. If we take the advice of our North African Church fathers, Cyprian and Augustine, prayer for ourselves would be limited to what's in the Our Father. In fact, it could be argued that everything in the list above is already covered in the Our Father. That's not to say we cannot pray for our own particular situations, but as we will see, if we follow the lead of the early Christians, we will keep our prayers as general as possible, in order to leave as much room as possible for God to answer our prayers and work in our lives according to His perfect will.

---

which were apparently meant to be prayed verbatim. However, this is a late development, and it is not clear to what extent these prayers were prayed by lay Christians. See *Apostolic Constitutions* 7.47–49.

[8] Tertullian, *On Prayer* 24; John Chrysostom, *Homilies on Philippians* 3. Chrysostom remarks, "How can one ask for future things, if one is not thankful for past?"

[9] John Chrysostom, *Homilies on Matthew* 23.

Praying for Others — Intercessions

In terms of intercessory prayer, early Christians were encouraged to pray for the healing of the sick, for the return to the Church of any who had gone astray, for protection for loved ones and fellow Christians, for the conversion of their neighbors, and for the growth of the Church (implied also is prayer for the clergy).[10] One of the most common admonitions is prayer for the well-being of government leaders — including those who were persecuting them (1 Tim. 2:2).[11] So they are praying for their persecutors, but not simply in the sense of praying for them to stop the persecution (they did that, but that would be in the category above). Rather, they were praying for their enemies in the way that we discussed in the last chapter.[12] Bishop Polycarp of Smyrna wrote in the early second century, "Pray also for kings, and magistrates, and princes, and for those that persecute and hate you, and for the enemies of the cross, that your fruit may be manifest to all, and that you may be perfect in him."[13] His colleague Bishop Ignatius of Antioch wrote that everyone should pray for the salvation of all, especially enemies and persecutors, and those who slander the Christians, and that these prayers must be backed up with good works that will witness to them so that they will be motivated to convert.[14]

Essentially, intercession is praying for God to show mercy on someone. As John Chrysostom pointed out, all answered prayer is an act of mercy on God's part, since God owes us nothing, and we deserve nothing.[15] But just as Jesus was motivated by compassion while in His earthly ministry, so God is still motivated by compassion to answer our prayers. And when we pray for someone else, we get to participate in God's mercy (cf. 1 Cor.

[10] See Cyprian of Carthage, *Treatise V: Address to Demetrianus* 20.

[11] Clement of Rome, *I Clement* 61. This prayer for the emperor comes during a time of persecution. See also Polycarp of Smyrna, *Letter to the Philippians* 12 (Polycarp himself was martyred not long after writing this), and Theophilus of Antioch, *To Autolychus* 1.11.

[12] Cf. Cyprian of Carthage, *On Patience* 16.

[13] Polycarp of Smyrna, *Letter to the Philippians* 12.

[14] Ignatius of Antioch, *Letter to the Ephesians* 10; John Chrysostom, *Homilies on Thessalonians* 1.

[15] John Chrysostom, *Homilies on Second Corinthians* 2.

3:9). In fact, the greater the number of people who pray for something, the more powerful the prayer is (as long as the people praying are sincere and virtuous), so when it comes to intercession, quantity matters.[16] Chrysostom went on to say how virtuous nations have won wars with prayer, so in this way, when enough people pray together, prayer can be a powerful weapon. He wrote, "Prayer is a mighty weapon if made with a suitable mind" (i.e., with sincerity and humility).[17] St. Cyprian went so far as to say that if the Church does not agree in prayer, their prayers may not be heard.[18]

The early Church had specially designated ministries of prayer. In addition to prayer (especially for the Church) being the duty of every Christian, the early Church had consecrated orders of virgins and widows, whose vocation it was to pray intercessions.[19] The widows, and the poor in general, were also expected to pray for those who gave them alms.

It is interesting to note the general absence of prayers for peace on earth.[20] The early Christians did not talk much about praying for peace on earth, since they seem to have thought that was covered under the prayer, "May your kingdom come." In other words, they did not believe there would be peace on earth until the return of Christ. The peace that early Christians hoped for was more along the lines of what we would call peace of mind — and that in spite of the lack of peace in the world. A Christian could have peace of mind by reconciliation with God through Christ and by His sacraments in the Church and could even hope to have joy in the midst of a hard and dangerous life.

Not All Prayer Is Worship: The Four Facets of Intercession

The early Christians believed that intercession happens in four "directions": The living pray for the living, the living pray for the dead, the dead pray for the living, and the dead pray for the dead.

[16] John Chrysostom, *Homilies on Second Corinthians* 2. He clarifies that a huge group of unrepentant sinners praying together would do no good.

[17] John Chrysostom, *Homilies on Hebrews* 27.

[18] Cyprian of Carthage, *Epistle* 73.

[19] *Didascalia* 3.5; *Apostolic Constitutions* 3.13.

[20] Tertullian is the exception to this; he does mention praying for world peace. Tertullian, *On Prayer* 29.

The Living Pray for the Living

We've already seen, in our survey of the intercessions in early liturgies and in the list above, what the Church fathers thought about living people praying for each other. And when we remember the very communal nature of the Our Father (that it is not "my Father"), we see that intercession is an important part of the prayer that Jesus taught us. Of course, Scripture is full of examples of people praying for each other, as St. James advised: "Pray for one another, that you may be healed. The [fervent] prayer of a righteous person is very powerful" (5:16). Incidentally, I've put the word "fervent" in brackets because that adjective is not actually in the Greek text. The point is *not* that "fervent" prayers are powerful, as if the power of the prayer is in the urgency or the sincerity of the prayer. The Church fathers understood the point of this passage — the point is that the prayers *of a righteous person* are powerful. The power of the prayer is, of course, ultimately in the power of God, but instrumentally it is in the *holiness* of the one praying. And as we have already noted, holiness requires forgiving others and doing good works.

So now we turn to the other facets of intercession: the intercession of the saints and prayer for the dead.

The Dead Pray for the Living

As we noted at the beginning of the book, not all worship is prayer. Praise (in the grammatical third person) is a form of worship that is not exactly prayer because we are not talking directly *to* God; we are addressing others, taking *about* God. Conversely, not all prayer is worship. When we pray *to God*, we are speaking to God, and by expressing our trust in God, it is a form of worship. But we can pray to others besides God — specifically, the saints of our Faith who have gone before us — and when we do this, we are not worshipping them; we are only asking them to pray for us.[21]

[21] Christians have never worshipped the saints. We do not try to discern their will for us or submit to their wills; we do not name them as divine persons in our creeds; and we do not conduct sacraments in their names. We do not ascribe divine attributes to them. We also do not ask them for information or power, and so the intercession of the saints is not a form of the occult, as would be forbidden under the Old Testament prohibition of necromancy

To pray to the saints assumes the simplest definition of the word *pray* — it just means to ask for something, and all we are asking for is prayer. We do not expect the saints to be able to *do* anything for us, other than pray for us.[22] We do not ascribe any divine power to them — only God can intervene. We do not even think they can hear our prayers on their own. They can hear our prayers only because God gives them the ability, as a result of their holiness and for the purpose of their ministry of intercession. The saints in Heaven are not omnipotent or omniscient. But by God's grace, they can hear our prayers, they can pray for us, and they can pray with us. The early Christians understood this, and they believed that the dividing line between this life and the next is not a barrier to prayer (cf. Luke 16:22–24). They saw biblical precedents for the intercession of the saints in Tobit 12:14 (Raphael, admittedly an archangel and not a deceased Christian, intercedes for people), 2 Maccabees 15:14 (Jeremiah, though long dead, prays for the people of Jerusalem), Baruch 3:4, and, of course, Revelation 5:8 and 8:4.[23] As Jesus said, God is the God of the living, and those who have passed on are not dead at all, but are more alive than ever (Matt. 22:31–32; Mark 12:26–27; Luke 20:38; cf. Phil 1:21).[24]

When their loved ones or other fellow Christians died, the early Christians continued the Roman tradition of the *refrigerium*, the memorial meal, often held at the grave site of the dearly departed.[25] And when the deceased

---

(Deut. 18:10). For more detail on the intercession of the saints in the early Church, see Papandrea, *Handed Down*, chap. 5, "The Communion of Saints."

[22] Even those traditional prayers to the saints that sound as if we are asking them to help us directly assume the implied, "through your intercession." On the other hand, it may be the case that those saints who are also archangels, St. Michael, St. Gabriel, and St. Raphael, may have some angelic powers of protection. But this would be the exception to the rule, since they are angels, not humans.

[23] There was also a tradition in Judaism that the matriarch Rachel prayed for her descendants, the people of Israel, during the exile. See Shane Kapler, *The Biblical Roots of Marian Consecration: Devotion to the Immaculate Heart in Light of Scripture* (Gastonia, NC: TAN Books, 2022), 99.

[24] See also Jerome, *To Vigilantius* 6, and Augustine of Hippo, *City of God* 20.9.

[25] See the *Didascalia* 6.22, and Cyprian of Carthage, *Epistle* 36.2. The *refrigerium* was held annually on the anniversary of the loved one's death. This is how we get our tradition of celebrating a saint's feast day, and in the case of

was a martyr, these memorial meals — the original feasts of the saints — often included the Eucharist as well as hymns, Scripture readings, the reading or telling of the story of the martyr's life and heroic death, and prayers. And these prayers included prayers directed to the martyrs in Heaven, asking for their intercession. At the *refrigerium* site in the excavations of the Catacombs of San Sebastiano in Rome, there are many examples of graffiti, where early Christians scratched prayers into the walls of the cemetery. These graffiti inscribe prayers to Mary, Peter, Paul, and other saints, asking them for their prayers. So we can see from the archaeological evidence as well as documents, that the early Christians practiced the intercession of the saints. Early Christians gathered at the catacombs and other cemeteries to commemorate those who had already finished the race and to ask for their prayers for those still in it (Heb. 12:1–3). St. Jerome wrote, "If apostles and martyrs while still in the body can pray for others, when they ought still to be anxious for themselves, how much more must they do so when once they have won their crowns, overcome, and triumphed?"[26]

Before long, the early Christians started to pray to certain saints based on the details of their lives (and deaths). Their occupation, an illness they suffered, or the way they were martyred all became things that the early Christians could connect to their own situations and their own lives — and this is how we got the idea of patron saints. People ask for the intercession of those saints with whom they feel they share some affinity. St. Sebastian was a soldier, so he is the patron saint of soldiers and first responders. St. Lawrence was executed by being burned alive on a grill, and so he is the patron saint of cooks. It may sound trivial, but it's been a part of the tradition of our Faith from the very beginning. The important thing is that those who are already in eternity with our Lord are ready and willing to pray for us, if we just ask them.

---

martyrs, this is usually the day they died. Because of the Christian doctrine of the resurrection, and the assumed eternal connection between the soul in Heaven and the body on earth, awaiting the resurrection, the presence of a saint's remains (relics) made the tomb or grave site holy ground. For more on the doctrine of the resurrection in the early Church, see Papandrea, *What Really Happens After We Die?*

26 Jerome, *To Vigilantius* 6.

St. Cyprian, writing in a time of persecution, even advised the living who might soon become martyrs, to remember that when they get to Heaven, they should pray for those still alive: "Let us relieve the burdens and afflictions by mutual love, that if any one of us by the swiftness of divine condescension, shall go hence the first, our love may continue in the presence of the Lord, and our prayers for our brothers and our sisters not cease in the presence of the Father's mercy."[27] Gregory of Nazianzus, in the eulogy for his father, said, "I am well assured that his intercession is of more avail now than was his instruction in former days, since he is closer to God."[28]

To give just one more example, Cyril of Jerusalem told his catechumen, as they were preparing for Baptism, "We commemorate also those who have fallen asleep before us, first patriarchs, prophets, apostles, martyrs, that at their prayers and intercessions God would receive our petition."[29] It's been said that the intercession of the saints is less about praying *to* the saints and more about praying *with* the saints. That is certainly true. When we ask the saints for their intercession, we are joining their prayers to ours and essentially asking them to pray with us for whatever we are praying for.

The Living Pray for the Dead

It is clear that the tradition of Masses for the dead goes all the way back to the beginning of the Church, in that same continuation of the tradition of the *refrigerium,* in which we find the origin of the feast of the saints. In those memorial meals, and, indeed, in the funeral Masses, the early Christians assumed that the intercession of the Mass would be focused on the departed person in whose memory they gathered, and of course they assumed that their prayers could benefit that person, even though he or she had already passed on.[30] After all, if St. Paul thought that someone could be baptized for

[27] Cyprian of Carthage, *Epistle* 56.5 (written in about AD 252).

[28] Gregory of Nazianzus, *Orations* 18.4 (ca. AD 374).

[29] Cyril of Jerusalem, *Catechetical Lectures* 23.9.

[30] *Didascalia* 6.22; *Apostolic Constitutions* 8.4.41. Cf. Cyprian of Carthage, *Epistle* 33.3.

the dead, how much more could the Sacrament of the Eucharist be celebrated for the benefit of the dead![31]

Tertullian said that prayer benefits the dead and that we should pray for the eternal rest of departed souls, and offer Masses on the anniversary of their deaths. In fact, he thought it was the solemn duty of every widow to continue to make sure that annual Masses were offered for their deceased husbands.[32] Cyril of Jerusalem wrote that prayer for the dead is of great benefit to the departed because we are asking Christ to have mercy on their souls.[33] And St. Augustine remarked that it was a universal teaching of the Church fathers that our prayers are of benefit to the dead.[34]

In the Old Testament book of 2 Maccabees, Judas Maccabeus organizes a sacrifice to atone for the sins of some of his dead soldiers. The narrator of the text comments, "In doing this he acted in a very excellent and noble way, inasmuch as he had the resurrection in mind; for if he were not expecting the fallen to rise again, it would have been superfluous and foolish to pray for the dead. But if he did this with a view to the splendid reward that awaits those who had gone to rest in godliness, it was a holy and pious thought"

31 1 Cor. 15:29. In spite of Paul's comment here, there is no evidence that early Christians ever practiced Baptism for the dead, though Didymus the Blind had heard that the Marcionites (a heretical sect) practiced it. He criticized them for it, saying they did not know that "baptism saves only the person who receives it." Didymus the Blind, *Pauline Commentary from the Greek Church*. If it was done at all in the New Testament era, the practice did not stand the test of time and was discontinued by the second half of the first century. Other Church fathers read Paul's statement as though it is simply a reference to Christian Baptism. Chrysostom said, "We are baptized in the hope that our dead bodies will be raised again," as if Paul's phrase "baptism for the dead" means "baptism for the resurrection from the dead." John Chrysostom, *Homilies on Corinthians* 40.2.

32 Tertullian, *On the Crown* 3; *On Monogamy* 10. By "monogamy," Tertullian means marriage only once, discouraging second marriages, even for widows. This text does not address polygamy *per se*.

33 Cyril of Jerusalem, *Catechetical Lectures* 23.9–10.

34 Augustine of Hippo, *Sermon* 173.2; *On Care to Be Had for the Dead* 7. Augustine also says that our alms can benefit the dead. On this point, see also John Chrysostom, *Homilies on Philippians* 3, and Jerome, *Epistle* 66.5. We will discuss almsgiving in the next chapter.

(2 Macc. 12:43–45).[35] The early Christians took this as biblical confirmation that it is appropriate to pray for the dead, though they did not believe that their prayers could atone for the sins of the dead in such a way as to bring them to salvation if they were not already going on to eternal life.[36] In other words, if someone was headed for Hell, no prayers of the living could change that, but the prayers of the living could help those who were on their way to Heaven.

The Dead Pray for the Dead

It is also true that the saints in Paradise can pray for the souls in Purgatory.[37] So it is a normal expression of concern for our loved ones who have passed on to ask for the saints to pray for them as well.

Have You Met St. Perpetua?

Perpetua was a young woman in her early twenties, living in Carthage, in North Africa, at the turn of the third century. She had entered into the catechumenate of the Church and was in preparation for her Baptism when, in the year AD 203, she and the rest of her catechism classmates were arrested by the local authorities and imprisoned for practicing the Christian faith. She was eventually martyred on March 7, which we now celebrate as her feast day. During her time in prison, awaiting her execution, she kept a diary, which was later completed (with the account of her martyrdom) and published — perhaps by Tertullian. Thus, she is another one of a very small number of early Christian women whom we can read in her own words.

While she was in prison, Perpetua spent a lot of time in prayer, and she records dreams and visions that she had, some of which were prophetic in nature, and apparently meant to give her and her friends courage to face the ordeal of their execution. In one of these dreams, Perpetua saw her younger brother Dinocrates, who had died at the age of seven. In her prayers, she

[35] See Augustine of Hippo, *On Care to Be Had for the Dead* 3, 22.

[36] Augustine of Hippo, *On Care to Be Had for the Dead* 6; *City of God* 21.13, 24. Augustine explains that prayers for the dead can help only those who were baptized and who were not so sinful that they were damned to Hell. See also Gregory the Great, *Dialogue* 4.41.

[37] Augustine of Hippo, *On Care to Be Had for the Dead* 7.

had been prompted to pray for him, and now she saw him in a dream, as she described in in her own words: "I saw Dinocrates going out from a gloomy place, where also there were several others, and he was parched and very thirsty, with a filthy countenance and pallid color, and the wound on his face which he had when he died."[38]

Perpetua prayed for her brother; she writes:

> I was upset, and knew that my brother was in suffering. But I trusted that my prayer would bring help to his suffering; and I prayed for him every day until we passed over into the prison of the camp ... and I made my prayer for my brother day and night, groaning and weeping that he might be granted to me. Then ... [presumably in another dream] this was shown to me: I saw that the place which I had formerly observed to be in gloom was now bright; and Dinocrates, with a clean body well clad, was finding refreshment. And where there had been a wound, I saw a scar.... Then I understood that he was translated from the place of punishment.[39]

Dinocrates was not in Hell — if he were, no prayers from his sister could help him. So what was the "gloomy place," the "place of punishment" that he was transferred out of because of her prayers? That place is Purgatory. The early Christians did believe in Purgatory, and the Church fathers did teach that our prayers could benefit the souls in Purgatory. Perpetua's prayers transferred her brother from Purgatory into Paradise.

St. Augustine wrote:

> Temporary punishments are suffered by some in this life only, by others after death, by others both now and then; but all of them before that last and strictest judgment. But of those who suffer temporary punishments after death, all are not doomed to those everlasting pains which are to follow that judgment; for to some, as we have already said, what is not remitted in this world is remitted in the next, that is, they are not punished with the eternal punishment of the world to come....

[38] Vibia Perpetua, *Diary of Perpetua* 2.3. According to Perpetua, he had died of some form of cancer.

[39] Vibia Perpetua, *Diary of Perpetua* 2.3–4.

> For some of the dead, indeed, the prayer of the Church or of pious individuals is heard; but it is for those who, having been regenerated in Christ, did not spend their life so wickedly that they can be judged unworthy of such compassion, nor so well that they can be considered to have no need of it.[40]

To paraphrase St. Augustine a bit, there are three categories of deceased people: those who were not Christians or who were bad enough to go to Hell (our prayers cannot help them), those who were martyrs or other saints who were so holy that they don't need our prayers (in fact, Augustine said we should not pray for them since they should be praying for us),[41] and those who were neither bad enough to go to Hell nor good enough to go straight to Heaven. This last, "middle" category would be the souls in Purgatory.

What Did the Earliest Christians Believe about Purgatory?

One could write a whole book on Purgatory, so this is not the place for a complete description of the doctrine of Purgatory or the Church's teaching on the subject.[42] All we can do at the moment is ask what the Church fathers taught and what the earliest Christians believed about it.[43] As we read in St. Augustine, Purgatory is a "temporary punishment" after a person's personal death but before the general resurrection and final judgment. To be in purgatory is to be "purified and melted by the fire of God's love."[44] Both Perpetua

[40] Augustine of Hippo, *City of God* 21.13, 24.

[41] Augustine of Hippo, *Sermon* 159.1; cf. *City of God* 21.24.

[42] For more detail on the subject of Purgatory in the context of the doctrine of the resurrection, see Papandrea, *What Really Happens After We Die?*, 76–80.

[43] Historically, there has been a perception that Eastern Christians did not believe in Purgatory. It is true that the Orthodox Church speaks of the purification after death in different ways than the West and that the later developments in the Western doctrine of Purgatory have been a matter of debate between East and West, but the essence of the belief as it was in the early Church (as I am describing it here) is the same and is based on the same Scripture texts and Church fathers. In particular, Gregory of Nyssa is evidence of an Eastern Church father who wrote about Purgatory. See *On the Soul and the Resurrection* and *On Infants' Early Deaths*.

[44] Augustine of Hippo, *Confessions* 11.29.

and Augustine describe it as a (gloomy) "place"; however, we should not push our conceptions of location, or, indeed, even punishment, too far into the literal, since Purgatory is outside the realm of space and time and those who are experiencing Purgatory are without their bodies.[45]

Nevertheless, Purgatory is understood to be a kind of suffering. As Augustine says, some people suffer mostly in this life and not so much in the next. Other people suffer in this life and in the next. And then there are people who don't suffer much at all in this life but do suffer in the next life. Again, we're talking only about people who are going on to salvation, so this suffering in the afterlife cannot refer to Hell. What, then, is this suffering, and what is the point of it?

In 1 Corinthians 3:11–15, St. Paul wrote:

> No one can lay a foundation other than the one that is there, namely, Jesus Christ. If anyone builds on this foundation with gold, silver, precious stones, wood, hay, or straw, the work of each will come to light, for the Day will disclose it. It will be revealed with fire, and the fire [itself] will test the quality of each one's work. If the work stands that someone built upon the foundation, that person will receive a wage. But if someone's work is burned up, that one will suffer loss; the person will be saved, but only as through fire.

Let's take note of a few significant aspects of the way the Church fathers and the earliest Christians interpreted this text.

First of all, the early (and medieval) Church did not teach a doctrine of "faith alone." In fact, the only place where the phrase "faith alone" appears in the Bible is in the letter of James, where he writes, "a person is justified by works and *not* by faith alone" (2:24, emphasis added). Jesus Himself, in His parable of the sheep and the goats (Matt. 25), makes it very clear that at least part of our individual judgment depends on our works, specifically whether we engaged in works of mercy.[46] So when we die, we come to the point of our personal judgment, having to take

45 Gregory of Nyssa, *On the Soul and the Resurrection*.

46 Augustine of Hippo, *Handbook on Faith, Hope, and Love* 69. Augustine remarked that because the "goats" did not give alms, they should not hope for any help from the living after their death.

responsibility for our works, whether good or bad. This is what is meant by the gold or silver (good works) or hay or straw (sinful works), though St. Chrysostom is quick to point out that the judgment of the works refers to the effort, not the results ("a teacher cannot be faulted merely because his pupils refuse to listen"!).[47]

In 2 Corinthians 5:10, St. Paul writes, "We must all appear before the judgment seat of Christ, so that each one may receive recompense, according to what he did in the body, whether good or evil." To "receive recompense" means more than simply a judgment of Heaven or Hell. It also means that, for those of us who are going on to Heaven, we must be purified of the residual effects of our sins.[48] St. Augustine said, "During the time which intervenes between a person's death and the final resurrection, the soul dwells in a hidden retreat, where it enjoys rest [Paradise] or suffers affliction [Purgatory] just in proportion to the merit it has earned by the life which it led on earth."[49]

This suffering of affliction is what it means for our works to be "burned up." But we need to be very clear: fire in this context is not a metaphor for

[47] John Chrysostom, *Homilies on Corinthians* 9.5. The Church would later develop a doctrine of the treasury of the Church, in which the good works of the most holy saints would accrue merit that could be applied to the living or to the souls in Purgatory. This is why St. Paul can talk about building on the foundation of Christ and "filling up what is lacking in the afflictions of Christ" (Col. 1:24). It is not that there is anything we can do to add to the all-sufficient suffering of Christ in His Passion but, rather, that we can participate in it by joining our suffering to that of Christ, either in the Mass, in prayer, or in good works. When we intercede for the souls in Purgatory, we join our intercession to Jesus' own (Rom. 8:17, 34; Heb. 7:25).

[48] The Church fathers did not clarify exactly what these residual effects are. However, they do seem to have assumed that this applies only to post-baptismal sin, since any sins committed before Baptism were already purified by the sacrament. The later Church developed a doctrine of the temporal effects of sin and clarified the difference between temporal and eternal punishment. The reader is encouraged to learn more about this, though it is outside the scope of the present book.

[49] Augustine of Hippo, *Handbook on Faith, Hope, and Love* 109. Translation adapted and bracketed terms added for clarification.

destruction; it is a metaphor for purification.[50] This is what the word *purgatory* means: a purging or purification. This is why St. Paul can say that a person is saved through fire.[51] To be confronted with our sins at the end of our lives would indeed be a painful moment, if only for the shame and regret.[52] But beyond that, those who are not martyrs will need to be purified before they can enter the heavenly realm of Paradise and the unveiled presence of God.[53] For St. Augustine, that means being purified of the earthly attachments that led us to sin.[54] Our good works are not burned up — we carry them into Paradise with us; but even though our sins are forgiven, there remains some corruption in us that needs to be purified. The point is that, according to St. Paul, in order for us to receive salvation and enter Heaven, this dross has to be burned off. We must be presented to the presence of God unblemished.[55] This is, in fact, the completion of our process of sanctification.

In Gregory of Nyssa's treatise *On the Soul and the Resurrection*, he relates to his readers the teaching of his sister St. Macrina:

> Just as those who refine gold from the dross which it contains not only get this base alloy to melt in the fire, but are obliged to melt the pure gold along with the alloy, and then while this last is being consumed the gold remains, so, while evil is being consumed in the purgatorial fire, the soul that is welded to this evil must inevitably be in the fire too, until the spurious material alloy is consumed and annihilated by this fire.

[50] See Ps. 17:3; 66:10; 119:140; Wisd. 3:1–7; Sir. 2:5; Ezek. 10; Zech. 13:9; Mark 9:49; James 5:3; 1 Pet. 1:7; Rev. 3:18.

[51] Augustine of Hippo, *Handbook on Faith, Hope, and Love* 68–69.

[52] Cf. the apocryphal 2 Esdras 7:78–87.

[53] Just as, in the Old Testament, those who found themselves to be "unclean" could not approach the presence of God in the temple until they performed the necessary cleansing rituals, so when we die, we cannot approach the presence of God in the Beatific Vision until we are purified. Martyrs are exempt from Purgatory because they are purified by their martyrdom, which the Church fathers called a baptism in their own blood.

[54] Augustine of Hippo, *Handbook on Faith, Hope, and Love* 69.

[55] Eph. 5:27; Rev. 21:27.

> If a clay of the more tenacious kind is deeply plastered round a rope, and then the end of the rope is put through a narrow hole, and then someone on the further side violently pulls it by that end, the result must be that, while the rope itself obeys the force exerted, the clay that has been plastered upon it is scraped off it with this violent pulling and is left outside the hole, and, moreover, is the cause why the rope does not run easily through the passage, but has to undergo a violent tension at the hands of the puller. In such a manner, I think, we may figure to ourselves the agonized struggle of that soul which has wrapped itself up in earthy material passions, when God is drawing it, His own one, to Himself, and the foreign matter, which has somehow grown into its substance, has to be scraped from it by main force, and so occasions it that keen intolerable anguish. Then it seems, I said, that it is not punishment chiefly and principally that the Deity, as Judge, afflicts sinners with; but He operates, as your argument has shown, only to get the good separated from the evil and to attract it into the communion of blessedness. That, said the Teacher [Macrina] is my meaning; and also that the agony will be measured by the amount of evil there is in each individual. For it would not be reasonable to think that the man who has remained so long as we have supposed in evil known to be forbidden, and the man who has fallen only into moderate sins, should be tortured to the same amount in the judgment upon their vicious habit; but according to the quantity of material will be the longer or shorter time that that agonizing flame will be burning; that is, as long as there is fuel to feed it.[56]

As St. Macrina shows us with this beautiful analogy of a rope encrusted with clay, this process of purification is painful in some way, considered a form of suffering, but it results in healing and purification. As far as the image

[56] Gregory of Nyssa, *On the Soul and the Resurrection*. See also *On the Early Deaths of Infants*. Note that for Gregory (and Macrina), Scripture passages that suggest different rewards for different people in the afterlife (such as the parable of the talents) are actually about Purgatory, not about different rewards in the Kingdom of Heaven (which would more appropriately be described by the parable of the workers in the vineyard, in which all the workers receive the same reward).

of fire goes, it is like a cauterization, so that, in Purgatory, the "punishment" for sin is also its cure (cf. Isa. 6:5–7).[57] Still, the suffering is significant enough that it is considered a work of mercy for us to pray that the suffering of the souls in Purgatory would be lessened.

This brings us back to St. Augustine's statement that some people suffer more in this life, and others suffer more in the next life. There seems to be an assumption among the early Christians that the more one suffers in this life, the less that person will suffer in Purgatory (cf. 1 Pet. 4:1–2). In terms of the practice of the Christian life, what this means is that the more one takes on penance in this life, the more one reduces the corruption of sin, and the less that person will have to experience the painful effects of the purification of Purgatory. In other words, penance is itself a purifier, perhaps as an act of reparation or perhaps simply as a result of the inherent self-sacrifice and patience it requires. The penance we do in this life is a kind of good work, and it contributes to our sanctification by getting us to "rid ourselves of every burden and sin that clings to us" (Heb. 12:1).[58] So although we are meant to do good works and penance all our lives, participating in the process of our own sanctification, that process is completed only after our death, in Purgatory. And we should not be so bold as to assume that we can become entirely sanctified in this life — we all should expect to experience Purgatory.[59] With that in mind, the early Christians believed that we can lessen the suffering of the souls in Purgatory through our prayers and even

[57] This is why Purgatory cannot be considered to be simply "temporary Hell." In Hell, one is separated from God. In Purgatory, God is there, since it is He who is doing the purifying. The suffering of Purgatory is, in fact, a hopeful suffering, whereas the suffering of Hell is a suffering that includes despair and hopelessness.

[58] Many of the Church fathers would also interpret Jesus' statements about pruning (such as John 15:2) as references to purification from sin, sinful desires, and the corruption of sin. Any necessary pruning that was not done in life through discipline, self-control, and penance would have to be completed in Purgatory. We will return to the idea of pruning as purification below.

[59] The exception is the martyrs, as I have noted, since their martyrdom completes their sanctification before their death. Another exception is the "Good Thief," called St. Dismas by tradition. Jesus could say to him, "Today you will be with me in Paradise" (Luke 23:43) because he had, in effect, availed

by doing penance and giving alms on their behalf. In fact, it could be said that prayer for the dead is a form of almsgiving, an act of generosity toward another person. And in this way, through our intercession even for the dead, we can participate in God's mercy and be God's co-workers (1 Cor. 3:9).

The Church fathers never really say exactly *how* our prayers help the souls in Purgatory, only that we should pray for them. Perhaps in part, our prayers help because the souls in Purgatory are given the gift of being aware that someone is praying for them. And for our loved ones especially, if they are aware that they are loved and remembered, that may do something to mitigate the pain that comes from the shame and regret of having to be confronted with a lifetime of sin. It's much more than that, and that takes us beyond the scope of this book, but if you want something concrete to hold in your mind as you pray for your loved ones who have passed on, perhaps this idea will be a starting point.

Less Is More

One more observation is in order before we close this chapter. There is a conspicuous brevity to the prayers of the early Church. Certainly, as time goes on, liturgical prayers develop to greater length, but when it comes to the prayers that laypeople might pray, early Christians were not encouraged to go on at length. For one thing, God doesn't need us to. As mentioned earlier, God is omniscient and therefore knows the situation better than we do (whether we are praying for someone else or for ourselves), and so God does not require us to give Him the whole backstory, let alone outline the details of what we think he should do about it. But in addition to that, there is a sense in the early Church that extemporaneous prayer was a "don't try this at home" situation. It was not meant to be done by laypeople — certainly not to lead prayer out loud in a group — since it was too easy to slip into unintentional heresy. Because praying out loud was considered a form of teaching (people learn by imitation), extemporaneous prayers were usually reserved for the clergy, or lay catechists who were authorized by the local bishop to teach. But even with private prayer, we do not see the Church fathers encouraging people (let alone teaching people) to pray in their own words. Of course, people *did*

himself of the Sacrament of Confession and Reconciliation with Jesus Himself on the Cross by his confession of faith in Jesus as the Christ.

pray in their own words — it would be absurd to assume that people used only prewritten prayers in their private devotions — but Jewish Christians especially would have continued the prayer practices of the synagogue, and as we will see, that mostly meant praying with the words of Scripture.

So as we can see, both in the intercessions of the Mass, and in the ways the Church fathers model other prayers, less is more. Prayer is not, in essence, about improvisation, but rather about putting one's trust in God for everything. Prayer is also not problem solving. It's simply a matter of presenting the problem to God, in the sense of "cast all your worries upon him" (1 Pet. 5:7) and leaving the solutions up to divine providence. We will have more to say about humility in prayer in a later chapter, but for now we note that the Church fathers did not value eloquence in prayer. Prayer in the early Church was not an exercise in rhetoric, focusing on the human creative act of putting thoughts together into prose.

This is the point of Jesus' critique of the Pharisee, in His parable of the Pharisee and the tax collector (Luke 18:9–14). The tax collector is praised for his humility, here expressed in his brevity, but the Pharisee exalted himself by relying on his eloquence (calling attention to himself) and on the length of his prayer. What's more, the prayer was all about himself! Prayer should not be self-focused, even when we pray for ourselves. Prayer is not introspection or self-reflection. It is not a time to explore our thoughts or argue a case before the Lord.[60] As St. Augustine said, "When you pray, you need piety, not wordiness."[61] Wordiness is the opposite of holiness.

As usual, the Church fathers' approach to prayer is to find the balance of a middle way between the extremes.[62] One extreme would be the method of the Pharisee in the parable — that is, a philosophical approach to prayer. This extreme is all about the creativity of the person — either through improvisation or prepared eloquence, but ultimately leaning too heavily on one's own words in prayer. This would be to assume that God is convinced by the same kinds of arguments that convince people, as if we think that if we are articulate enough, we can force God to do something through the power of

[60] Augustine of Hippo, *Our Lord's Sermon on the Mount* 2.3.

[61] Augustine of Hippo, *On the Lord's Prayer* 6.4.

[62] Clement of Alexandria, *Exhortation to the Greeks* 2; Augustine of Hippo, *Confessions* 7.7.

our logic or, worse, that we could teach God something.[63] The philosophical (or Pharisaical) approach assumes that the value of the content of a speech is directly related to the eloquence of the speaker.[64] It attempts to prove devotion through obsequiousness, to cajole God into granting one's wish, as if He were somehow reluctant to want to care for us, or we fear He can't be bothered to pay attention to us unless we get His attention with a lot of words. This approach is flawed because it is not the quantity of words, or even the quality of the prayer, that matters. What matters is the motivation for the prayer, whether we are coming to God in humility, gratitude, and trust, and in the desire to serve Him and do His will above our own.

The other extreme is a pagan approach to prayer, in which the person praying thinks that the prayer will be answered positively only by saying precisely the right words. There is no room for variation or even any personal expression. It's both a kind of legalism and a superstitious approach to prayer. It's a fearful way of praying, ironically also based on the assumption that God is predisposed not to want to give us good things, and so He waits to hear if we will say exactly the right words in the right order. The person praying in this way — and this is pretty much how the pagans prayed — treats the prayer no differently than a spell or an incantation. Perhaps this is because some pagans thought of their deities as less personal, lacking compassion, or as ruled by the laws of nature. Unfortunately, this kind of praying has also crept into Christian practice through the centuries. Some Christians even blur the line between prayer and occult practices. But God does not have to be appeased by our saying just the right words, and He cannot be made to submit to our will through some magic spell.

The Church fathers model a way of prayer that takes the middle way, the balance between the extremes. Prayer is neither a pagan obsession with the exact words nor a philosophical obsession with eloquence. When you pray, you do not have to get the words just right because God knows the need better than you do. You could never add to His understanding of the situation. And God is not so mean as to answer prayer only when it's perfect. On the other hand, you do not have to go on and on, or make up

[63] Augustine of Hippo, *Our Lord's Sermon on the Mount* 2.3; *Confessions* 5.3, 5.6.

[64] This seems to be the assumption of those who claimed to follow Apollos rather than Paul (Acts 18:24; 1 Cor. 3:4).

a lot of words, or put all the burden on yourself even to know what to pray for. The good news is that the burden is not on you to come up with all the right words. As the author of Ecclesiastes says, "God is in heaven and you are on earth, therefore let your words be few" (5:1). And John Cassian said, "We ought to pray often, but briefly."[65]

There are some who teach that we should pray specifically, if we want our prayers to be answered specifically.[66] This is entirely opposite of what the Church fathers modeled and the early Christians practiced. The prayer of the early Church was intentionally very general, so as not to presume to tell God how to answer the prayers. God does not need the kinds of explanations that we are often tempted to give, and to think that we can come up with words that are any better than words that have been prayed before us is considered a form of pride. To pray "specifically" is to make the prayer all about ourselves, but to leave it open for any answer God chooses to give is to admit that we can't see the future and only God knows what's best. In fact, it would seem that growth in spiritual maturity goes hand in hand with growth toward greater trust in God, which would mean that increasing sanctification does not mean that our prayers get more eloquent — rather, it would mean that our prayers become simpler over time, perhaps, we could even say, more childlike (Matt. 18:2–4).

So don't worry about what kind of prayer you are praying. And don't worry about having the right words to say, or having to explain everything to God. And especially when you don't know what to say in prayer, ask the saints to pray for you.

We'll conclude with a very early prayer for the intercession of the Blessed Virgin Mary. This comes from the third century, during the time of persecution. It's called by its Latin title, *Sub Tuum Praesidium,* which means "under your protection."[67] There is a Greek version and a Latin version, so

[65] John Cassian, *Conferences* 9.36.

[66] This concept is especially present in the so-called prosperity gospel but is present in other segments of the Protestant world as well. In 1982, the Christian group Daniel Amos critiqued this approach to prayer in their satire song "A New Car" on the *Doppelgänger* album.

[67] Notice that the traditional prayer known as the Memorare is somewhat based on this earlier prayer.

for the sake of comparison, I'll put English translations of the Greek and Latin versions side by side, then give the traditional (Catholic) version, and finally my own translation, which I made from a combination of both the Greek and Latin versions of the prayer. It's meant to be a more modern translation, to make the meaning and significance more clear.

Greek Version
Under your compassion we take refuge
O Mother of God
Do not reject our petitions
In times of need
But rescue us from dangers
Only pure, only blessed one

Latin Version
We fly to your protection
O holy Mother of God
Do not reject our petitions
In times of trouble
But deliver us always from all dangers
O glorious and blessed Virgin

Traditional Version
We fly to thy protection (*or:* patronage)
O Holy Mother of God
Despise not our petitions
In our necessities
But deliver us always
From all dangers
O glorious and blessed Virgin

My Translation[68]
Holy Mother of God
Uniquely pure and blessed
We take refuge
Under your compassion
Do not ignore our prayers
In our time of need
But free us from danger

Therefore, to pray like the earliest Christians:

1. **Don't worry about what kind of prayers you're praying.** Let go of all those acronyms (ACTS) and other shortcuts. You don't need that anymore. With every prayer, come to God in a spirit of gratitude for all that He has done for you and given you. Be that one leper who returns to Jesus. Also, come to God in a spirit of contrition (humility) and trust in God's omniscience and benevolent providence. This will allow you to let go of having to tell Him how to answer your prayers.

[68] My translation is a combination of both the Greek and Latin versions of the prayer. It was first published in James L. Papandrea, *Praying a Christ-Centered Rosary: Meditations on the Mysteries* (Notre Dame, IN: Ave Maria Press, 2021), 134–135.

2. **Remember that less is more: keep your prayers brief.** As Cassian said, "Pray often, but briefly." Don't put a burden on yourself to have to be eloquent or convincing (avoid the philosophical approach). Also, don't worry that your words will be "wrong" or inadequate (avoid the pagan approach). Remember that God *wants* to answer your prayers. There's nothing wrong with pouring out your heart to God (1 Pet. 5:7), but God doesn't need backstory, explanation, or embellishment. He already knows. If you have prayed the Our Father, your prayer is already complete. Let that be good enough, and prefer to let the Holy Spirit pray within you and for you (Rom. 8:26–27).

St. Faustina had a vision of Jesus in which He said to her, "My daughter, don't be exerting yourself so much with words. Those whom you love in a special way, I too love in a special way, and for your sake, I shower my graces upon them. I am pleased when you tell me about them, but don't be doing so with so much effort."[69] On another occasion Jesus said to her, "The simpler your speech is, the more you attract me to yourself."[70] Keep in mind that early Christian prayer for someone requires only remembering the person in prayer, just calling to mind the person's name.

3. **Pray for anyone you love, or are concerned about, including those who have passed away.** Pray for anyone who needs healing or encouragement. Pray for anyone who is in mourning or who is suffering. Pray for your clergy and for your church or parish — especially if there are people in preparation for Baptism. Pray for the troops, for allies, for an end to wars, and for protection of Christians from persecution. Pray for prisoners. And don't forget to pray for government leaders — the ones you agree with and the ones you don't (or maybe you already covered those when you prayed for your enemies!). If you are so inclined, pray for all the souls in Purgatory. As Jesus said in another vision to St. Faustina, "It is in your power to bring them relief."[71]

4. **Keep your prayers for yourself to a minimum.** Whenever possible, let the Our Father be sufficient for prayer for yourself. If you expand on that, focus

[69] Kowalska, *Divine Mercy in My Soul*, 295.

[70] Kowalska, *Divine Mercy in My Soul*, 315.

[71] Kowalska, *Divine Mercy in My Soul*, 441–442.

on prayers for whatever will keep you on track toward sanctification and salvation — for grace, for discernment, and for the fruit of the Spirit in your life (Gal. 5:22–23). Keep prayers for yourself as short as possible, too, resisting the temptation to tell God how to answer the prayers. Don't let your prayers become problem-solving. Prayer is supposed to be problem-surrendering, not problem-solving. As you progress in your prayer life, practice making your prayers less specific, and use fewer words.

5. **Ask Mary and the other saints for their intercession.** Pray the *Sub Tuum Praesidium*. Ask the saints to join you in your prayers to God. The intercession of the saints augments our prayer to God, so you should always pray to God first and then ask the saints to pray for you and with you. Praying with the saints must never replace prayer to God, of course, but if you find that there are times when it's hard to talk to God, it's okay to begin by talking to Mary or another saint and asking for their intercession to help you in your prayers. Just remember that the help comes from God, not from the saint. Don't ascribe divine power or divine attributes to the saint. It's not St. Anthony who helps you find your car keys; it's God.[72] But it's okay to ask St. Anthony to pray to God on your behalf, for *God* to help you find the lost keys. Just don't fall into the habit of talking to Mary and the other saints more than you talk to God.

6. **Find your patron saint(s).** As you practice asking the saints for their intercession, find the saints with whom you share some affinity. You may already know that you are named after a saint, or you may have a Confirmation saint. Find the saint whose feast day is your birthday. Look up the patron saint of your occupation, or if you have a particular chronic illness, find the patron saint for that. I was born into a family with a particular devotion to St. Padre Pio. It's good to identify with one or more particular saints and to cultivate a special devotion to that saint; however, don't become so obsessed with a saint that you spend more time reading about that saint than you do reading Scripture or reading about God. It can be fun to research all the different patron saints, and while you do that, you learn a bit of Church history along the way. Just don't take it too far.

[72] St. Anthony of Padua is the patron saint of lost items.

To Go Deeper

Primary Sources

Vibia Perpetua, *The Diary of Perpetua* (written in AD 203), https://www.newadvent.org/fathers/0324.htm.

Clement of Rome, *I Clement* (*Letter to the Corinthians*) (written about AD 95), https://www.newadvent.org/fathers/1010.htm.

Secondary Sources

Mike Aquilina, *Mothers of the Church* (Huntington, IN: Our Sunday Visitor, 2012).

Maria Faustina Kowalska, *Divine Mercy in My Soul: The Diary of Saint Maria Faustina Kowalska*, 3rd ed. (Stockbridge, MA: Marian Press, 2019).

James L. Papandrea, *Handed Down: The Catholic Faith of the Early Christians* (El Cajon, CA: Catholic Answers Press, 2015).

James L. Papandrea, *What Really Happens After We Die?: There WILL Be Hugs in Heaven* (Manchester, NH: Sophia Institute Press, 2019).

Insight 5

How to "Pray without Ceasing"

(And the goal of prayer is not your comfort, but your sanctification)

You cannot plumb the depths of the human heart
or grasp the workings of the human mind;
how then can you fathom God,
who has made all these things,
or discern his mind, or understand his plan?
No, my brothers, do not anger the Lord our God....
He has it equally within his power to protect us at such time as he pleases,
or to destroy us in the sight of our enemies.
Do not impose conditions on the plans of the Lord our God.
God is not like a human being to be moved by threats,
nor like a mortal to be cajoled
So while we wait for the salvation that comes from him,
let us call upon him to help us,
and he will hear our cry if it pleases him.

—Judith, Judith 8:14–17

Rejoice always. Pray without ceasing.
In all circumstances give thanks,
for this is the will of God for you in Christ Jesus.

— St. Paul, 1 Thessalonians 5:16–18

As I have already noted, the Church fathers do not give us much in the way of a concrete definition of prayer or instructions on how to pray. They do, however, have something to say about what prayer is for (and what it is not for). And once again, this is one of those things that we *think* we know, or we go about our lives as though we know, but we rarely think about it, much less examine our assumptions. It's easy enough to say that prayer is a conversation with God, but we as humans often fall into the trap of turning that conversation into something too utilitarian, as though the purpose of the conversation is *what results from it*. We talk to God when we want something. I'm sure you've heard this analogy, but if you called your parents only to ask for money, that wouldn't be much of a relationship; and so it is that if we pray only when we want something from God, that, too, is not much of a relationship with Him. So yes, prayer is a conversation with God, but not for the purpose of getting something from Him — prayer is conversation with God, for the purpose of connecting with Him. The primary purpose of prayer is for what happens *in the prayer*, not for what happens after the prayer.

Now, of course we will pray for things we need, and we will pray for others who need help, but if we want to grow spiritually and progress in our prayer life toward greater union with God, we will need to move beyond thinking of prayer as a means to an end and will make the prayer an end in itself; this means spending time in the Divine Presence, without the distractions of the world getting in the way. We will need to move beyond prayer as asking for things and think of prayer as a means of grace in and of itself. We will need to spend less time praying for God to change our circumstances and spend more time praying for God to change us.[1] Even when it comes to praying for the end of an injustice, the purpose of prayer is not to change the world but to change hearts. Of course, changing hearts will change the world, but not because prayer changes "systems"; rather, it is because prayer changes individuals, and those individuals become more Christlike. So if you wanted to fight injustice in the style of the Church fathers, you wouldn't rely on protest, and you wouldn't pray for the defeat of your enemies; you would pray for your enemies and evangelize them until they were converted — and then *their own prayers* would change their hearts until their consciences convicted them, and they made changes in the systems over which they have power.[2]

Prayer Is Not Giving God Advice

If we think about prayer on the spectrum from philosophical prayer to pagan prayer, philosophical prayer attempts to validate the person praying by his calling attention to himself and impressing others with his eloquence, while pagan prayer attempts to say just the right words to compel the gods to act in a way that is in accordance with the will of the one praying. Needless to say, both of these extremes are flawed, and both of them fail to take into account that the person who prays doesn't really know what's best in the situation. In the case of pagan-style prayer especially, there is an assumption that if the one praying says all the right words in just the right way, it is guaranteed that the gods will do what is being asked. We can be quick to dismiss this kind of prayer as something no Christian would ever engage in; however, many Christians approach this kind of prayer when they assume that if God doesn't answer their prayers in the way they hope, they must be doing something wrong.[3]

1 Notice that, even in the Our Father, the Church fathers interpreted "lead us not into temptation" not as a request to remove temptation from our lives but as a request for strength in the midst of temptation.

2 There is no doubt that sometimes protest works, as in the civil rights movement and in the work of closing down abortion clinics. However, when protest works, it is because it is accompanied by prayer and is nonviolent.

3 This is at the heart of the prosperity gospel movement. The foundational assumption is that if you are "doing it right," then God will bless you materially.

You already know that God is not a vending machine nor our own personal ATM, and we should not pray as though we assume that simply putting in a prayer will result in getting what we want. We all know this, but we all forget it when we are actually praying for things and when we become disappointed that we don't get what we ask for. I would go so far as to say that prayer is not really about asking for things at all. Of course, in the context of prayer, we might ask for things (and this is the very definition of the verb *to pray*, "to ask for something"), but if God is a vending machine, He is not a very good one, because often that thing we really want — that thing we think will solve the problem or make our life complete — just never drops down into the bin. We will discuss the concept of unanswered prayers below, but for now, we have to admit that all prayer should be undertaken with the acknowledgment that God knows our needs better than we do. As St. Augustine wrote:

> When we pray we ask for what we need, yet the Truth himself has told us, "Your heavenly Father knows well what your needs are before you ask him." So by confessing our own miserable state, and acknowledging your mercy towards us, we open our hearts to you, so that you may free us wholly, as you have already begun to do.[4]

God is also not *the Godfather*, a well-connected patron whom we can ask to fix things for us, even at the expense of the free will of our enemies. Being a Christian is not simply a matter of having a friend in high places who can intervene for us. Again, we know this on an intellectual level, but it's very easy to fall into the habit of treating prayer this way, as if the purpose of prayer is to get *God* to do *our* will. But prayer is not about what we *get*; it's about what we *become*. It's not about making God our servant; it's about becoming a better servant of God. And to that end, prayer is a power source — less like going to the ATM and more like plugging in to charge a battery. It's a means of grace by which we become empowered to live the Christian life and to grow in sanctification.

As I noted above, the Church fathers did not believe in praying "specifically." They did not model a kind of prayer in which the person praying tells

[4] Augustine of Hippo, *Confessions* 11.1, quoting Matthew 6:8. Note that in the *Confessions*, Augustine is writing as if he is speaking to God.

God how to answer the prayer. They did not pray as though they presumed to know what was needed to fix a situation. In other words, they did not treat prayer as though they were giving God advice. This is because they were absolutely convinced in such attributes of divinity as God's omnipresence, omniscience, omnipotence, and omnibenevolence. To put it simply, God is omnipresent — eternally present in the past, present, and future — so He knows everything (is omniscient), including what is best for us in the long term. God is also omnibenevolent (all-good) and omnipotent, so He wants what's best for us and is able to accomplish what's best for us. In other words, *God does not need us to pray.*

Then why do we pray? We pray for two reasons. First, *we need to pray* — we need to be plugged into the power source, to be empowered by the Holy Spirit, who forms our consciences and gives us strength to resist temptation. Second, it is God's design that we participate in our own sanctification and salvation and in the sanctification and salvation of others. This participation in, or cooperation with, what God is doing in the world is called *synergy.* It means working along with, collaborating. And although many more recent approaches to theology would put everything on God, as though there is no part we play in anything from good works to our own salvation, that is not how the early and medieval Christians saw it. The Church fathers believed that everything begins with God's grace, but then we cooperate with grace through our own free will.[5] And when it comes to prayer, there are things we need to bring to the table, so to speak — things we need to supply for our prayers to be effective.

There are three things we need to contribute to our prayer. These are what I call "meta-virtues," and I've already covered two of them. We have

[5] To be fair, those who reject the concept of synergy, including those who follow the theology of John Calvin, are getting their ideas from one Church father in particular — and one of the most important at that — St. Augustine. But we must keep in mind that although St. Augustine contributed much to the development of doctrine in the later part of the early Church, Church fathers are not infallible, and when it comes to Augustine's teachings that influenced some of the Protestant reformers toward Calvinism, Augustine was an outlier — he did not speak for the consensus of the Church fathers — and, in fact, these were the very teachings that the Church rejected. See Papandrea, *Reading the Church Fathers,* chap. 11.

seen that before we even begin to pray, we need to make sure that we are not holding a grudge against anyone. We need to come to prayer forgiving all those who have wronged us and making sure that there is no one holding a grudge against us if we can help it. That is, if there's something we could do to reconcile with that person, we should do it so that our prayers are pure. So the first meta-virtue is forgiveness. In the Our Father, we have promised to forgive those who have sinned against us, and Jesus Himself said this is a *requirement* if we want God to forgive us.

We've also covered the second meta-virtue, which is thanksgiving. As I've noted, thanksgiving is not a type of prayer but is the attitude with which we should pray all of our prayers. The most important prayer, the Eucharistic Prayer, is called *the* Thanksgiving, and everything else flows from there. Every prayer we pray has to be motivated by gratitude for the Incarnation and the Passion of Jesus Christ, which makes our reconciliation with God, our sanctification, our salvation, and our eternal life possible. Prayer *is* being the one grateful ex-leper who returns to thank Jesus (Luke 17:11–19). Later in this chapter we will get into how to "pray without ceasing" (1 Thess. 5:17), but for the moment it's enough to note that praying without ceasing means going through all of daily life with an attitude of gratitude.

I hinted at the third meta-virtue above when I mentioned contrition and noted how contrition or confession is also not a particular kind of prayer (at least not for private prayer) but that all prayer requires a spirit of contrition and that the Church fathers expected that people would prepare themselves for Mass by confessing their sins. It is also evident in Jesus' praise of the tax collector's prayer. The third meta-virtue is humility, which warrants its own chapter, below. So the three meta-virtues are forgiveness, gratitude, and humility. They are called meta-virtues because all the other virtues subsist in them and flow from them. Therefore, these meta-virtues are the foundation of all prayer.

This means that if you feel as if your prayers are not "working," it might be because you are expecting God to do everything for you, and you're not bringing anything to the prayer — in other words, if your prayers always seem to go unanswered, if your prayer time seems fruitless, if it seems impossible to get any peace or have any patience, it could be because you are refusing to forgive or reconcile with someone, or you are not praying in a spirit of thanksgiving and humility. Just as there are channels of grace (the sacraments, sacramentals, and prayer itself), there are also grace-blockers. These include the opposites of the meta-virtues, such as pride (one of the mortal sins), the refusal to forgive (the mortal sin of anger), and forgetting to be thankful (often motivated by another mortal sin, greed), and this includes complaining and failing to count your blessings.[6] All of these things, along with the other mortal sins, will get in the way of your prayers.

When I was in college, I took a course in jazz composition. I thought it would be fun to know how to write jazz music. The course turned out to be an independent study (I was the only student) taught by a teaching assistant. When I asked the instructor to define *jazz*, he couldn't do it. He could only say, "I know it when I hear it." So I wrote some music and gave it to him, and he said, "This isn't jazz." I asked again, "So what *is* jazz?" And he replied, "I'll know it when I hear it, but this isn't it." And so I wrote some more, and turned it in. And he said, "This isn't jazz." And around and around we went, and at the end of the semester, he took pity on me and gave me a C for the effort. I never wrote any jazz. It's like this with the things of God. Often it's easier to define something by saying what it is *not* rather than by trying to come up with a concrete definition of what it is.

Prayer is not giving God advice about how to do His business. Prayer is not informing God of your will so that He can follow you. It's not even giving God suggestions — prayer is not Heaven's suggestion box. Even with intercession, as we have already seen, prayer is not telling God *how* to answer your prayers for someone or even *what* to do at all. Intercession is really only about lifting up people to God in your spirit and giving them over to His care, entrusting them to His mercy. You don't need to tell God what to do for them or even explain the situation. God already knows. And this is good news because it means the pressure is not on us to get it right. Whether praying for yourself or someone else, it's better to leave it up to God what to do about it.

One last thought about what prayer is not. Prayer is also not daydreaming. That might seem obvious, but how many times do we give in to the temptation to let our prayers morph into daydreaming? We fantasize about

[6] St. Faustina wrote that she had discerned how "grumbling interiorly," complaining, and gossiping were blocking grace in the lives of some of her sisters. Kowalska, *Divine Mercy in My Soul*, 282.

things we wish we had said to that person who humiliated us. We fantasize about winning the lottery as a solution to all our problems. We rehash the regrets of the past and make plans for the future. All of these are traps that prevent us from being in the present moment and actually praying.

So if that's what prayer is not, what is prayer? Or rather — since we already noted that the Church fathers don't answer that question for us — what is prayer for? What does it do? What is the purpose of prayer?

The Goal of Prayer Is Not Your Comfort but Your Sanctification

We could summarize what we know so far by saying *it's not about you*. When Jesus criticized the Pharisee in His parable of the Pharisee and the tax collector, a big part of His criticism had to do with the fact that the Pharisee made the prayer all about him. It literally was about him ("I fast twice a week ..."), but it was also all about him in the sense that the whole purpose of his prayer was to draw attention to himself and to impress with his eloquence those who would hear it (the philosophical approach to prayer) (Luke 18:9–14).[7] But that's the wrong approach to prayer, and that's not what prayer is for. When you pray, it's not *about* you, but it is *for* you — in other words, for your benefit. But remember that *we* don't really know what's best for us. And when we think we do, it's often shortsighted, focusing on the short-term (which we know) rather than on the long-term (which we don't). An eye-opening example of those who left the short-term up to God in favor of the long-term is the early martyrs, such as St. Polycarp of Smyrna and St. Ignatius of Antioch, who did not pray to be spared from execution; instead, they prayed that they would be sanctified through their martyrdom and saved for eternal life and that their experience would be an encouragement to other believers.[8]

Clement of Alexandria wrote that the Christian "makes his prayer and request for the truly good things which appertain to the soul, and prays, he himself also contributing to his efforts to attain to the habit of goodness, so as no longer to *have* the things that are good ... but to *be* good."[9] Prayer is

[7] See Cyprian of Carthage, *Treatise IV: On the Lord's Prayer* 6.

[8] *Martyrdom of Polycarp* 14; Ignatius of Antioch, *Letter to the Trallians* 12 and *Letter to the Romans*.

[9] Clement of Alexandria, *Miscellanies* 7.7 (emphasis added). Clement actually says that "the gnostic makes his prayer ..." but he was not speaking of the

not for what we get, but for what we become. The very act of praying itself contributes to our sanctification and to character building (that is, the fruit of the Spirit).

St. Cyprian wrote that the purpose of prayer is preparation for Heaven, and that includes detaching from the things of the earth.[10] When we pray (in the Our Father) for help in resisting temptation, we are praying for the strength to resist the attractions of the "kingdom of the world," which is always seeking to entice us with things that will drag us down. For Cyprian, this is what Jesus meant when He said to seek the Kingdom of God first (Matt. 6:33; Luke 12:31). He meant to be primarily looking for the things that will elevate our spirits toward the heavenly realm, as opposed to the things that create attachments to the material world.

The desert fathers (the early hermits and monks) taught a kind of detachment from the world that they called *dispassion,* in the sense that one who is dispassionate is not drawn by the passions of the body and life in the world. This dispassion, which they understood to be achieved through prayer, led to the kind of peace that comes from detachment — a peace that surpasses understanding (Phil. 4:7) — and that allows one to be free from the temptations and frustrations of the world.

And so prayer is not meant to be about asking for comforts in this material world. In fact, we should prefer discomfort in this world if it means we are more able to detach from the things of the world and orient our priorities toward the things of God (not to mention that discomfort may be a penance that contributes to our purification — i.e., sanctification). St. Augustine wrote of attachment and detachment in terms of what we love in this life. If our love is directed at God first and foremost, then we have our priorities right. If our love is directed at anything (or anyone) else over God, then not only is that a form of idolatry, but it results in our own frustration because we will always live in fear of losing what we are obsessed with (or of never having what we covet) and that fear will always lead us into sin and away from God.

---

heretical sects of gnosticism; he had a rather odd way of refuting gnosticism by saying that Christians are the true "gnostics" (i.e., the ones with the knowledge), so he is talking about Christians there.

[10] Cyprian of Carthage, *Treatise IV: On the Lord's Prayer* 13, 20.

Of course, this dispassion or detachment does not mean that we should abandon responsibility and caring for our loved ones. But it does mean that our goal in prayer is not material comforts but sanctification leading to salvation — for us and for others. Even when it comes to praying for justice in the world, the point is not simply to improve the quality of life for people (though that is obviously a good thing) but to draw them closer to God in Jesus Christ, through His Church. So if we pray for an end to injustice, it should be oriented toward reconciling people with God primarily — both the perpetrators and the victims — and secondarily with each other. And this brings us back to praying for our enemies.[11] St. Polycarp wrote that we should pray for our enemies *so that* we can be perfect.[12] Not that praying for our enemies makes us perfectly holy, but perfect in the sense of complete. A prayer life that does not include prayer for enemies is incomplete. Don't stop with praying for your loved ones; take it all the way, and pray also for your enemies (Matt. 5:46–48). It may be uncomfortable to pray for our enemies, but the goal of prayer is not our comfort. In fact, the desert fathers taught that prayer for one's enemies is itself a penance that purifies us toward sanctification.

If prayer is done right, it is a means of grace and a source of peace, leading to our own sanctification and empowering us to participate in what God is doing in our lives and in the lives of others. Prayer for others is simply to set them before God and ask for His mercy, with their sanctification and their salvation in mind. Prayer calms our hearts, reorients our priorities, purifies our desires, and opens us up to receive God's grace.[13] We pray primarily for spiritual blessings (which God is always ready to give), not for material things. And if we pray only when we want something from God, then that's like saying we don't need prayer at other times. That would be like a sick person who thinks he's healthy and refuses medicine.[14] We know that

[11] As Jesus said, those who cause His children to sin are in real danger of Hell, and we should pray for their salvation (Matt. 18:6–7; Mark 9:42). And as for the victims of these enemies, prayer for victims should be primarily that they be shown God's love so that they feel at home in the Church, since only there will they find true healing. Cf. Sirach 38:9: it is God who heals.

[12] Polycarp of Smyrna, *Letter to the Philippians* 12.

[13] Augustine of Hippo, *Our Lord's Sermon on the Mount* 2.3.

[14] Augustine of Hippo, *Sermons on New Testament Lessons: Sermon 30 on Matthew 17:19* 4.

the primary way we remain connected to God and receive grace for daily life (i.e., are plugged into the power source) is by receiving the Eucharist regularly. But even if we cannot receive the Eucharist daily, we cannot go a whole week, or even a few days, without prayer. That's too long to go without plugging in. As St. Gregory of Nyssa wrote, anyone "who does not unite himself to God through prayer is separated from God."[15]

The Development of Private Prayer, or "Personal Devotion"

So if prayer is primarily a discipline that contributes to our sanctification, we should pray as much as possible — not only in church but also at home and on the road. In fact, St. Paul famously said that we should "pray without ceasing" (1 Thess. 5:17). But how do we do that? Obviously, we can't be at Mass 24-7. And yet we don't have much recorded evidence from the early Church in terms of the personal prayer lives of laypeople outside of the liturgy. As I have noted, the prayers from the early Church tend to be written as though the person praying is part of an assembly or at least part of a group; they are written from the first-person-plural perspective: *we* and *us*, not *I* and *me*.

We assume that the earliest Christians continued at least some of the private prayer practices of Judaism, but we don't know much about what that looked like either. The early Christians kept some things from Judaism and abandoned others. They certainly continued the practice of praying the psalms, and there are many psalms written in the first person singular (*I* and *me*), but we have very little evidence to tell us whether the earliest Christians made a habit of praying the psalms at home. We know that they did pray at home, and they could see from the Gospels that Jesus Himself practiced private prayer (Matt. 14:23; Mark 1:35; 6:46; Luke 4:42; 5:16; 6:12; 22:39–46). We also know that eventually Celtic Christianity gave the Church a collection of prayers prayed in the first grammatical person — that is, *I* and *me* prayers — such as the Breastplate of St. Patrick (see the appendix).

In the fourth century, the desert hermits were the inspiration for the formation of the first monastic communities.[16] Most of the monks "prayed without ceasing" by praying all 150 psalms every day. Some were less strict

[15] Gregory of Nyssa, *Sermons on the Lord's Prayer,* Sermon 1.

[16] See Papandrea, *Reading the Church Fathers,* chap. 12.

and prayed all the psalms in a week. Before long, the great monastic leaders, such as Basil of Caesarea and Benedict of Nursia, wrote rules for their communities that formalized a rhythm of prayer hours throughout the day — what we call the Liturgy of the Hours, or the Divine Office (I'll have more to say about the development of the prayer hours below).

Those laypeople who were not called to the monastic life but wanted to imitate the monks in their prayer habits started praying the psalms as well, and because many of the psalms are written from that first-person-singular perspective, people discovered that they are very conducive to private prayer.[17] At first, this practice was available only to the wealthy, since it required being able to buy and own a personal copy of a book of the psalms (known as a Psalter), not to mention the fact that it required a certain amount of free time in one's schedule to pray the Psalms systematically. But eventually lay Christians developed a lifestyle of prayer — that is, a rhythm of prayer that punctuated each day, week, and year. And so with the developments of first-person prayers from the Psalms and Celtic Christianity, and the imitation by laypeople of the prayer hours of the monks, we can see the development of what we might call personal devotion, or a private prayer life.

For private devotions, St. Cyprian recommended silent prayer, holding up as an example the Old Testament figure Hannah, who prayed with her lips moving, but without making a sound (1 Sam. 1:13). She prayed "within the very recesses of her heart," and so becomes a foreshadowing of the Church.[18]

Have You Met St. Basil the Great?

Basil of Caesarea was another brother of St. Macrina, younger than Macrina but older than their brother Gregory. As the bishop of Caesarea (in Cappadocia, modern Turkey), Basil, his brother Gregory of Nyssa, and their friend Gregory of Nazianzus, would become known as the *Cappadocian Fathers,*

[17] For a contemporary take on using the psalms for personal prayer, see the companion volume to this book: James L. Papandrea, *Praying the Psalms: The Divine Gateway to* Lectio Divina *and Contemplative Prayer,* also from Sophia Institute Press.

[18] Cyprian of Carthage, *Treatise IV: On the Lord's Prayer* 5.

and together they were very influential in the continuing clarification of the doctrine of the Trinity after the Council of Nicaea, especially with regard to pneumatology (the doctrine of the Holy Spirit).[19]

Macrina had inspired both of her younger brothers to enter monastic life, and Basil would become known as the father of Eastern monasticism — not because he was a pioneer of monasticism (he wasn't) but because he was the Eastern father who did the most to formalize the life of monks and to make sure that that life included more than just introspection. He famously criticized the hermits by saying, "If you live alone, whose feet will you wash?"[20] For Basil, the goal of monastic life was not only to embrace poverty as a means of sanctification but also to help those who were involuntarily poor, and in this, he was a pioneer in the ways that monastic communities would become hostels, hospitals, and hospices. His ideal for the monastic life was a life in community, a life of service, and a life devoted to prayer. To that end, Basil and his contemporaries created a rhythm of life, in which they lived up to St. Paul's advice to "pray without ceasing" by returning to prayer at regular intervals during every day. These are the prayer hours, or the Divine Office. In one of his homilies, Basil gave his answer to the question of how we are to "pray without ceasing." He said:

> Ought we to pray without ceasing? Is it possible to obey such a command? These are questions which I see you are ready to ask. I will endeavor, to the best of my ability, to defend the charge. Prayer is a petition for good addressed by the pious to God. But we do not rigidly confine our petition to words. Nor yet do we imagine that God requires to be reminded by speech. He knows our needs even if we do not ask Him. What do I say then? I say that we must not think to make our prayer complete by syllables. The strength of prayer lies rather in the purpose of our soul and in deeds of virtue reaching every part and moment of our life. It is said, "whether you eat or drink, or whatever you do, do everything for the glory of God [1 Cor. 10:31]."

[19] For more details on the life of Basil, the Cappadocians, and their contribution to the development of doctrine, see Papandrea, *Reading the Church Fathers,* chap. 11.

[20] Basil of Caesarea, *Long Rule,* Question 7.

As you take your seat at the table, pray. As you lift the loaf, offer thanks to the Giver. Whenever you sustain your bodily weakness with wine, remember the One who supplies you with this gift, to make your heart glad, and to comfort your infirmity. Has your hunger gone away? Do not let the thought of your Benefactor go away too. As you are putting on your tunic, thank the One who gave it to you. As you wrap yourself in your cloak, feel even greater love for God, who has given us coverings convenient for us, both in summer and in winter, both to preserve our life and to cover what is unseemly. Is the day done? Give thanks to the One who has given us the sun for our daily work, and has provided for us a fire to light up the night, and to serve the rest of the needs of life. Let night give the other occasions of prayer. When you look up to heaven and gaze at the beauty of the stars, pray to the Lord of the visible world, pray to the original architect and maker of the universe, who has made them all in his wisdom. When you see all nature sunk in sleep, then again worship the One who gives us release from the continuous strain of toil — even against our wills — and by a brief refreshment restores us once again to the vigor of our strength.

But do not let the night belong to sleep alone. Do not let half of your life be useless through the senselessness of slumber. Divide the time of night between sleep and prayer. Even let your sleep itself be an exercise in piety, for it is only natural that our sleeping dreams should be for the most part echoes of the anxieties of the day. Our dreams will inevitably follow our conduct and pursuits. In this way, you will pray without ceasing, if you pray, not only in words, but by uniting yourself to God through all the course of life, and so your life will become one ceaseless and uninterrupted prayer.[21]

How to Pray without Ceasing

And so it becomes clear that, for the Church fathers, the way we should pray without ceasing is by organizing our lives around a rhythm of prayer (and fasting, as we'll see). But before we begin to look at the development of a

[21] Basil of Caesarea, *Panegyrical Homily V: On the Martyr Julitta*, quoted in *Nicene and Ante-Nicene Fathers*, Second Series, vol. 8 (Peabody, MA: Hendrickson Publishers, 1994), lxix (translation adapted for clarity).

rhythm of prayer, it's important to say up front that the point of making one's whole life "one ceaseless and uninterrupted prayer" is not to complicate life but actually to simplify it, through organization — creating order out of chaos, as God does. Although the Church fathers understood prayer to be a duty, they did not see it as a burden. Sometimes prayer is difficult, and sometimes it is a penance, but overall, prayer leads to more peace, not less. A rhythm of prayer in everyday life allows us to organize our lives around our relationship with God, which should be our number-one priority anyway, and in this way, we put everything in life in the proper order; we are seeking first the things of the Kingdom.

But don't mistake rhythm for routine. The prayer rhythm we create with our lives is not going to feel as if we're in a rut or that we're going through the motions of a routine; if we are paying attention, it will give our lives more meaning by punctuating each day, each week, and even each month and year with spiritual highlights. As we have seen, the Eucharistic Prayer is our primary prayer (even though we as laity don't verbally pray it), and so the Mass should be the main thing that punctuates our life's rhythm. The Mass is the point in our rhythm at which the grace and the hope of the heavenly realm breaks through into the mundane, at least once each week, on the Lord's Day.

But needless to say, the Church fathers believed that we should pray every day, not only on special days or only at Mass.[22] In fact, many of the Church fathers would look at 1 Thessalonians 5:16–18 and assume that rejoicing, giving thanks, and praying are all one and the same thing. It is true that Basil speaks of giving thanks at specific times, but this does not mean that there must be specific prayers of thanksgiving. All prayer is an act of thanksgiving. So Basil implies that we can be always in prayer, even in our sleep. Not all prayer requires words, since it is possible to act with an attitude of thanksgiving toward God. St. Augustine advised that monks should sing Christian songs while they work, the way rowers might chant as they row a boat.[23] In fact, he said that the prayers you want to memorize can be recited while you work to help commit them to memory.

[22] For example, see Clement of Alexandria, *Miscellanies* 7.7, and Tertullian, *On Chastity* 10.

[23] Augustine of Hippo, *Of the Work of Monks* 20.

The truth is that we all *need* daily prayer, to resist temptation and to maintain peace of mind. St. Augustine quotes Matthew 26:41 to emphasize the need for vigilance against temptation: *Watch and pray that you may not undergo the test. The spirit is willing, but the flesh is weak.*[24] And when it comes to peace in life, peace is not something you achieve and just settle into, as if now you can relax; peace also requires vigilance to avoid the things that rob us of peace. The world wants to take away your peace and replace it with chaos and drama and complications and temptations toward imbalance in life, and so, although this sounds counterintuitive, we all need to continually *strive* for peace, by constantly renewing our commitment to be detached from the things of the world.[25] And the only way to do this is through daily prayer.

Our earliest advice on daily prayer comes from the *Didache*, which says that Christians should pray the Our Father three times each day.[26] By the time of Tertullian, at the turn of the third century, this idea of praying the Our Father three times a day had been expanded to the concept of three specific *prayer hours* per day, which ideally were the third hour (between 8:00 and 9:00 a.m.), the sixth hour (between 11:00 a.m. and noon), and the ninth hour (between 2:00 and 3:00 p.m.).[27] Tertullian says that this

[24] Augustine of Hippo, *On the Good of Widowhood* 21.

[25] See Cyprian of Carthage, *Treatise IV: On the Lord's Prayer* 13, and *Treatise VII: On the Mortality* 18.

[26] *Didache* 8.

[27] Tertullian *On Fasting* 10. On the Roman reckoning of the hours of the day, see "Times and Seasons," in James L. Papandrea, *A Week in the Life of Rome* (Downers Grove, IL: IVP Academic, 2019), 22–23. The original three prayer hours of the early Christians was, no doubt, patterned after the Jewish tradition of praying three times each day. See, for example, Daniel 6:11. Jews prayed at the third hour, the ninth hour, and at sunset, at which times they prayed their primary prayers, the Shema (their "creed," from Deuteronomy 6:4–9) and the Eighteen Benedictions. There are some who believe that the Our Father is Jesus' summary and "boiling down" of the Eighteen Benedictions, just as His two greatest commandments are a summary and condensing of the original Ten Commandments. On this, see Shane Kapler, *The Biblical Roots of Marian Consecration: Devotion to the Immaculate Heart in Light of Scripture* (Gastonia, NC: TAN Books, 2022), 185–186.

tradition goes back to the apostles and is based on the Old Testament precedent of Daniel's praying three times a day.[28] However, Tertullian also says that Christians should pray before eating, and he implies that some also pray during the night.[29] Therefore, we can already see that the three prayer hours per day are going to be further expanded. Clement of Alexandria remarked that "some" Christians prayed the three prayer hours, but he suggests that, in his opinion (and we remember he was on the very strict side of things), three is not enough. He cited Psalm 119:164, which says, "Seven times a day I praise you because your judgments are righteous," hinting that Christians should be praying seven prayer hours per day.[30]

St. Cyprian wrote that the three original prayer hours are "ancient" (apostolic) and are "a sacrament of the Trinity" and that "the perfect Trinity is numbered every three hours."[31] He says that the three prayer hours were chosen because the Holy Spirit came at the third hour (Acts 2:15), Peter had his vision of the "unclean" foods at the sixth hour (Acts 10:9), and Jesus died at the ninth hour (Matt. 27:46; Mark 15:34). Nevertheless, Cyprian adds to the ancient practice a morning and an evening prayer — the morning for the Resurrection, and the evening as a vigil to pray for the return of the Lord.[32] Thus, we see the development of the total number of prayer hours into five.

By the time of the latest additions to the Church order manual known as the *Apostolic Tradition*, we read of six prayer hours. In addition to the original three hours, we now have a formal morning prayer, which was meant to be prayed as soon as one wakes up, before going to work (though if there is Mass or catechetical instruction on that day, one should go there).

[28] Tertullian, *On Fasting* 10; *On Prayer* 23, 25. Cf. Dan. 6:11. Notice that Daniel prayed kneeling, facing Jerusalem (which, for him, would have been facing west).

[29] Tertullian, *On Prayer* 25; *To His Wife* 5.

[30] Clement of Alexandria, *Miscellanies* 7.7.

[31] Cyprian of Carthage, *Treatise IV: On the Lord's Prayer* 34–35.

[32] Cyprian of Carthage, *Treatise IV: On the Lord's Prayer* 35. In fact, Cyprian remarked that the Church's prayers are ongoing, "day and night," by which he must have meant the personal prayers of the laity. See *Treatise V: Address to Demetrianus* 20.

This is presumably the first hour of the day, between 6:00 and 7:00 a.m.[33] And then we have a formal evening prayer, meant to be at bedtime; and a midnight prayer, sometimes called "cockcrow" (assumed to be three hours before sunrise, so perhaps between 3:00 and 4:00 a.m.). In addition, the *Apostolic Tradition* mentions a mealtime (dinner) prayer.[34] We should note, however, that it is unlikely that most laypeople actually prayed for a whole hour at these times. For most Christians, praying throughout the day probably meant stopping for a moment to pray the Our Father, and perhaps a few other prayers, at some time during the designated hour.

Cyril of Jerusalem recommends that if a Christian wakes up in the middle of the night, he should use that time to pray, especially to call to mind his sins before God. The nighttime is an especially good time for prayer, says St. Cyril, because it becomes a vigil.[35] It is also a good time to read the Scriptures, especially the psalms, and we will see below how the reading of the psalms or other Scriptures becomes a form of prayer.

In the monastic communities like the ones led by St. Basil of Caesarea and St. Benedict of Nursia, the monks eventually adopted a very standardized *Liturgy of the Hours*, also called the Divine Office. And with that, Clement of Alexandria finally got his way — and then some — since the number of prayer hours was expanded to not seven but eight. As they developed at their peak, here are the eight prayer hours (the times are not specific, the point is to spread them out to sanctify the entire day):

- Dawn Prayer (*Lauds*) — Traditionally anticipates the dawn, 3:00 to 4:00 a.m.
- Morning Prayer (*Prime*) — Traditionally the first hour of the day, 6:00 to 7:00 a.m.
- Midmorning Prayer (*Terce*) — Traditionally the third hour, 8:00 to 9:00 a.m.
- Midday Prayer (*Sext*) — Traditionally the sixth hour, 11:00 a.m. to noon
- Midafternoon Prayer (*None*) — Traditionally the ninth hour, 2:00 to 3:00 p.m.

[33] *Apostolic Tradition* 35–36.

[34] *Apostolic Tradition* 7.49.

[35] Cyril of Jerusalem, *Procatechesis* 16; *Catechetical Lectures* 9.7.

- Evening Prayer (*Vespers or Evensong*) — Traditionally at sunset
- Bedtime Prayer (*Compline*) — Traditionally before going to bed
- Midnight Prayer (*Matins*) — Traditionally in the middle of one's sleep time

Eventually, the hours were cut back to seven, as (for all practical purposes) Dawn Prayer and Morning Prayer were combined into one, meant to be prayed at sunrise. But the reality is that this kind of commitment to prayer was never expected of the laity. This was always for the clergy and those in religious communities. As we will see below, however, there were ways that the laity followed the example of the monks by creating prayer rhythms of their own, suited to their lifestyle and their responsibilities in the world. The development of private devotion among the laity will combine elements from Jewish prayer, Celtic Christian prayer, and the practice of the monks. But before we can get to that, we have to talk about how the Church fathers were adamant that a lifestyle of prayer could not include *only* prayer.

The Two Wings of Prayer

St. Augustine wrote that if you want your prayers to fly up to God, you must give them the two wings of fasting and almsgiving.[36] In fact, all the Church fathers would seem to agree that prayer with fasting and almsgiving is much more likely to be heard and answered than prayer that is not accompanied by these two "wings." St. Cyprian drew attention to the archangel Raphael's advice in the book of Tobit: "Prayer with fasting is good. Almsgiving with righteousness is better than wealth with wickedness. It is better to give alms than to store up gold, for almsgiving saves from death, and purges all sin. Those who give alms will enjoy a full life" (12:8–9). St. Cyprian interprets this as follows: "Our petitions become efficacious by almsgiving, life is redeemed from dangers by almsgiving, [and] souls are delivered from death by almsgiving."[37] He further says that no one should expect God to hear his prayers if he does not hear the prayers of the poor (Prov. 21:13).[38] Cyprian said that our prayer

[36] Augustine of Hippo, *On the Psalms* 43.7.

[37] Cyprian of Carthage, *Treatise VIII: On Works and Alms* 5.

[38] Cyprian of Carthage, *Treatise VIII: On Works and Alms* 5.

must not be "naked," that is, unclothed by good works.[39] And he speaks for the consensus of the Church fathers when he assumes that the concept of "good works" in general is what we mean when we talk about almsgiving.[40]

St. John Chrysostom wrote that praying is not separate from doing. Jesus taught us how to pray, and then immediately taught us what to do.[41] Chrysostom goes so far as to say that "not by grace only, you see, ought we to become [God's] children, but also by our works."[42] He names the good works he has in mind, giving them as a list of remedies or medicines for the salvation of the soul. In addition to prayer, the list includes the meta-virtues of forgiveness, thanksgiving, and humility, as well as repentance and confession of sins, and "showing mercy in alms and actions."[43] In fact, he says, "there is no pardon, no, none for the one who does not do works of mercy."[44]

All this is to say that when it comes to a lifestyle of praying without ceasing, prayer itself is only one leg of a tripod — the other two legs being equally necessary for stability: fasting and almsgiving. Pope St. Leo the Great wrote that there are three duties of every Christian — three things, in fact, that literally define what it means to be religious (in the sense of pious, or devoted) — and these are the three traditional disciplines of prayer, fasting, and almsgiving. These three are the foundation of all virtue and the catalyst for all sanctification.[45]

Fasting

Jewish believers incorporated fasting into the observance of the Hebrew religion, and Jesus assumed that His followers would continue that practice (Matt. 6:16–18; cf. Matt. 9:15; Mark 2:20; Luke 5:35). Jesus Himself would have been raised with regular fasting, and so, for Him, there is no "if," only "*when* you fast ..." (Matt. 6:16). We know from multiple sources that the

[39] Cyprian of Carthage, *Treatise IV: On the Lord's Prayer* 32–33.

[40] Cyprian of Carthage, *Treatise VIII: On Works and Alms* 5.

[41] John Chrysostom, *Homilies on Matthew* 23.

[42] John Chrysostom, *Homilies on Matthew* 19.

[43] John Chrysostom, *Homilies on Matthew* 42, *Homilies on Second Corinthians* 4.

[44] John Chrysostom, *Homilies on Hebrews* 31.

[45] Leo of Rome, *Sermon* 15.4. See also Augustine of Hippo, *On Man's Perfection in Righteousness* 8.

early Christians were expected to fast two days a week, on Wednesdays and Fridays.[46] This is already assumed in the *Didache*.[47] According to the Church order manual, the *Apostolic Constitutions*, Christians fast on Wednesdays because that's when Jesus was betrayed by Judas, and on Fridays because that's the day of the Crucifixion.[48] Since fasting is originally an act of mourning,[49] we commemorate these two events with fasting. However, it seems that when a saint's feast day fell on a Wednesday or a Friday, the fast was suspended.[50] So right from the beginning we can see that the practice of fasting is not only about the deprivation; it is part of a rhythm of fasting and feasting, as appropriate to the day and season.

For the early Christians, fasting was more than just about food. It was a way to discipline the body, and so, even early on, we can see that the definition of *fasting* could be much broader than simply going without eating. In some places, and at some times, there was an expectation that married couples fast from intimacy for twenty-four hours before receiving the Eucharist — and in the West, this became one of the justifications for the development of a celibate clergy. A priest who is expected to celebrate Mass every day, cannot be married because he would also be expected to abstain from marital intimacy for twenty-four hours before each Mass. In any case, fasting was seen as an act of sacrifice, in humility,[51] which, as we will see, is the key to everything in the life of prayer.

Beyond this, we don't get any real consensus from the Church fathers as to what fasting looked like, exactly. In the *Apostolic Tradition*, bread and water seem to be a concession for those who are sick or pregnant, so this must mean that the expectation (or the ideal, in the mind of the author) was normally a complete fast from all food.[52] However, we also get the sense

[46] Tertullian refers to these two days as the "station" days. The assumption is that the fasting is accompanied by prayer. Tertullian, *To His Wife* 4.

[47] *Didache* 8.

[48] *Apostolic Constitutions* 5.15.

[49] See Dan. 9:3.

[50] Once the season of Lent developed, Lent took precedence over the feast day, so that if a saint's feast day fell on a Wednesday or a Friday during Lent, the fast was kept.

[51] See Ezra 8:21.

[52] *Apostolic Tradition* 33.

that, in most cases, the day's fasting ends at the ninth hour (by 3:00 p.m.), which would mean that it was over before dinnertime (or for those early Christians who were using the Jewish reckoning of the day, a meal could be taken after sundown).[53]

Eventually the rhythm of fasting and feasting was expanded beyond a weekly rhythm to a seasonal rhythm.[54] Seasons of mourning and humility for one's sins came to precede the feasts of the Resurrection (Easter) and the Incarnation (Christmas) as a time of preparation for them. And so the seasons of Lent and Advent developed as whole seasons that included fasting, and eventually the Lenten fast emerged as an expectation for all Christians.

For Lent in particular, Good Friday was a fasting day from the very beginning. Then, but still very early on, that one-day fast was expanded to two days, to include Holy Saturday.[55] In some places, it was expanded to three days, to include Holy Thursday, but of course, in those cases, the fasting day was ended in time to celebrate the Lord's Supper in the evening of Holy Thursday. By the third century, the fast lasted all of Holy Week, and from there, it was expanded to three weeks and then to forty days, in commemoration of Jesus' forty days in the desert during His temptation.[56] The longer fasting season may also have been influenced by, or coincided with, the times of catechesis in preparation for Baptism, since the most popular times to be baptized in the early Church were Easter and Christmas. There was a general expectation that preparation for Baptism included fasting, and even as early as the *Didache*, it is recommended that the whole congregation

[53] We do see a bit of a controversy over the Montanists, who were the exception to this. They were keeping their fast beyond the ninth hour, perhaps shaming the mainstream Christians with their strictness. See the appendix on charismatics in the early Church.

[54] With regard to feasting, it is worth noting that in Jerusalem, when Lent was over, fasting was actually prohibited from Easter to Pentecost, even for those monks who fasted all year round the rest of the year.

[55] *Apostolic Tradition* 33.

[56] Socrates Scholasticus, *Ecclesiastical History* 5.22. These forty days were calculated differently in different places, depending on whether Sundays were excluded, etc. In the time of Egeria's pilgrimage, Jerusalem had an eight-week Lent because Saturdays were also excluded (except Holy Saturday).

fast along with those preparing for their Baptism.[57] So the Lenten fast also functions as a way of praying for those preparing for Baptism at the Easter vigil.

But again, there does not seem to be any consensus about what the Lenten fast meant for people. Based on Egeria's description of Lent in Jerusalem, people do what they can, but there are no universal rules that everyone must follow, and no one is criticized for what he or she cannot do. We might assume that the same expectation applied, that a fasting day meant no food at all until the ninth hour, and Egeria does say that no leavened bread is allowed, but she mentions something like an oatmeal or gruel ("flour soup") that is allowed.[58] The *Didascalia* says that bread and water (and salt) are allowed throughout Lent (though a day's fast seems to last through the night until the next morning), and it is only on Good Friday that the expectation is to eat no food at all. The *Apostolic Constitutions* allows that bread with salt may be eaten on the Monday through Thursday of Holy Week, but again, no food at all on Good Friday. So we do not get any universal consensus from the Church fathers about exactly *how* to fast, and in Jerusalem at least, it seems to have been up to one's own discernment the level of discipline one could follow. The most rigorous fasting we hear of (apart from a few unhealthy outliers) was a group of monks called *Apotactitae* who fasted every day of the year, which essentially meant that they ate only one meal per day, after the ninth hour. But even these were required to suspend their fast during certain days of feasting.

The point of this is not to be concerned about the specific rules for fasting in the early Church — except perhaps to note that there were no universal rules — and in any case, the Church continues to advise people with regard to fasting, and so we have our Magisterium to guide us in fasting now. Rather, the point is to notice that, for the Church fathers and the early Christians, prayer and fasting go hand in hand, and both figure into a rhythm of a life of practicing the Faith. The Church fathers were certain

[57] *Didache* 7; Justin Martyr, *I Apology* 61. Keep in mind, however, that infant and child Baptism was practiced in the early Church, so not everyone who was baptized went through catechesis or was expected to fast. On infant Baptism, see Irenaeus of Lyons, *Against Heresies* 2.22.

[58] Egeria, *Diary of Egeria* 28.4.

that fasting enhances prayer.[59] Fasting facilitates resisting temptation, and it is a form of penance when we fail to resist temptation.[60] The author of *II Clement* goes so far as to say that "fasting is better than prayer"![61] Though to be fair, he might be exaggerating to make his point, really meaning to say that fasting with prayer is better than prayer *alone,* and in any case, we don't really know who this author is, and he might not be speaking for anyone but himself.

Nevertheless, the Church fathers all believed that fasting is not just a matter of "not eating" or even "going hungry." It isn't just a negative, in the sense of going without or giving up something. There has to be a positive aspect to it — not leaving an emptiness but filling the lack with something more significant.[62] The food we refuse has to be replaced by something, and so fasting is a discipline in which one embraces something: sorrow for sin, humility, devotion to God, and works of mercy, including almsgiving.[63] In this way, we turn our gratitude into discipline.

Almsgiving

We don't use the word *almsgiving* much anymore. We assume it's synonymous with "giving to charity" or something like that, and, to a large extent, it is. But the word itself, in the Greek, is based on the same root word as the word for *mercy*. To give alms is to show mercy or to have compassion. Usually we mean it in the specific sense of giving to the poor, but it can be thought of in a broader sense, to include any act of kindness or sharing of resources or even giving our time. For the Church fathers, almsgiving is a work of mercy, as it is to this day, though, for the early Church, the concept of almsgiving would include everything on the Church's list of corporal works of mercy: feeding the hungry, giving drink to the thirsty, sheltering the homeless, and even giving up time to visit the sick and imprisoned — pretty much everything Jesus

[59] Tob. 12:8; Jth. 4:13; Joel 2:12–13; Jon. 3:7–10; Acts 13:2–3; 14:23.

[60] Polycarp of Smyrna, *Letter to the Philippians* 7.

[61] *II Clement* 16.

[62] I am reminded of the parable about a demon who is cast out of a man but returns to find the man has not replaced the demon's presence with anything, and so there is room for the demon to return along with seven of his friends! (Matt. 12:43–45; Luke 11:24–26).

[63] Cf. Isa. 58:6–11. See Augustine, *Confessions* 13.23, 13.25.

mentions in Matthew 25. For the Church fathers, almsgiving is a concrete way of making a spiritual sacrifice (1 Pet. 2:5) and a sacrifice of praise — as Ben Sira said, "one who gives alms presents a sacrifice of praise."[64]

In the same letter referenced above, the author of *II Clement* goes on to say, "Fasting is better than prayer," but "almsgiving is better than both … for almsgiving relieves the burden of sin."[65] Again, I would interpret this as though he is saying that *prayer with* almsgiving is better than prayer and fasting together *without almsgiving.* The point is that if fasting enhances prayer, almsgiving does too (see Acts 10:1–6, 31). We have already seen how St. Cyprian said that we should not expect God to hear our prayers if we do not hear the prayers of the poor. Almsgiving is our way of answering the prayers of the poor. It is a sacrifice we make but one that benefits us as well, for the way to make a deposit in the storehouse of Heaven is to put food into the belly of a hungry person.[66] Pope St. Leo the Great said, "Nothing is so much a person's own as that which he spends on his neighbor."[67] To give alms is another way (besides forgiving one another) to avoid being the "unmerciful servant." We receive the generosity of God, and out of gratitude, we pay it forward, offering generosity to others. There is a sense in which we cannot really keep the gifts of God unless we share them. In fact, the Church fathers called forgiving those who wrong us a kind of spiritual almsgiving.

Almsgiving demonstrates not only our gratitude toward God, through a concrete action, but also our trust in God's providence, since we give away something we may potentially need, trusting that God will provide for us anyway. It's an act of faith that says we believe that God has always provided for us and always will. Recognition of past blessings informs our faith and trust in God for the future, and almsgiving demonstrates that faith (cf. James 2:18).

[64] Sir. 35:1–5. The phrases "spiritual sacrifice" and "sacrifice of praise" are often interpreted as though they refer only to worship in the assembly, but the Church fathers would understand that good works are in a way the Christian sacrifice that replaces the animal sacrifices of the temple. Cf. Matt. 9:13; 12:7.

[65] *II Clement* 16.

[66] Cf. Augustine of Hippo, *On the Lord's Prayer* 6.6, where he says, "Store up alms in the heart of the poor."

[67] Leo of Rome, *Sermon* 16.2.

In a way, this brings us back to the concept of synergy, participating in what God is doing in the world. Any prayer for God to help the less fortunate would seem empty and hypocritical if it does not include something to the effect of asking God how *we* can help the less fortunate (James 2:15–16). We must be ready to participate in God's answering of our own prayers to the extent that we can. Prayer in relation to the poor begins with gratitude for all we have, acknowledging that there is no reason we should have anything that they don't have — and without claiming we've earned it because, by one stroke of bad luck, the roles could be reversed. We should always say, *There but for the grace of God go I.* There is nothing wrong with hard work and earning, but so many people work hard and don't earn much because they struggle with hardships we don't have. Economic earning is not the same thing as moral deserving, and no one deserves to eat less than anyone else. All resources, gifts, blessings, and good health ultimately come from God, and we cannot presume to know why He has given us something that He has not given others, except for the certainty that if He has given us a surplus, the purpose is to share it.[68] Don't ask, *Why didn't God give them more resources?* Instead ask, *Why didn't God give me more hardships?* It may be that God has given us more because we more desperately needed to learn how to share. It may be that when we pray for God to help the poor, God's answer is, *I gave you the resources to help the poor.* Therefore, almsgiving is not an option for the Christian, it is the third leg of the tripod (James 2:13).

In addition to benefiting the one who receives the alms, almsgiving also benefits the giver because the Church fathers would all agree that almsgiving is a form of penance. The book of Tobit provides the Old Testament background for Christian almsgiving: "Almsgiving delivers from death and keeps one from entering into Darkness. Almsgiving is a worthy offering in the sight of the Most High for all who practice it" (4:10–11). And Sirach tells us, "As water quenches a flaming fire, so almsgiving atones for sins" (3:30; see 29:8–13). In fact, even before the Sacrament of Confession and Reconciliation was standardized, almsgiving was the primary penance to atone for post-baptismal sin. In the second century, Bishop Irenaeus of Lyons said that "possessions distributed to the poor do annul former

[68] Clement of Alexandria, *Who Is the Rich Man That Shall Be Saved?*

covetousness."[69] St. Cyprian wrote that "every man, in proportion to his wealth, ought by his patrimony rather to redeem his transgressions than to increase them."[70] In other words, he's saying that the best thing we can do with wealth is to use it to do penance because other uses of wealth risk increasing our sins. John Chrysostom said that the way to wash away the pollution of sin is "by tears, by prayers, and by works of mercy."[71] St. Augustine said that almsgiving cleanses us of venial sins, though not mortal sins — at least not habitual mortal sins — since almsgiving works as a penance only if a person is willing to change and turn away from sin (otherwise, it would be reduced to buying forgiveness).[72] And Pope St. Leo the Great wrote, "By alms we redeem our sins."[73]

All of this may seem shocking to Christians who were brought up in the Protestant tradition. But remember that the Church fathers all assumed that when they wrote these things, their audience knew what they had already been taught: that, on the one hand, we are not saved by works, but on the other hand, we do not persevere without them (Matt. 24:13; Mark 13:13; Luke 21:19).

Finally, there is something I will call *intercessory almsgiving*, for just as the reality of vicarious faith allows one person to be baptized on the basis of the faith of another (parents and sponsors), and building on the tradition of prayer for the dead, it is possible to give alms for the dead — that is, to benefit a soul in Purgatory.[74] You can give to the poor on behalf of someone else as an act of intercessory prayer. It may seem obvious to us that we can make a donation in honor of someone, but for the Church fathers, the donation really does benefit the one in whose honor it is made, especially if that person is a soul in Purgatory. You may already be thinking that the abuse of this doctrine (the sale of indulgences) in sixteenth-century Germany became one of the sparks that ignited the Protestant Reformation, and that is true. But that was an *abuse* of the doctrine that came along much later. Our point

[69] Irenaeus of Lyons, *Against Heresies* 4.12. He gives the example of Zacchaeus, who vowed to give back more than he took.

[70] Cyprian of Carthage, *Treatise II: On the Dress of Virgins* 11.

[71] John Chrysostom, *Homily on Hebrews* 31.

[72] Augustine of Hippo, *On Man's Perfection in Righteousness* 9; *Handbook on Faith, Hope, and Love* 70.

[73] Leo of Rome, *Sermon* 15.4.

[74] See Jerome, *Epistle* 66.5, and John Chrysostom, *Homilies on Philippians* 3.

for the present is to underscore that, for the early Christians, almsgiving enhances prayer and is an important part of the life of prayer. It is, in fact, part of what it means to "pray without ceasing."

Almsgiving in general was seen by the Church fathers as creating a kind of symbiotic relationship between those with surplus resources and those without. The specific ministry of the wealthy was to give to the poor, and the specific ministry of the poor was to pray for the rich, since, after all, the rich have more distractions and attachments, making it harder for them to go on to salvation (Matt. 19:23–26; Mark 10:23–27; Luke 18:24–27). And although Jesus said His followers should give alms secretly (that is, without making a show of it [Matt. 6:1–4]), the Church fathers did believe that the ones receiving the alms should know who gave them so that they could pray for their patrons.

One Church father, Clement of Alexandria, even wrote a whole treatise called *Who Is the Rich Man That Shall Be Saved?* to show that it is not a sin to be rich, *per se*, but it is a sin to hoard wealth, and that although it is as difficult for a wealthy person to enter the Kingdom of God as it is for a camel to go through the eye of a needle, nevertheless it is not impossible, since nothing is impossible for God. But the point is that the way the rich man will get through the eye of the needle is by giving alms and by the intercessory prayers of the poor to whom he gave.

And so prayer flies on the two wings of fasting and almsgiving, which is to say that prayer is supported and enhanced by the disciplines of self-denial and self-sacrifice, motivated by gratitude. Some in the early Church believed that the money saved by fasting should be given directly to the poor.[75] In a way, all sin is an expression of selfishness, and both self-denial and self-sacrifice train us in unselfishness, thereby moving us away from sin. In fact, one could probably define spiritual growth and sanctification entirely in terms of decreasing in selfishness and increasing in generosity.

Prayer is good, but prayer with fasting is better, and prayer with fasting and almsgiving is the best, because it completes the tripod of spiritual disciplines. And all three of these disciplines are (ideally) a part of a rhythm of life that incorporates a balance of both fasting and feasting; both counting our blessings and giving them away.

[75] *Didascalia Apostolorum* 19.

Lectio Divina

You may have heard it said that prayer should be at least as much listening to God as talking to God. The sentiment is well-meaning, but in the early Church (and especially before the development of contemplative prayer), "listening to God" meant only one thing: listening to Scripture. No one in the early Church would have tried to just sit there quietly and hear the voice of God. People did hear the voice of God, to be sure — visionaries such as St. Perpetua. But for most people then — as it is today — God speaks to us when we read the Scriptures.

St. Cyprian wrote, speaking of reflection on certain Scripture passages, "The mind must be strengthened, beloved brethren, by these meditations. By exercises of this kind it must be confirmed against all the darts of the devil. Let there be the *divine reading* in the hands, the Lord's thoughts in the mind. Let constant prayer never cease at all, let saving labor persevere."[76] So by the third century, we can see what became a fourth prayer discipline emerging alongside the original three. For Cyprian, another way to engage in prayer without ceasing, another saving discipline, is meditation on Scripture, what he calls "divine reading." Although it's too early in the Church's history to expect any kind of precise definition of the word *meditation* relative to prayer, what we have here is the tradition of praying the words of Scripture.

We know that the Church inherited from Judaism the practice of praying (or chanting) the psalms in the liturgy. And we know that the monks would develop the practice of praying the psalms in their daily and weekly prayer rhythms and that this would become the heart of the Liturgy of the Hours. The *Apostolic Tradition* advised that those who owned copies of the Scriptures should read them every day.[77] St. Augustine included the reading of Scripture in a list of what he called the "spiritual delights" (to be pursued in order to replace the "carnal delights" in one's life).[78] Of course, at first, only the wealthiest laypeople could afford to own books of the Scriptures. But for those who had the free time, they began to find ways to imitate the monks in their commitment to praying the psalms. All of this developed

[76] Cyprian of Carthage, *Treatise X: On Jealousy and Envy* 16 (emphasis added).

[77] *Apostolic Tradition* 41.

[78] Augustine of Hippo, *On the Good of Widowhood* 26.

into the practice of praying the words of Scripture, as if they were one's own, making the words one's own, and mentally applying them to one's own situation.[79] By praying in this way, a person reads the words of the Psalms or other Scriptures: words directed toward God become the person's own prayers, and words directed toward God's people become God's own loving message to the person praying — thus, listening to God.

By the end of the early Church period, St. Benedict of Nursia formalized this practice into what we now call *Lectio Divina*. A good description of how *Lectio Divina* is done can be found in the letters of the great spiritual director Jean-Pierre de Caussade, who wrote:

> Begin by placing yourself in the presence of God, and by begging his help. Read quietly, slowly, word for word, to enter into the subject more with the heart than the mind. At the end of each paragraph that contains a complete meaning, stop for the time it would take to recite a Pater [the Our Father] or even a little longer, to assimilate what you have read, or to rest and remain peacefully before God. Should this peace and rest last for a long time it will be all the better. But when you find that your mind wanders, resume your reading, and continue thus, frequently renewing these same pauses.... Above all, drop all anxious thoughts, abandoning to Divine Providence all that might become a subject of preoccupation for you.[80]

The goal is to read slowly, not to understand or overthink the meaning but just to own it. Then as one reads, one will naturally find a phrase or a few words that stand out as particularly relevant or as summarizing the rest in the mind. Then the object is to focus on those words and read them again, praying them as a prayer. Go back to those few words or that phrase as many times as it seems appropriate and pray them. This is *Lectio Divina*, divine reading. For more detailed instructions on the practice of *Lectio Divina*, see the companion volume to this book, *Praying the Psalms: The Divine Gateway to* Lectio Divina *and Contemplative Prayer.*

[79] John Cassian, *Conferences: Second Conference of Abbot Isaac, On Prayer* 11.

[80] De Caussade, *Letters on the Practice of Abandonment* 2.35. This same method can be used to read other edifying books, though that should not replace the reading of Scripture.

Therefore, to pray like the earliest Christians:

1. **Make time to pray every day.** On the days you go to Mass, that counts, and that could be enough for that day, but on the days you don't go to Mass, you'll need to decide when to pray. If you can do the whole Liturgy of the Hours, then, by all means, go for it. I know laypeople who have taken their prayer life to the next level by incorporating the Divine Office. Others take it up for Lent or for a certain period of time. But for the most part, it's the clergy and religious who do all the prayer hours. What will be your prayer hour? Do you have time in the morning? It seems like a good idea to start the day with prayer, but if you don't have time in the morning, then make it in the evening or at night or at noon — whatever works for you so that you can set aside significant time for prayer every day. If you don't already have the habit of praying before meals, try to cultivate that habit. Pray whenever you eat (*and drink*, says St. Basil!). And if you wake up in the middle of the night, especially if you find it hard to get back to sleep — don't waste that time — use it to pray. I find that breathing prayers (see the next chapter) are perfect for these times of prayer in the middle of the night.

2. **Beware that your prayers are not too focused on yourself.** Don't let prayer become an exercise in trying to make God do your will. In fact, as much as possible, try to avoid asking for anything for yourself in your prayers. Remember that God does not need you to pray and does not need your advice. And just as in the Mass, it's not about what you get from the prayer after the prayer is over; it's about what you become from the prayer itself and how the prayer contributes to your sanctification. Make sure you are bringing to your prayer the meta-virtues of forgiveness, thanksgiving, and humility. And when you pray for others, try to avoid telling God what to do for them. Work on limiting your prayers of intercession to simply remembering others in prayer and lifting them up to God's care. Leave it to God to decide what to do for them. And don't forget to pray for your enemies — that also contributes to your sanctification, so don't neglect it. Pray for your enemies to become your friends.

3. **Be intentional about creating a rhythm of fasting for your life.** For many people, this will overlap with dieting, or trying to get into shape, and there's nothing wrong with that, but don't make fasting all about trying to lose weight.

The motivations are different. But do make a plan to fast regularly. Certainly make sure you understand the Church's expectations for Lent, but beyond that, find ways to incorporate the discipline of fasting into the rest of the year as well. This may require some trial and error, to see what you can handle, and that's okay, but do it. Figure out how to organize your life around a balance of feasting and fasting. Not only your fasting days, but also what are your holy days, saints' days, or other holidays on which you will celebrate? Create order out of chaos by organizing your daily, weekly, monthly, and even yearly rhythms. Maybe even think about how often you will go on pilgrimages to holy sites. And although the Church fathers don't talk about this, I would add: incorporate regular exercise into your weekly rhythm to be a good steward of the gift that is your body.

4. **Be intentional about your almsgiving.** Many of us give to charity, but it's too easy to do it randomly or to let it be so minor that it doesn't really make it a sacrifice. Look at your budget (and yes, that might mean you need to create a budget — but that's a good discipline too: to be a good steward of your resources). What can you afford to give that will be a sacrifice but still be within the bounds of responsibility for your family? In general, the early Church fathers did not worry about amounts or percentages, and they did not mandate tithing (only one of the Church order documents recommends it). Like fasting, giving to those less fortunate is a matter of one's personal ability and conscience. Just don't think you can wait for opportunities to present themselves. They may, and you should be ready to give when they do, but there should be some regular giving as well, over and above doing your part for your parish or local church. We all need to express our gratitude by paying God's gifts forward in self-sacrifice. Also remember that almsgiving is not limited to giving money to the poor. For all practical purposes, all of the works of mercy count as almsgiving. Think about how you will balance giving money versus volunteering time or offering up other resources. Can you step up your game with regard to the works of mercy?

5. **Think about the concept of spiritual almsgiving.** This includes forgiving others, giving others the benefit of the doubt, having compassion and empathy for others, not being judgmental, and refusing to gossip. Could you do a better job with spiritual almsgiving? Pray for the grace to have the presence of mind and the strength to do that.

6. **Read Scripture every day using the practice of** Lectio Divina. If you want to listen to God, understand that God speaks to you primarily through the Scriptures. Begin with the psalms, since they are especially conducive to personal prayer. Use the companion volume to this book: *Praying the Psalms: The Divine Gateway to* Lectio Divina *and Contemplative Prayer*. Then branch out into other Scriptures. This will take some time, but make a point to incorporate *Lectio Divina* into your prayer hour every day.

To Go Deeper

Primary Sources

James L. Papandrea, *Praying the Psalms: The Divine Gateway to* Lectio Divina *and Contemplative Prayer* (Manchester, NH: Sophia Institute Press, 2023).

Who Is the Rich Man That Shall Be Saved? by Clement of Alexandria (late second century), in the Ante-Nicene Fathers Series, vol. 2, https://www.newadvent.org/fathers/0207.htm.

Secondary Sources

James L. Papandrea, *A Week in the Life of Rome* (Downers Grove, IL: IVP Academic, 2019).

James L. Papandrea, *Reading the Church Fathers: A History of the Early Church and the Development of Doctrine* (Manchester, NH: Sophia Institute Press, 2022).

Insight 6

The Truth about Repetition

It's a good thing!

When you pray, do not be like the hypocrites,
who love to stand and pray in the synagogues
and on street corners so that others may see them.
Amen, I say to you, they have received their reward.
But when you pray, go to your inner room,
close the door, and pray to your Father in secret.
And your Father who sees in secret will repay you.
In praying, do not babble like the pagans,
who think that they will be heard because of
their many words.
Do not be like them.
Your Father knows what you need
before you ask him.

—Jesus, Matthew 6:5–8

As I said above, it's surprising how little the Church fathers and mothers said about prayer. They mostly talk about how important it is, but they don't really *teach* people how to pray, because they believed that Jesus had already done that. His primary teaching on prayer was, of course, the Our Father — his response when his disciples asked him to teach them how to pray. And as we have noted, Jesus' intention for the Our Father was that it be repeated verbatim — in fact, St. Augustine said that Jesus didn't just teach the Our Father; he *dictated* it.[1] And very early on, quite possibly based on Jesus' instruction, the Church set the expectation that Christians should pray the Our Father three times a day. And so, from the very beginning, the early Christians assumed that prayers were meant to be repeated.

Of course, Jesus had a few other lessons on prayer as well, and one of these is the passage above, from Matthew's Gospel. However, in modern times, that passage has created a problem — or rather, a bad translation of that passage, which became very well known, and often memorized — created the problem. In what is perhaps one of the worst cases of bias affecting translation, the Greek phrase rendered above as "do not babble like the pagans" (verse 7) was translated, in some very influential versions of the Bible, as though it says, "do not use *meaningless repetition*," or worse, "*vain repetition*." This gave people the impression that Jesus was saying that repetition itself is meaningless or vain.[2] But as I have shown in my book

[1] Augustine of Hippo, *On the Lord's Prayer* 9.1.

[2] For example, the King James Version (KJV and NKJV) as well as the NASB. The so-called Living Bible is even worse, doubling down on the addition to the text with: "Don't recite the same prayer over and over as the heathen do,

Reading Scripture Like the Early Church, the word *repetition* never occurs in the Greek text of that verse![3] The word was added by translators who had a bias against repeating prayers. This same kind of bias is responsible for the idea that the Our Father was meant to be a template for prayer, demonstrating the various kinds of prayer — but as we have seen, we now know that all of that is a myth.

The passage above, Matthew 6:5–8, begins with a warning against prayer for show, such as we have already seen in the parable of the Pharisee and the tax collector (Luke 18:9–14). Prayer is not meant to call attention to ourselves or to try to impress others. The only answer you will ever get to that kind of self-aggrandizing prayer is, perhaps, attention. Maybe people *will* be impressed with you. But God will not, because He cannot be impressed. So then Jesus goes on from that to say that, by the way, God is also not impressed with a lot of words. As we noted above, God does not need you to go on and on about situations, backstories, and certainly not about excuses and justifications. All this is to say that Jesus warns us against falling into the trap of praying like the unbelievers, either with the philosophical approach (eloquence) or the pagan approach (cajoling), and so He advises His followers not to "babble on" with "many words" (that's the NABRE). Or another way to translate that might be, "do not heap up empty phrases" (as in the NRSVCE).

The point is that Jesus did not say, "Do not use repeated prayers"; He is saying, "Do not pray long prayers."[4] Keep it short, because *Your Father knows what you need before you ask Him*. This brings us back to the point that, as laypeople, we are off the hook from having to compose prayers in our own words. In fact, it turns out that it's not about our words at all, really; it's about what's in our hearts — our "inner room" — and God already knows

---

who think prayers are answered only by repeating them again and again." This is not at all what Jesus said. Note that the phrase even finds its way into some English translations of the Church fathers, even though it was not in their text, so the problem has a ripple effect when people read biased translations of the Church fathers. Thankfully, some of the revisions of older translations (of both the Bible and the Church fathers) are correcting the mistake.

[3] Papandrea, *Reading Scripture Like the Early Church*, 70–71.

[4] Augustine of Hippo, *Letter* 130.

that intimately. And even when we want to pour out our hearts before God (as Hannah did)[5] well, on the one hand we could never do that adequately or find the right words to do our hearts justice; and on the other hand, we don't need to, because God knows our hearts better than we do. This is why sometimes the prayers that express our needs best are the ones that go beyond words, when the Holy Spirit prays for us (Rom. 8:26–27). The hard truth is that we are most in danger of babbling on and on with "many words" and "empty phrases" when we try to pray in our own words.

Repetition Is a Good Thing!

So to go on and on about situations and needs in prayer is a form of babbling, and it's exactly what Jesus warned against. As we noted above, we do not need to give God advice about how to answer our prayers. On the other hand, repeating simple prayers is not babbling. In fact, Jesus Himself repeated His prayers. As a faithful Jew, He would have repeated the traditional Hebrew prayers. And when He was praying in the Garden of Gethsemane on the night of His arrest, at the moment of His greatest anxiety, we are told that He prayed the same prayer three times. Both Mark and Matthew point out that He prayed repeatedly, "saying the same thing" (Mark 14:35–36, 39, 41; Matt. 26:39, 42, 44). Of course, this is not due to any lack of faith on Jesus' part, and it's not because the Father didn't hear Him the first time or didn't know the situation.

So why did Jesus repeat His prayers? For the Church fathers, the key to answering this question is in the last part of Jesus' prayer, where He practiced what He preached. Just as He had told His disciples to pray to the Father, *Your will be done*, so Jesus now does that, saying, "Your will be done" — in

[5] 1 Sam. 1:15. As it turns out, the Old Testament is not very helpful for telling us *how* the Jews (let alone the early Christians) prayed, since most prayers recorded in the Old Testament are the prayers of a king or prophet asking God for discernment in matters of war and diplomacy. Those prayers tend to be answered by God directly, sometimes with the use of the Ephod, which is a kind of casting lots. And although the apostles did choose a replacement for Judas with this method in the book of Acts, the early Church did not encourage it as a method of private prayer, for obvious reasons. We should, in fact, avoid at all costs any kind of looking for signs, which quickly becomes a form of testing God.

Matthew 26:42, the same exact phrase as in the Our Father. In the Latin, the word is *fiat*, making this Jesus' *fiat*. Remember that Mary had her moment of *fiat* (Luke 1:38), and in the Our Father, Jesus had taught His disciples to follow her example and say *fiat* as well. Now it was His turn. And the point here is that Jesus repeated His own prayers as a way to align His human will to the divine will and participate in the will of the Father. Apparently, one time through the prayer was not enough for Him.

Incidentally, at this same time, Jesus told His sleepy disciples that they should pray as well — specifically that they "may not undergo the test," which, in Greek, is the exact same phrase as "lead us not into temptation" in the Our Father. I believe that Jesus was using this phrase as a shorthand for the whole prayer and that He was actually telling His disciples to pray the Our Father. So Jesus taught His disciples to pray repeated prayers, He instituted the Sacrament of the Lord's Supper, with its repeated Eucharistic prayers, and He Himself prayed the same prayers repeatedly. Clearly, He was not against repetition in prayer. And the apostles got the message. St. Paul prayed repeatedly (three times) for his "thorn in the flesh" to be removed — a prayer that was not answered with a yes, by the way (2 Cor. 12:8).

St. Augustine wrote about a friend whom he described as "a Christian and faithful servant" of God. He said of this friend, "Time and again he knelt before [God] in church repeating his prayers and lingering over them."[6] In fact, Augustine wrote that repeating prayers is a good way to make sure that we really pray the words, rather than just rushing through them or just going through the motions of prayer.[7] This may seem counterintuitive — in other words, it might seem like repeating prayers can too easily slip into mindless mouthing of words, and there are those who would argue against repetition in prayer by saying that repetition *makes* the words meaningless. But experience shows that this is not the case. The truth is that we are easily distracted no matter how we pray, so our minds wander in any case. But with repeated prayer, if our minds wander, we come back to the prayer, and we get another chance to really pray the words and make them our own. So if your mind wanders at the beginning of a short prayer, you will pick it up in the next round. If your mind wanders at the end of the prayer, you get that

[6] Augustine of Hippo, *Confessions* 8.6.

[7] Augustine of Hippo, *On the Lord's Prayer* 8.13.

next time. By repeating the prayer, you truly pray the whole prayer, and it sinks into your heart.

And to the objection that God hears you the first time, remember that we do not pray because God needs us to pray or because God needs information from us to care for us. We pray because we need to pray and because prayer is one way we participate in what God is doing in the world, and by praying we prepare ourselves to cooperate with God's grace. The truth is that repeated prayers contribute to our sanctification more than one-off prayers because the words become part of the formation of our consciences. And Gregory of Nyssa wrote (in the context of the Our Father), "Through frequent repetition, we may be given to understand some of its hidden meaning."[8]

Not Persistence, but Patience

Another place in the Gospels where Jesus teaches us about prayer is in the parables of the friend at midnight (Luke 11:5–8) and the unjust judge (Luke 18:1–8, which comes right before the parable of the Pharisee and the tax collector). In both of these parables, we see a person who is praying (asking) for something, and the person who is being asked (an annoyed neighbor and a corrupt judge) is unwilling to give it. Luke introduces the parable of the unjust judge by saying, "Then he told them a parable about the necessity for them to pray always without becoming weary." So Luke tells us up front the point of the parable: keep praying, and don't become weary — don't get tired of praying. In other words, don't be afraid to (or think you shouldn't have to) repeat your prayers. In fact, it would be impossible to "pray without ceasing" if every prayer had to be unique.

At the end of the parable of the friend at midnight, Jesus tells us the moral of the story, when He says that the prayer was answered "because of his persistence." That's what my Bible says, but the Greek word that is translated "persistence" does not quite mean *persistence* in the way we might think of it. It really means something like "because of the fact that he was willing to humiliate himself by being so annoying, at such an inconvenient time." The point is that Jesus is not telling us to be "persistent" in prayer, if that conjures up images of obstinacy, stubbornness, or forcefulness. Jesus is telling us to be humble enough to approach God repeatedly in prayer,

[8] Gregory of Nyssa, *Sermons on the Lord's Prayer*, Sermon 2.

without any feelings of entitlement (like saying, "I shouldn't have to ask twice"). In other words, these parables are not really about persistence; they are about patience. We know this because although it might appear as though the sleepy friend and the grumpy judge are playing the role of God in an allegory in these parables, God is obviously not being compared to an annoyed friend who can't be bothered to help us, much less a corrupt judge who finally answers our prayers only to shut us up.[9]

God *can't wait* to bless us (Matt. 7:9–11; Luke 11:11–13). But sometimes God does wait to bless us, so that we will enter into a deeper participation in Him and in what He is doing. And it is from that deeper participation that the fruit of the Spirit grows.[10] For the Church fathers, these parables are Jesus' teaching behind Paul's advice to "pray without ceasing." Jesus tells us to pray day and night and not to give up praying — even if that means praying the same prayer over and over again. It's not that God needs to hear it again but that we need to keep praying. And it could be that what we really need — and what the prayer is giving us — is patience. That might be what God is growing in us as we pray repeated prayers. As we have seen, prayer is not ultimately about asking for things (let alone getting things); prayer is about communion with God, for the purpose of sanctification and the goal of salvation.

Patience is, in fact, the active manifestation of trusting God. Both St. Cyprian and Tertullian wrote treatises called *On Patience,* though Cyprian mostly copied Tertullian's and added some of his own thoughts. With regard to prayer, patience means being willing to make time for prayer in the first place and then being willing to take it slow and not rush through your prayer. On those occasions when I've been blessed to pray with members of a religious community, it's surprising how slowly they go through their

[9] As St. Augustine pointed out, these parables are not technically allegories; rather, they are to be interpreted anagogically, in the sense of a contrast: "If it's like this on earth, how much more in Heaven." In other words, if people who are reluctant to answer a request will eventually give in, how much more does the God who is generous and merciful want to give us what we ask. Augustine of Hippo, *Our Lord's Sermon on the Mount* 15.

[10] This comes from Galatians 5:22–23: "The fruit of the Spirit is love, joy, peace, patience, kindness, generosity, faithfulness, gentleness, self-control." Here we are focusing on patience.

prayers, such as the Our Father. But this is their way of making sure it doesn't become mindless. They go slowly and really pray — that is, they think through and really *mean* — every word. In our own private prayers, we may not need to go quite as slowly as monks and nuns do, though we could probably go slower than we usually do. I will get back to that thought later in this chapter, but the point for now is that we often go too fast, thinking more about what we're planning to do when the prayer time is over than about the prayer. Prayer is meant to be prayed in the present, without dwelling on the past or planning the future, and to maintain this kind of presence in the moment requires patience.

The early Christians believed that Jesus' parable of the ten bridesmaids (sometimes called the ten virgins) set a precedent for the monastic lifestyle of watching and waiting (Matt. 25:1–13). The moral of the story is that the five wise bridesmaids were ready for the return of the groom at any time, but they were also prepared to be in it for the long haul — they were willing to be patient, even if the groom would not return for a long time. But this kind of vigilance through prayer is not for only for monks and nuns. For all Christians, trusting in God often means being willing to wait for what we want — or even for what we need. And sometimes the purpose of the waiting is specifically so that we might grow in patience. Patience is a sign of sanctification (it is a fruit of the Spirit), but it is also true that patience increases sanctification.

I think that most modern people have a hard time with the idea of waiting and with how much of the Christian life has to do with waiting and being vigilant. Jesus said we are to live one day at a time and not worry about tomorrow and that "seeking first" the Kingdom of God means focusing on the present (Matt. 6:25–34; Luke 12:22–31). But we are often so focused on planning that we fall into the trap of trying to control our future — which demonstrates a lack of faith in God.[11] We'll return to this issue of living in the present, as opposed to planning the future, in another chapter; for now, it must be said that "waiting," in the Christian sense of vigilance in prayer, is anything but passive. It does not mean inaction; it means active attention to the present and not short-changing faithfulness in the moment by focusing too much on the future. So although we may be tempted to think of patience

[11] De Caussade, *Letters on the Practice of Abandonment* 6.9.

as something passive, perhaps even irresponsibly so, true prayerful patience is active and contributes to our spiritual growth.

In fact, real patience requires courage and endurance. It is not simply refraining from complaining (though it is that); it is an active effort at keeping a positive attitude in the face of the crosses we have to bear. It is not simply keeping silent when we want to speak angry words; it is also having the courage and the trust in God to speak well of others even at the risk of our own reputation. Jean-Pierre de Caussade, the eighteenth-century spiritual director, wrote, "Let us always distrust our eagerness.... To take things patiently is to do a great deal.... Make your courage consist in patient endurance and resignation."[12] But the bottom line is that, for the Christian, being patient is active because being patient means praying. Prayer is how we stay vigilant against temptation. Prayer is what we do while we are waiting. Prayer is hope in action.

Have You Met St. Monica?

St. Monica was the mother of the famous St. Augustine, and we know of her through her son's autobiography, the *Confessions*. In that book, we read how she prayed for both her husband and her son to come to faith in Christ — prayers that were answered, but not quickly. I have made the point elsewhere that in some ways Monica represents God's grace personified in the *Confessions* because she followed Augustine from North Africa to Rome, from Rome to Milan, and back to Rome, where she passed away in the port city of Ostia on the way back to North Africa. And just as she followed her son around Italy, St. Augustine would later write about God's grace in a similar way — that it is an active force that pursues a person, coaxing and inspiring that person toward the will of God. There is no doubt that Monica cooperated with the grace of God through her prayers, and that her prayers (and her witness) played a significant role in the conversion of Augustine to Christianity.

St. Monica is known as a patron of people who pray for their wayward husbands or sons, or other loved ones. But I would submit that she is also the patron saint of patience and perseverance in prayer. She never gave up, and she never stopped praying. She never thought to herself, "Well, God has heard my prayer, so now I just wait." She kept on praying. And all the

[12] De Caussade, *Letters on the Practice of Abandonment* 2.28, 4.14, 4.15.

while, she practiced the Christian faith, going to Mass faithfully (daily) wherever she was. The story is that when they got to Milan, she complained to the bishop there, who was St. Ambrose, and asked him what to do about the fact that the liturgy and fasting expectations in Milan were not exactly the same as those in Rome. His reply was to coin the famous line *When in Rome, do as the Romans do.*

Although it does not seem as though Monica had any education beyond what most women got in her day, she could hold her own in theological discussions with her brilliant son. Their last discussion, and St. Augustine's description of her passing, is the most poignant part of the *Confessions*. A few days before she passed, she said to her son:

> My son, for my part, I find no further pleasure in this life. What I am still to do, or why I am here in the world, I do not know, for I have no more to hope for on this earth. There was one reason, and one alone, why I wished to remain a little longer in this life, and that was to see you a Catholic Christian before I died. God has granted my wish, and more besides, for I now see you as his servant, spurning such happiness as the world can give. What is left for me to do in this world?[13]

God had granted her prayers, but it took years, and it took the patience necessary to repeat her prayers many times.

Patience Leads to Peace and Joy

Both Tertullian and Cyprian, in their treatises on patience, talk about how patience is a prerequisite for the other fruits of the Spirit, including peace and joy.[14] Everyone wants peace and joy in life, but we often don't know how to hold on to them. The answer is prayer and, specifically, patient prayer. With regard to peace, the Church fathers taught that patience is the foundation of peace. Practicing patience in prayer will lead to a better ability to have patience in life, and that, in turn, will lead to more peace in life — more peace of mind

[13] Augustine of Hippo, *The Confessions* 9.10, trans. R. S. Pine-Coffin (New York: Penguin, 1961), 198–199.

[14] When St. Paul says that love "endures all things," he's talking about patience. Notice that when he makes his list of things that define love, he begins with "love is patient" (1 Cor. 13:4–7).

and more peace with other people. Patience is the "mother of mercy" and is required if we are going to have empathy for others (or kindness, another fruit of the Spirit) and forgive those who wrong us. And as we have seen, the Church fathers understood forgiving others to be a kind of spiritual almsgiving, so patience with others is a form of generosity (another fruit of the Spirit) and forms us in a generous spirit in our lives. As Jesus said, our response to insult, injury, and injustice must be generosity — but there's no way to respond in that way without first having patience.

With regard to joy, patience is the path to real joy in life. Patience is required for joy because true joy is not about being happy all the time, and it's not about getting everything we want. Quite the opposite: true joy is about contentment, and to be content requires being willing to let go of wanting what we don't have. So patience does not mean forcing yourself to wait for what you want; it means letting go of what you want and being content without it. And contentment does not mean getting what you want so you can arrive at contentment; it means learning to be satisfied with what God has given you, learning to wait for what He hasn't given you yet, and learning to be okay with the idea that He may never give you what you don't have. Never forget that God knows what we need better than we do, and He knows the future, so His refusal to give us something we want may be His way of protecting us from something that will harm us or waste our time in the long run (Rom. 8:28). Our response to any lack should be not disappointment but patience.[15]

Again, it's easy to say we should count our blessings, but true contentment comes from caring less about the things we don't have than about the things we do. This is not being careless; it's being carefree. And by the way, joy is our best tool of evangelism, because everyone wants joy. To be a joyful Christian is to be an attractive witness. Joy is contagious. But there is no joy without patience. Patience and joy are not mutually exclusive (they are both fruits of the Spirit), and they are not in some kind of inverse relationship, as though the more patience you have to have, the less joy you'll have, or as if you have to have patience *until* you have joy. Patience makes joy possible.

On the other hand, both Tertullian and Cyprian wrote that impatience is not only the opposite of patience, but it is the opposite of peace and is the

[15] De Caussade, *Letters on the Practice of Abandonment* 3.1, 3.16.

gateway to anger and other mortal sins, especially lust, envy, covetousness, and resentment and the desire for revenge.[16] They said that the devil is the author of impatience and that impatience is the exact opposite of self-control, which we need to resist temptation. In prayer, impatience leads us to babble on and on, while patience allows us to keep our words to a minimum. In life, if the choice I face is to have patience or to be impatient, experience tells me that I'm more likely to regret impatience than patience. But with that, I'm getting ahead of myself. For now, I will just say that as much as patience is one virtue required for all the other virtues, there is one thing that is required first, before we are able to grow in patience. That one thing is the meta-virtue of humility, and that will be the subject of our next chapter.

Now here's what all this has been leading to: If you want to practice patience in prayer, and to have that patience in prayer lead to patience in life as well as peace and joy, the teachings of the Church fathers and mothers and the prayer practices of the earliest Christians suggest that *it is better to pray short prayers repeatedly than long prayers only once*. And *it is better to pray with words given to us by God in Scripture than with our own words*. In the most important prayer (the Eucharistic Prayer), our priests pray the words of Jesus that He used to institute the Sacrament of Communion and that now effect the miracle of transubstantiation. In the most powerful prayer (the Sign of the Cross), we pray the words of Jesus that He revealed to us as the name of the Blessed Trinity: the Father, Son, and Holy Spirit. In the most perfect prayer, we pray the words of Jesus that He dictated to His apostles as the primary Christian prayer to be repeated daily. Now we turn to another prayer, in which we pray, not only the words of Scripture, but the name of Jesus.

The Jesus Prayer

St. Paul tells us that no one can say "Jesus is Lord" except by the Holy Spirit (1 Cor. 12:3). What this implies is that one who says "Jesus is Lord" or who "calls on the name of the Lord," is indwelt by the Holy Spirit; that is, this person is a baptized and confirmed Christian who is going on to salvation, since there is no other name by which anyone can be saved (Rom. 10:13; Acts 4:12).

16 In addition to Tertullian and Cyprian's treatises *On Patience*, see de Caussade, *Letters on the Practice of Abandonment* 6.14. For de Caussade, patience is its own means of grace, which means that impatience blocks grace.

The Jesus Prayer is a prayer in which a person simply, and repeatedly, calls on the name of Jesus. And true to the ideal of early Christian prayer, this prayer is not asking for anything specific, only for the Lord to have mercy, trusting that He knows what is best and wants to do what is best.

We don't know just how ancient the Jesus Prayer is. It seems to come from the practice of the desert hermits, perhaps as early as the fourth century. The first mention of it in the primary sources seems to associate it with a disciple of St. John Chrysostom named Neilos the Ascetic, who died around AD 430. In the sixth century, it was known to be practiced by, among others, an Egyptian hermit named Abba Philemon, and he promoted its use among the desert fathers. They believed that the prayer was useful to ward off distraction and guard against temptation and that it increased one's love for God. Later, the prayer became associated with a collection of sayings known as the *Philokalia*. Although the earliest layers of tradition in the *Philokalia* go back to the fourth century, the collection as we know it was not published until the eighteenth century, so the Jesus Prayer has only become widely known in the modern age — though it is an early Christian prayer tradition.

The content of the prayer seems to be built on the prayer that Jesus Himself praised in His parable of the Pharisee and the tax collector. The tax collector prays — repeatedly, it seems — "God, be merciful to me, a sinner" (Luke 18:13).[17] This prayer is also included at the beginning of the ancient Liturgy of St. James. But the Jesus Prayer specifically addresses Jesus, using the words apparently adapted from St. Peter's confession, "You are the Christ, the Son of the living God" (see Matt. 16:16). Putting it all together, the Jesus Prayer goes like this:

Lord Jesus Christ, Son of God,
Have mercy on me, a sinner.[18]

Notice that this is a "me" prayer, so while it does come from the time of the early Church, it makes sense that it would develop out of the monastic

[17] Some early versions of the Jesus Prayer do not include the words "a sinner."

[18] There are a few early variations on this prayer; for example: "Lord Jesus Christ, have mercy; Son of God, help me." Some variations did not include the phrase, "Son of God" but used a shorter version of the prayer: "Lord Jesus Christ, have mercy on me."

movement, which incorporated the "me" prayers from the psalms and from Celtic Christianity. Needless to say, the point of the Jesus Prayer is to pray it repeatedly, over and over. In fact, Eastern Christianity has a tradition of using a string of a hundred beads to say the Jesus Prayer a hundred times.

Breathing Prayer

In the prayer practice of some, by the end of the early Church period, the Jesus Prayer developed into something called *breathing prayer*. It seems that in an attempt to "pray without ceasing" (and taking that perhaps a bit literally), some of the desert fathers and mothers tried to figure out a way to pray the Jesus Prayer (or, in some cases, simply pray the name of Jesus) while breathing in and out. To be clear, everything we've talked about so far can apply to both vocal prayer (out loud) and mental prayer (silent prayer). But breathing prayer assumes that one is praying silently, in one's heart and mind, but not out loud.

The way breathing prayer works is simple. One prays a line of prayer while breathing in, and then prays the next line of the prayer while breathing out. This can work with longer prayers just fine, though it helps if there is an even number of lines, but for the early monastics, most seem to have focused on two-line prayers, such as the Jesus Prayer. So to pray the Jesus Prayer as a breathing prayer, one prays silently, while breathing, like this:

Breathe in: *Lord Jesus Christ, Son of God*
Breathe out: *Have mercy on me, a sinner*

We've talked about how, in the Mass, our whole bodies are involved because, as Christians, we don't believe in a disembodied faith — that is, our faith is not only in our minds. Now, here in private prayer as well, we have a way to involve the body with the spirit at prayer. The breathing prayer aligns the body with the spirit, but more important, it facilitates our slowing down in prayer. Matching our prayer to our breathing is the best way to find the perfect pace for our prayers.

You can also use the practice of *Lectio Divina* to lead you into breathing prayers. As you read Scripture and reflect on the words, you can pick out specific lines that speak to your heart and pray those lines as a breathing prayer. The companion volume to this book, *Praying the Psalms: The Divine Gateway to* Lectio Divina *and Contemplative Prayer*, is organized with this in mind.

Now, a disclaimer. On one hand, breathing prayer can lead us into contemplative prayer. Contemplative prayer is outside the scope of this book, since it wasn't really practiced in the early Church; though it is a valid prayer form, it developed later. On the other hand, breathing prayer and contemplative prayer should not be confused with non-Christian forms of meditation. They are also not to be confused with "mindfulness" or "centering prayer" which are inventions of the twentieth century and can be quite problematic, possibly even dangerous.

Praying repeated prayers such as the Jesus Prayer, and even breathing prayer and contemplative prayer, always remains *Christian* prayer — that is, the prayers are Christ-centered, and through Christ, they facilitate a relationship with the triune God that remains in submission to God and leads to obedience to God in life. Remember that the purpose of prayer is our sanctification, and that includes influencing us toward faithfulness when we are not in prayer. So while prayer is a lot about what happens in the prayer time, it is not about chasing after feelings in prayer, or about trying to achieve an altered state of consciousness.

Eastern meditation tends to involve focusing on the self, or going deeper into the self, often with the assumption that one will find enlightenment or encounter the Divine *deep within*, as if God is really just a part of you that you need to connect with. Needless to say, this is not Christian. When we pray, no matter how we pray, we are not going inward so much as reaching out to the Holy Trinity — or perhaps a better way to say that is that we are opening ourselves up for the Holy Trinity to reach out to us — but the point is that we never blur the line between us and God. This is a relationship with God, not "finding the god within." Sometimes Eastern meditation involves emptying the mind — this is something we would never want to do as Christians. We don't want to empty our minds; we want to use our minds and fill our minds with the things of God and focus our minds on God in Christ. That's a far cry from an empty mind. And it must be said that an empty mind is very susceptible to being occupied by evil. To empty your mind is to invite the demonic.[19] Eastern meditation often depersonalizes

[19] Note Jesus' parable of the unclean spirit (Matt. 12:43–45; Luke 11:24–26), and think of the house as a metaphor for the mind or spirit.

God, but we know a personal God. We do not want to reduce God to an impersonal "cosmic absolute" or, worse, simply personify "the universe." We are in a relationship with God, and prayer should be quality time that we spend with the one who loves us more than any human could; it is not a mindless trance.

When it comes to modern practices like "mindfulness" or "centering prayer," these are also based more on Eastern (non-Christian) meditation than on Christian prayer, so they are to be avoided as well. Centering prayer, in particular, has been called a form of self-hypnosis, which again, focuses more on the self than on God. And any practice that involves a mantra is usually using that word or phrase to "zone out," with the goal of moving into a state of mind that, in some ways, separates the mind from the body because the senses are numbed. The Jesus Prayer, breathing prayer, and other Christian repeated prayers, are not mantras because our goal in praying them is not to mindlessly mumble them while we become catatonic but, rather, to *mean the words every time we say them*. Our goal is neither mindlessness nor "mindfulness" (mindful of what?) but communication with the God who is distinct from us. Simply put, non-Christian forms of meditation, including those that claim to be Christian but are really based on Eastern religion, are too self-centered. Christian prayer, including breathing prayer, is always Christ-centered, and it draws us into a deeper relationship not with ourselves but with the Blessed Trinity.

Having said that, any real benefits of relaxation and peace that are promised by secular or non-Christian meditation techniques are present in Christian prayer, especially breathing prayers. We just have to be careful that we aren't taken in by the promises of things that are not really benefits, such as "getting in touch with yourself." The goal of prayer is to get in touch with God. And if what you really need is rest, then just take a nap.

So for example, if you wanted to pray the Our Father as a breathing prayer, it would go like this (remember to go slowly, at your regular breathing rate, or you'll hyperventilate!):

Breathe in: *Our Father*
Breathe out: *Who art in Heaven*

Breathe in: *Hallowed be Thy name*
Breathe out: *Thy Kingdom come*

Breathe in: *Thy will be done*
Breathe out: *On earth as it is in Heaven*

Breathe in: *Give us this day*
Breathe out: *Our daily bread*

Breathe in: *And forgive us our trespasses*
Breathe out: *As we forgive those who trespass against us*

Breathe in: *And lead us not into temptation*
Breathe out: *But deliver us from evil*

Breathe in: *For the Kingdom, and the power, and the glory are yours*
Breathe out: *Now and forever*

If you want to pray the Glory Be as a breathing prayer, it would go like this:

Breathe in: *Glory be to the Father*
Breathe out: *And to the Son*

Breathe in: *And to the Holy Spirit*
Breathe out: *As it was in the beginning*

Breathe in: *Is now, and ever shall be*
Breathe out: *World without end*

What About the Rosary?

The Rosary as we know it did not come into use until the Middle Ages, but in many ways, it was the natural development of early Christian private devotional practice that began with laypeople imitating the prayers of the monks.[20] As the monks were praying all 150 psalms every day, or every week, laypeople also started praying the psalms. But for those who could not afford to own Psalters, or for those who could not read, it was enough to pray the Our Father 150 times. Needless to say, no one objected to the idea of repeated prayers. But they did have a problem keeping count of how many times they had said the prayer. This led to the development of, first, ropes with 150 knots, and then strings with 150 beads. Later, the 150 beads were divided into "decades"

[20] On the Rosary, see Papandrea, *Praying a Christ-Centered Rosary.*

or groupings of ten beads, and the different prayers were added to the Our Father, and the Rosary was born.

Although the Rosary, as it is now, was not prayed yet in the early Church, it does contain some of the most ancient of the repeated prayers: the Our Father and the Glory Be, as well as the Creed. As we have seen, the *Didache* documents the expectation that Christians pray the Our Father three times each day, and St. Augustine considered the Creed to be a prayer and said that Christians should pray that every day as well, in the morning and in the evening.[21]

In addition, the Rosary is based on the very ancient practice of praying the words of Scripture. The Hail Mary (or Ave Maria) combines the archangel Gabriel's greeting to Mary in Luke 1:28 ("Hail, grace-filled one, the Lord is with you") with Elizabeth's greeting to Mary in Luke 1:42 ("Blessed are you among women, and blessed is the fruit of your womb").[22] Then it calls Mary what Elizabeth called her: "And how does this happen to me, that the *Mother of my Lord* should come to me?" (Luke 1:43, emphasis added),[23] but using the more formal ancient title that we saw in the *Sub Tuum* prayer, that she is Mother of God.[24] Finally, in the early Christian tradition of the intercession of the saints, it simply asks for Mary to pray for us, both "now and at the hour of our death."

[21] In context, Augustine meant the Nicene Creed, but the Apostles' Creed is even more ancient. The Apostles' Creed is the result of the coming together of several Western regional creeds, which probably happened by the third century. The Nicene Creed was written at the Council of Nicaea in AD 325 and then revised at the Council of Constantinople in 381. As it turned out, the Apostles' Creed came to be associated with Baptism, while the Nicene Creed came to be associated with the Eucharist, and so the Nicene Creed is the one we say in Mass, and the older creed, the Apostles' Creed, is the one normally prayed with the Rosary. See Augustine of Hippo, *On the Lord's Prayer* 8.13.

[22] Cf. also Mary's Magnificat, and the line, "from now on will all ages call me blessed," Luke 1:48.

[23] See Shane Kapler, *The Biblical Roots of Marian Consecration: Devotion to the Immaculate Heart in Light of Scripture* (Gastonia, NC: TAN Books, 2022), 141.

[24] This title for Mary was confirmed as appropriate and theologically correct at the Third Ecumenical Council of Ephesus in AD 431.

If you are new to the Rosary, I encourage you to read my book *Praying a Christ-Centered Rosary*, in which I go into detail about the history of the Rosary and how to pray it, along with theological meditations that help you meditate on the life and Passion of Christ while you pray. If you are not new to the Rosary but would like to take your Rosary devotion to the next level, consider that some of the saints in more recent history have highlighted the benefits of meditating on the Passion of Jesus in prayer.[25] By praying the Sorrowful Mysteries of the Rosary and combining them with meditations on the Stations of the Cross (another medieval prayer practice that naturally developed from the practices of the early Church), you can meditate on the Passion of Christ in ways that will facilitate your ability to live the virtues and produce the fruit of the Spirit. In this way, you can — to quote the concluding prayer of the Rosary — "imitate what they [the mysteries] contain and obtain what they promise."

For example, in meditating on the Agony in the Garden (the first of the Sorrowful Mysteries), we see that Jesus suffered extreme *anxiety* and *disappointment* (at His betrayal and His disciples' failure to stay awake with Him), and yet He was willing to submit His human will to the will of the Father. And so you might ask for the grace to set aside your own will and put all your trust in the divine will, and have peace. You might begin that decade by praying:

> *Lord Jesus, in the garden, You suffered extreme stress, when You were betrayed by a friend, disappointed by those who could not stay awake with You, and arrested unjustly. And yet You did not retaliate, You did not lose Your peace, and You did not fail to trust in the will of the Father. I want to be more like You. I want to imitate Your ability to handle stress by trusting*

[25] For example, St. Faustina said that if we want to imitate Christ, we should mediate on His Passion. In a vision, the Blessed Virgin Mary said to St. Faustina, "I am mother to you all, thanks to the unfathomable mercy of God.... Be courageous. Do not fear apparent obstacles, but fix your gaze on the passion of my Son, and in this way you will be victorious." Kowalska, *Divine Mercy in My Soul*, 198–199. St. Faustina assumed that this meditation on the Passion of Jesus is exactly what we should be doing during Eucharistic adoration.

> *completely in divine providence and the divine will. Give me the grace I need to say "fiat" in all circumstances.*

Then keep this in mind as you pray the prayers and meditate on the mysteries.

In meditating on the Scourging at the Pillar (the second sorrowful mystery), we see that Jesus suffered extreme *pain* and *injustice,* and yet He had the patience and self-control to absorb the pain and not spread it to others. And so you might ask for the grace to set aside anger and resentment and protect your loved ones by having the discipline to accept what comes to you for the sake of the bigger picture. You might begin this decade by praying:

> *Lord Jesus, at the column, You suffered extreme pain, which You did not deserve. And yet You did not despair, and You did not reflect that pain onto others. You absorbed the pain for the sake of the will of the Father. I want to be more like You. I want to imitate Your discipline by not echoing my pain or frustration to my family and friends. I want to be the bulletproof vest for my loved ones and not let that suffering get through to them. Give me the grace I need to absorb it all and offer it up to You.*

In meditating on the Crowning with Thorns (the third sorrowful mystery), we see that Jesus suffered extreme *humiliation* and *disrespect,* and yet He not only didn't lash out at His enemies; He did not even defend His pride, and He eventually forgave His tormentors. And so you might ask for the grace to set aside your pride and to have the humility you need to accomplish God's purpose for you, even if that does not lead to fame and good reputation — even if it should lead to humiliation. You might begin this decade by praying:

> *Lord Jesus, at the hands of the soldiers, You suffered extreme humiliation, and You responded with forgiveness. I want to be more like You. I want to imitate Your rejection of pride and Your empathy for others, even those who lash out at me. I want to be content with whatever it is Your will for me to have, no matter how modest or humble that is. Give me the grace to live quietly and peacefully.*

In meditating on the Carrying of the Cross (the fourth sorrowful mystery), we see that Jesus suffered extreme *exhaustion* and *sadness* (mourning over the holy city, and seeing the suffering of His Mother), and yet He never complained. And so you might ask for the grace to carry your much smaller crosses without complaining. You might begin this decade by praying:

> *Lord Jesus, on the road to Calvary, You suffered extreme exhaustion and sadness when You carried Your Cross. You have asked me to carry much lighter crosses. I want to be more like You. I want to imitate Your willingness to lean into the cross and carry it as a labor of love. I want to accept my crosses without complaining, for the sake of my loved ones.*

And in meditating on His Crucifixion (the fifth sorrowful mystery), we see that Jesus suffered *defeat* and *death*, holding nothing back, not even His very life. And so you might ask for the grace to set aside selfishness, to be "all in" with your faith, holding nothing back and offering your whole life in the service of God. You might begin this decade by praying:

> *Lord Jesus, on the Cross, You gave Your life for me and for my family and my friends. I want to be more like You. I want to imitate Your total commitment to love and to the will of the Father. I want to be all in, for the service of You and Your Church.*

These are just suggestions, but you get the idea. You can add the meditations on the Stations of the Cross to the meditations on the Rosary, to create a deeper meditation, allowing you to meditate on the Passion in a way that will deepen in you the meta-virtues of gratitude, humility, and forgiveness. See the chart at the end of this chapter for more detail on how you might use the Rosary to meditate on the Passion of Christ.

And if you choose to pray the Rosary as a breathing prayer, you will slow down and deepen your prayer experience even more. It will take a bit longer to pray the Rosary as a breathing prayer, but if you have the time, it will help prevent you from rushing through the memorized prayers. As a breathing prayer, the Hail Mary would go like this:

Breathe in: *Hail Mary, full of grace*
Breathe out: *The Lord is with thee (you)*

Breathe in: *Bless art thou (are you) among women*
Breathe out: *And blessed is the fruit of thy (your) womb, Jesus*

Breathe in: *Holy Mary*
Breathe out: *Mother of God*

Breathe in: *Pray for us sinners*
Breathe out: *Now and at the hour of our death*

Therefore, to pray like the earliest Christians:

1. **Keep in mind that it's better to pray the words of Jesus** (the Sign of the Cross, the Our Father) **or the words of Scripture** (the Jesus Prayer and even the Rosary) **than to pray in your own words.** It's also *better to pray short prayers and repeat them than to pray long prayers just once.* As the great spiritual director Jean-Pierre de Caussade wrote, "May others, Lord, multiply their prayers and supplications. I ask but one thing. I offer this prayer to you: Grant me a pure heart."[26] When it comes to prayer, less is more. Less of us and more of God (John 3:30). In fact, it would be fair to say that as we progress in prayer and grow in sanctification, we would pray less and less with our own words and more and more with the words of Sacred Scripture. This is, of course, what *Lectio Divina* is.

2. **Remember that repeated prayers are a gift to you.** Repeated prayers allow you to let the Holy Spirit pray for you (Rom. 8:26–27) because they allow you to pray without worrying about coming up with all the words or getting the words just right. If you get distracted, repeated prayers allow you to get another chance at praying whatever parts of the prayers you missed when your mind wandered. You can also let yourself off the hook for those times when your mind does wander. This is not a sin (as long as your mind doesn't wander into sinful thoughts), and you don't need to beat yourself up over it or dwell on it. Just move on to your next round and your next chance at praying the words you missed. Of course, this means you need to focus and really pray the words, and not let them become mindless or rote. Repeated prayers actually prevent you from babbling on and on in prayer. If you are used to praying only extemporaneously in your own words, if you have not yet found your rhythm for praying repeated prayers, try again, only slow down, and really pray the words.

[26] Jean-Pierre de Caussade, *The Sacrament of the Present Moment* (San Francisco: Harper, 1982), 34.

3. **Slow down.** Don't rush your prayers. Work on increasing your patience in prayer, both in terms of how you pray (slower) and in how you wait for an answer. *Try praying some breathing prayers.* The pace of your regular breathing will help you slow down to the right speed, so you're not rushing through your prayers. This takes a bit of time, and it does mean that you will need to set aside a bit more time for prayer than just the bare minimum, but that's also a gift. It forces you to incorporate a rhythm of prayer into your daily life, and it develops patience. Use the companion volume, *Praying the Psalms: The Divine Gateway to* Lectio Divina *and Contemplative Prayer*, to practice *Lectio Divina* and pray the words of Scripture as breathing prayers. For more, see the list of suggested breathing prayers in the appendix.

4. **Try the Jesus Prayer**, either as a breathing prayer, or not. You don't need to count how many times you say it, but you could count on Rosary beads — two times around the Rosary would be one hundred Jesus Prayers, the number the Eastern monks pray.

5. **Pray the Rosary.** It's true that the early Christians did not pray the Rosary, but it's a great prayer for every day because it already contains a day's worth of Our Fathers as well as a Creed. Remember that the Rosary developed out of laypeople's imitation of the prayer rhythms of the monks, so in a way, the five decades are like mini prayer hours, all put together. If you are already used to praying the Rosary, try combining the Sorrowful Mysteries with the meditations on the Stations of the Cross (see the chart below) for a deeper meditation on the Passion of Christ.

To Go Deeper

Primary Sources

St. Augustine, *The Confessions* (written around the turn of the fifth century), in the Nicene and Post-Nicene Fathers, Series 1, vol. 1, https://www.newadvent.org/fathers/1101.htm.

The Philokalia: The Eastern Christian Spiritual Texts, selections compiled and annotated by Allyne Smith (Nashville: Skylight Paths Publishing, 2006).

Secondary Sources

Mike Aquilina, *Mothers of the Church* (Huntington, IN: Our Sunday Visitor, 2012).

Jean-Pierre de Caussade, *Letters on the Practice of Abandonment*.

Shane Kapler, *The Biblical Roots of Marian Consecration: Devotion to the Immaculate Heart in Light of Scripture* (Gastonia, NC: TAN Books, 2022).

James L. Papandrea, *Praying a Christ-Centered Rosary: Meditations on the Mysteries* (Notre Dame, IN: Ave Maria Press, 2021).

James L. Papandrea, *Reading the Church Fathers: A History of the Early Church and the Development of Doctrine* (Manchester, NH: Sophia Institute Press, 2022).

James L. Papandrea, *Reading Scripture Like the Early Church: Seven Insights from the Church Fathers to Help You Understand Scripture* (Manchester, NH: Sophia Institute Press, 2022).

James L. Papandrea, *Praying the Psalms: The Divine Gateway to* Lectio Divina *and Contemplative Prayer* (Manchester, NH: Sophia Institute Press, 2023).

Using the Rosary to Meditate on the Passion of Christ

The Sorrowful Mysteries (Traditional Rosary)	**Jesus prays in the garden**	**Jesus is whipped at the pillar**
Scriptural Rosary and Stations of the Cross biblical texts	Ps. 22:13–14; Isa. 53:3, 8; Matt. 26:1–56, 69–75; 27:1–10; Mark 14:1–51; Luke 22:1–65; John 13; 18:1–18, 25–27	Ps. 22:15; Isa. 53:4–5; Matt. 26:57–68; 27:1–26; Mark 15:1–15; Luke 22:66–23:25; John 18:19–24, 28–19:16
Stations of the Cross: Traditional Stations (S) and Pope St. John Paul II's Ecumenical (Scriptural) Way of the Cross (W)	Jesus prays in the Garden of Gethsemane (W1). His friends fall asleep. Jesus is betrayed by Judas and arrested (W2). Jesus is denied by Peter (W4).	Jesus is tried by the Sanhedrin and condemned to death by Pilate (S1, W3, 5). Jesus is scourged and generally mistreated (W6).
Meditate on what Jesus suffered	**Stress** **Disappointment**	**Pain** **Injustice**
To imitate Jesus	Submission to the divine will	Discipline
For grace to produce	Peace Joy	Patience Self-control

Jesus is crowned with thorns	**Jesus carries His Cross**	**Jesus dies on the Cross**
Ps. 22:7–8; Isa. 53:7; Matt. 27:27–31; Mark 15:16–20; Luke 22:63–65; 23:6–12; John 19:2–5	Ps. 22:15–16; Isa. 53:6; Matt. 27:31–32; Mark 15:20–21; Luke 23:26–32; John 19:17, 26–27	Ps. 22:8–9, 17–19; Isa. 53:5, 8–12; Matt. 27:33–66; Mark 15:22–47; Luke 23:33–56; John 19:18–42
Jesus is crowned with thorns, mocked, and humiliated (W6).	Jesus carries His Cross (S2, W7). Jesus falls three times (S3, 7, 9). Jesus meets his Blessed Mother (S4). Simon helps Jesus carry His Cross (S5, W8). Veronica wipes the face of Jesus (S6). Jesus prays over the women of Jerusalem (S8, W9).	Jesus is stripped of His garments (S10). Jesus is nailed to the Cross (S11, W10). Jesus promises the Kingdom to the Good Thief (W11). Jesus entrusts Mary and John to each other (W12). Jesus dies on the Cross (S12, W13). Jesus is taken down from the Cross (S13). Jesus is laid in the tomb (S14, W14).
Humiliation **Disrespect**	**Exhaustion** **Sadness**	**Death** **Defeat**
Humility	Carrying our crosses without complaining	Self-sacrificing servanthood
Kindness Gentleness	Faithfulness	Love Generosity

Insight 7

Humility Is the Key . . . to Everything

For you do not desire sacrifice or I would give it;
a burnt offering you would not accept.
My sacrifice, O God, is a contrite spirit;
a contrite, humbled heart, O God, you will not scorn.

— Psalm 51:18–19

Tertullian wrote that "nothing is more dear to [God] than humility."[1] So much of what we have discovered about prayer in the early Church has led us to this point — it all comes together here. To be in a rightly ordered relationship with God, we have to recognize certain truths — and really live with them in the front of our minds. These truths include the fact that we are not in a reciprocal relationship with God. We are not entitled to anything from God; we only have the duty to submit to Him. We are not God's equals, and although we know that intellectually, we often talk to God as though He's a buddy or, worse, as though He's our caddy. God is our power source, and He is unlimited in power and in knowledge. We should come to God in prayer, with the full acknowledgment that we do not know what is best for us in any situation, and we really have no idea how God should answer our prayers — even if we are thinking in terms of our own best interests.

Have You Met St. Benedict?

Benedict of Nursia (modern Norcia, Italy) was born toward the end of the fifth century and was about twenty years old when the year 500 rolled around. By that time, he had already gained a reputation as someone who was so holy that he could perform miracles, and his holiness had led him to become disillusioned with life in society and even regular friendships. Just like the Eastern desert hermits, Benedict had decided to leave the city behind and live a life of prayerful solitude. And just like the desert fathers, his desire for solitude only enhanced his reputation as a holy man, and that led others to seek him out, which effectively meant that the solitude wasn't going to last.

[1] Tertullian, *On the Veiling of Virgins* 16.

The whole trajectory of Eastern monasticism — from solitude to community and eventually to hospitality — can be seen in a microcosm in St. Benedict. In the year 529, what started as a loose community of hermits looking for a spiritual director became the first Benedictine monastery: Montecasino. In time, one monastery became a dozen, and Benedict would become known as the father of Western monasticism — not because he was the first, but because (like Basil in the East) he was so influential on all that would come after him.

The *Benedictine Rule* that he wrote for his monasteries formalized the life rhythm of the monks as never before and standardized the prayer hours. To be fair, much of the rule is based on what had come before it, incorporating material from St. Basil and the East (at least partly transmitted to the West by John Cassian) and from St. Augustine in North Africa. But Benedict made important additions and expanded on how the monks should pray. The Benedictine motto is *Ora et labora,* that is, *Pray and work,* in a daily and weekly rhythm of life that helps the monks keep their priorities straight — always seeking first the Kingdom of God, and always praying without ceasing. Most important for our purposes at the moment, Benedict included a long section on humility in his *Rule,* and there he shows how humility is the key to everything.

What Is Humility, Really?

Humility is one of those concepts we often think we understand better than we really do. To define and describe humility, I want to begin with a definition from an excellent book about St. Benedict, and then I will add some thoughts based on my own reading in St. Benedict, the other Church fathers, and some later interpreters. Michael Casey, in his book, *A Guide to Living in the Truth: Saint Benedict's Teaching on Humility,* says this:

> Humility is, above all, a respect for the nature of things, a reluctance to force reality to conform to subjective factors in ourselves.[2]
>
> . . . We can define humility as the capacity for receiving grace and the gift of final salvation. It is not, in essence, a particular attitude in

[2] Michael Casey, *A Guide to Living in the Truth: Saint Benedict's Teaching on Humility* (Liguori, MO: Liguori Publications, 2001), 18. Note how humility's opposite, pride, is often precisely the attempt to force reality to conform to the subjective personal experience of individuals.

> social dealings but a fundamental stance before God: a willingness to be saved, an openness to God's action, an assent to the mysterious processes by which God's plan is realized in the hearts of human beings. Humility is not an action, nor a sequence of actions, nor a habit formed by the repetition of actions. It is, rather, a receptivity or passivity; a matter of being acted upon by God.[3]

So, at its core, *humility* means acknowledging our proper place before God and not overstepping that. It is maintaining a healthy "fear of God" in the biblical sense, which is always to hold God in reverence and to fear the consequences of ignoring or offending Him. But it is not simply groveling, as though God needs that from us. It is a submission to God that is born out of dependence on Him. It means really believing that everything good comes from God and then opening ourselves up to receive from the only One who can give us anything of value. St. Augustine, writing of his life before his conversion, said, "My sin was this, that I looked for pleasure, beauty, and truth, not in him, but in myself and his other creatures, and the search led me instead to pain, confusion, and error."[4]

Often we try so hard to put our trust in things that we can control, but that only gets in the way of putting our trust in God. We try so hard to find security, and ultimately peace, in tangible things, but those things become idols that take God's place in our lives. Our fatal flaw as humans is that we try so hard to put our trust in our own ability to control our futures (an ability that does not exist) that we fail to trust in God's providence as completely as we should.[5] Not only do we have no merit to deserve anything from God, but we also have no power to get anything for ourselves. We have

3 Casey, *A Guide to Living in the Truth*, 56. Note the phrase "a willingness to be saved." It can be argued that the unforgivable sin is the refusal to accept the invitation of forgiveness. The motivation for this refusal is often pride, but *humility* means being willing to admit that we need salvation in the first place and then being willing to admit that only God can offer it.

4 Augustine of Hippo, *Confessions* 1.20.

5 The irony of this fatal flaw is acknowledged throughout history in the mythology of many cultures, in stories such as *Oedipus Rex*, which is a cautionary tale about a man who tried too hard to control his destiny, and in trying to prevent what he feared, he actually made it happen.

nothing to bring to the table — except humility — and we are completely depending on God's mercy.

So although there is a horizonal component to humility — that is, the way we interact with other people — the vertical component is primary, and it is the vertical component — our relationship with God — that makes any good and healthy relationships with others possible.

Humility as a Meta-Virtue

When we look at St. Paul's list of the fruit of the Spirit in Galatians 5:22–23 (love, joy, peace, patience, kindness, generosity, faithfulness, gentleness, and self-control) we might notice that humility is missing. This is because humility is the foundation for all of them. It's more root than fruit. The medieval Scholastics, such as St. Thomas Aquinas, said that humility is not a virtue like the other virtues, but it's the one overarching virtue that should be the foundation of all the others, ordering one's whole life. This is why I refer to humility as one of the meta-virtues, along with gratitude and forgiveness. I suppose we could also call them "root virtues." Gratitude and forgiveness are also not listed among the fruit of the Spirit, but like humility, they are essential as a prerequisite for prayer. St. Francis of Assisi would later teach that it is humility that leads to patience, peace, and joy, as we have already noted — but the point is that it all begins with humility.

The truth is, humility and gratitude are interdependent. It is difficult to be humble when one is feeling entitled to something one doesn't currently have. We have to be grateful enough to have the humility to admit: *I do not deserve more than I have; I deserve less than I have; in fact, I deserve nothing, and yet I have so much.* To be humble is to reject entitlement and replace it with gratitude. To be grateful is to reject covetousness and replace it with contentment and then generosity. St. John Chrysostom said that if you're not thankful for everything, don't bother praying for anything.[6]

Therefore, humility is not simply an attitude, or even a state of mind, but a lifestyle and a whole worldview. If we truly believe that God can (and does) turn anything to the good for those who are in relationship with Him (Rom. 8:28), we have to live in submission to His omniscience and omnipresence. But when we reserve the right to be skeptical about God's

[6] John Chrysostom, *Homilies on Philippians* 14.

providence, we presume to know more than we do, and we presume to be able to control more than we can. So humility is the refusal to assume too much about yourself, and the refusal to assume too little about God and what He can do.

When Jesus said, "Blessed are the poor in spirit" (Matt. 5:3), the Church fathers all understood this to be a reference to humility.[7] To be poor in spirit is to be poor in self-will — that is, submissive to the will of God.[8] To be poor in spirit is to resist the temptation to ask why and simply to say *fiat*, that God's will might be done — not just in the moment but, rather, as a lifestyle. A person who is rich in the things of the world is tempted to think that he has earned his wealth and, thus, to ascribe to himself too much ability to control his circumstances or to believe too much in his own independence. To be poor in spirit is to have a clearer path to the Kingdom, not so much because of the lack of possessions (though that does mean fewer distractions) but, more so, for the lack of pride, entitlement, and willfulness.

For St. Benedict, humility as a lifestyle means living in contentment with what we are given: contentment with our work, contentment with modest living, contentment with anonymity. Of course, this contentment requires a certain gratitude that recognizes that there is not a single good thing in our lives that is not a gift from God, but this only emphasizes the overlap of the meta-virtues of humility and gratitude — each one energizes the other. In fact, our gratitude and humility should combine to the extent that we can admit to ourselves that if God never gave us another good thing for the rest of our lives, we would already have more than we deserve. Contentment

[7] With regard to Luke 6:20, where Jesus says, "Blessed are the poor" (without adding "in spirit"), most Church Fathers believed that Matthew, writing later, had clarified Luke or was writing a more complete version of the sermon. In any case, for the Church fathers, the meaning is the same, since those who are literally poor also tend to be humble. They have fewer distractions from the spiritual life (Matt. 19:23–24; Mark 10:23–25; Luke 18:24–25; cf. Sir. 20:21), and they are already used to the idea of not being entitled. This is part of the reason monastics take a vow of poverty. The renunciation of ownership is also the renunciation of control over things.

[8] John Cassian, *Conferences* 10.11. Cassian says that to be poor in spirit is to be totally dependent on God.

means living in the present, without letting thoughts of what we don't (yet) have take over too much of our minds.

To be humble in this way — in a lifestyle of contentment — is to be open to receiving God's grace. Both James 4:6 and 1 Peter 5:5 quote Proverbs 3:34 as saying that *God gives grace to the humble,*[9] so for the Church fathers, humility itself is a means of grace. Conversely, pride is a grace blocker, and the self-righteous feeling of entitlement is effectively a refusal of God's grace. We noted how the goal and purpose of prayer is the sanctification of ourselves and those for whom we pray, and so as a prerequisite for prayer, humility is the foundation of sanctification.[10] St. Augustine said that no one reaches the Kingdom of God except by humility.[11]

Love Yourself Enough to Tell Yourself the Truth

Jesus said to "love your neighbor as yourself," so doesn't that mean we should love ourselves (Matt. 22:39; Mark 12:31; Luke 10:27)? Without getting into the precise interpretation of the second greatest commandment, we do need to clarify that humility is not self-loathing, and it is not intentionally having low self-esteem. On the other hand, it is the opposite of pride, which — let's not forget — is one of the deadly sins. Pride encompasses many of the things already mentioned as attitudes to be avoided: entitlement, self-congratulation, willfulness, and the illusion of independence. We may think we don't suffer from pride, but when we put more trust in ourselves and our attempts to control things than we put in God, that is a symptom of pride. And all of these attitudes block God's grace from flowing into our lives. But humility is the renunciation and rejection of these attitudes. Yet sometimes the only way to get pride out of the way is to starve it out, by depriving it of what feeds it — whatever feeds the ego.[12] Sometimes this requires a reality check.

9 The Greek is the same in James and 1 Peter, though it is interesting that some translations of the New Testament render the two verses differently. For example, the NABRE renders James 4:6 as "gives grace to the humble," but 1 Peter 5:5 is translated, "bestows favor on the humble." No doubt this is the result of different people translating the two documents, but the inconsistency is lamentable.

10 De Caussade, *Letters on the Practice of Abandonment* 4.2.

11 St. Augustine probably has in mind Sirach 3:18.

12 De Caussade, *Letters on the Practice of Abandonment* 7.14.

So what is required for humility is not a self-hatred, but a resignation and a willingness to see ourselves as we really are.[13] We don't hate ourselves; in fact, we have to love ourselves enough not to lie to ourselves and pretend we're something we're not. We have to be honest with ourselves — more than honest — brutally honest: less concerned with our accomplishments and more concerned with correcting our flaws; less concerned with the faults of others and more concerned with our own.[14] Humility is realizing that we live in the gap between reality and perfect faithfulness.[15]

In the prayer of confession found in Psalm 51, quoted at the beginning of this chapter, the psalmist offers the sacrifice of a humble heart, sometimes translated "sincerity of heart." I like the use of the word *sincerity* there because it emphasizes that the humble person is the one who is sincere in his or her heart — that is, the person who is honest with him- or herself. To be humble is to be honest with yourself about your sins, imperfections, impurities, and failures — not to dwell on the past but to grow toward faithfulness in the future. It's being able to admit who we really are — that person in us whom we don't want other people to get to know very well but whom God knows intimately. It's about being able to confront our sins and confess them with a sincere desire not to repeat them.

In the parable of the prodigal, when the son comes to his senses, in some translations it says he "came to himself." The point is that he was willing to open his eyes and see the reality check.[16] He was less than he was meant to be — not simply because he was poor but because he was *alone*. But he did not shrug it off, giving himself permission to be a "work in progress" or justifying himself by saying "nobody's perfect"; he got to that point where he was willing to humble himself — first, to refuse to live in denial and admit to himself the reality of the situation and then to *do* something, to get up and go home.

Now, it is true that some of the early monastics and other Church fathers go so far as to talk about humility as though it is a deep distrust of

[13] De Caussade, *Letters on the Practice of Abandonment* 5.15.

[14] De Caussade, *Letters on the Practice of Abandonment* 2.6.

[15] De Caussade, *Letters on the Practice of Abandonment* 2.11.

[16] Cf. Augustine of Hippo, *Confessions* 8.7: "I stood naked before my own eyes."

the self, calling it "self-reproach," but that's not the same thing as hating oneself. To distrust oneself is to recognize that even if we could control our circumstances (which we can't), we would certainly make a mess of things because we can't see the future. So humility is not a lack of self-esteem; it is holding ourselves in the right amount of esteem — not too little, but also not too much.[17] It is ultimate self-awareness because it is truthful. When we are humble, we are constantly aware of the ways we have fallen short of faithfulness, without diminishing them in our minds or making excuses.

And when we avail ourselves of the Sacrament of Confession and Reconciliation, it forces us to confront our weaknesses, name our sins, and put ourselves in a position of accountability to the Church. When we listen to whatever the priest might have to say in the way of spiritual direction, we grow in self-awareness and honesty with ourselves. Sometimes the only way to really be honest with ourselves is to have to be honest with someone else. And sometimes a reality check is painful. But that is how we put ourselves back into a rightly ordered relationship with God when that relationship gets out of whack. This kind of truthful self-awareness is a gift from God. St. Faustina wrote in her diary, "Jesus gave me the grace of knowing myself."[18] In short, humility means never letting yourself say, "I'm good enough" or "I'm basically good." These are lies we tell ourselves to excuse ourselves from self-improvement.

Humility as a worldview means looking at the universe with a readiness to see God's hand in creation everywhere, to see evidence of God's activity even in small things, and to think of oneself as small enough and simple enough to be open to the miraculous and to giving God the credit for all that is good in the world. This includes a refusal to become cynical — a refusal to believe that evil can overcome good.[19] Since God is everywhere, the one who sincerely seeks God will find Him, but it will require humility to recognize Him when you do. It may require the humility to admit that when you do find God, He might not be what you expect or act as you want him to. To say, "The God I worship wouldn't..." is often a symptom of

[17] Cf. Augustine of Hippo, *Confessions* 7.20: "I was full of self-esteem, which was a punishment of my own making."

[18] Kowalska, *Divine Mercy in My Soul*, 132.

[19] De Caussade, *Letters on the Practice of Abandonment* 7.8.

pride, specifically the attempt to make God in one's own image. A humble worldview means being willing to see the work of God in other people more than in yourself. It may even mean being willing to remain insignificant by the world's standards while you watch others get all the praise, trusting that God doesn't always ask us to accomplish great goals. For most of us, God asks us to be faithful only in small things. And so humility is being content with the small things, not presuming that they are too small for us, or that we are too good for them, or that we have to know how they fit into the bigger picture in order to be willing to put in the effort.

Self-Reliance Is a Trap

In some ways, American culture is built on the supposed ideals of personal independence and self-reliance. So anyone (including me) who grew up in this culture lives with the constant temptation to value things such as "making it on your own" and "pulling yourself up by your own bootstraps." The problem with these concepts is that they always lead to one of two things: disappointment or pride. If we fail, we fall into despair, because we have convinced ourselves that we should be able to control our own destiny. If we succeed, we mistakenly give ourselves all the credit. Neither of these outcomes is healthy. *The only way to win,* as the saying goes, *is not to play.*[20]

To live a lifestyle of humility is to opt out of the attempt to be self-reliant, and to own up to the fact that we are *children* of God (not colleagues of God) and as such, we are meant to be reliant on God (not to mention on each other, especially in the Church). To have a childlike faith (Matt. 18:3–4) is to be, not independent, but dependent on God. Even when we are on the right path of spiritual growth, we are tempted to try to force it, and then, if we do see any progress, we congratulate ourselves, as if we earned something, rather than seeing everything as a gift. In any case, there is no such thing as self-sanctification, and as we have already noted, the purpose of prayer — indeed, the goal of the whole spiritual life — is sanctification.

Self-reliance is a form of pride, and, as such, it is in an inverse relationship with humility. The more you try to rely on yourself, the less you are relying on God. The more you trust in your own ability, your own control,

[20] Lawrence Lasker, Walter F. Parkes, and Walon Green, *WarGames* (1983), dir. John Badham.

your own resources, the less you are trusting in God and His providence. Even trusting in your good works is fraught with problems because it's very difficult to separate good works from selfish motives.[21] It is one of those paradoxes of Judeo-Christian wisdom that, in order to receive strength and wisdom from God, one must first admit that one is weak and foolish. Another way to say that is, true humility means distrusting your own strength and wisdom. If you want the gifts of God, you have to admit you need them.

We are often tempted to think that self-reliance is the way to peace. We think, *if only I could save enough money to be financially independent*, or *if only I could buy that bigger house*, or whatever the goal is that's out there, we think that if we can just "get there," we can arrive at peace. But one of the many problems with this approach to life is that it quickly becomes competitive. For one person to get that job or promotion, another has to be denied it. And so a worldview in which it's "you and me against the world" leads only to fear and anxiety, born of the reality that we might not get what we worked so hard for and we think we deserve. That fear and anxiety is expressed outwardly in judgmentalism and criticism of others, which is the dark side of self-reliance. This is the temptation to live and act as if, in order for me to be raised up, I need to knock someone else down.[22]

Again, the only way to win that game is to refuse to play it. In truth, we are not supposed to lift ourselves up at all. Jesus said, "Whoever exalts himself will be humbled; but whoever humbles himself will be exalted" (Matt. 23:12). We are supposed to humble ourselves, in imitation of Jesus. St. Paul tells us, that just as Jesus humbled Himself in His Incarnation, so we should be ready to humble ourselves to follow Him — or at least accept the humiliation that can come with following Christ (Phil. 2:5–11). Humility, as a lifestyle, is precisely the way we are meant to live as followers of Jesus. It is the way we "work out our salvation" (Phil. 2:12, the very next verse). This humility is what allows us to stop focusing on ourselves long enough so see Jesus in others and have empathy and compassion for others (Matt. 25:35–36, 42–43). It's fair to say that if you see someone who does not have compassion for others or show mercy to others, you are seeing someone who lacks humility.

[21] De Caussade, *Letters on the Practice of Abandonment* 7.1.

[22] De Caussade, *Letters on the Practice of Abandonment* 2.11.

And so the self-reliant worldview does not lead to peace at all but to its opposites, fear and anxiety. In fact, St. Augustine pointed out that, in a way, all sin comes from fear: either the fear of losing what we have, or the fear of not getting what we want.[23] Humility undercuts that fear and allows us to live in peace because we are so grateful for all that we have, that we know we don't deserve more, we trust God to provide for us, even if we should suffer loss, and we are content with what we have, so that we are not obsessed with some future acquisition.

Peace does not come from achieving self-reliance. Peace doesn't come from achieving anything — because if it did, that would mean peace is not possible in the present. But peace *is* possible in the present precisely because it is not focused on the future. We will explore this concept more in the final chapter, but for now, the point is that peace comes from letting go of the attempt to control the outcome of things and relying on God instead. In fact, we should see our own inability to control our lives as a gift and give ourselves permission to have the peace that comes from not having to be responsible for everything.[24] This may also require letting go of concern for what others think of us, but then, that is a part of humility.

But we often don't let go of control, or we don't give ourselves permission to let go and have peace, because we worry about being irresponsible or being perceived as lazy. In fact, some of us are conditioned to feel a little guilty about being at peace, as if we are shirking something, or as if enjoying peace in life by surrendering our own agenda is somehow a lack of ambition.[25] So it needs to be said that to let go of self-reliance is not the same thing as irresponsibility or laziness. As always, we strive for the balance between extremes. Peace is found in neither independence nor irresponsibility. Peace is living between the extremes: taking responsibility and planning appropriately for the future, balanced with a healthy distrust of one's ability to control the future — neither lazy nor driven.

Finally, humility as a lifestyle means that it is not a temporary thing. It is not something that gets us somewhere, except in the sense that it facilitates sanctification. To see humility as a temporary means to an end is

[23] Augustine of Hippo, *Confessions* 2.5.

[24] De Caussade, *Letters on the Practice of Abandonment* 4.7, 6.7.

[25] In some ancient writers, ambition is considered a sin.

to turn humility itself into a form of self-reliance, as if to say, *I will practice humility until I achieve another goal and move beyond it.* But humility is not a work we do, as if we could someday stop doing it. Humility is a means of grace, and we will always need God's grace. And God's grace is not like training wheels, to help us along until we don't need it anymore. Our weakness and insufficiency are the rule, not the exception — our default status, not a temporary problem that can be fixed. To live in humility is to realize that what is needed is not overcoming inadequacy but resigning ourselves to our permanent state of inadequacy and surrendering to our permanent state of dependence on God.

No Complaining

Complaining is a symptom of pride; it's as simple as that. Complaining demonstrates a lack of gratitude for what God has already given and a lack of faith in God's providence to come. A complaint is an outward expression of entitlement — that is, the belief that one deserves better than whatever is happening in the moment or in the past, which is usually *not* true.[26] Now, here one might protest, holding in the mind something that happened and thinking, *Surely I didn't deserve to be treated like that, if only for the sake of human dignity!* We all think like this. But when we do, we are forgetting the many times we treated someone else disrespectfully or unfairly. We are forgetting our own sins while we hold the sins of others against them. We are being like the unmerciful servant and demanding to be treated better than we have treated others. And this may be one of the most difficult aspects of the lifestyle of humility (it is for me), but that does not make it any less true. Complaining is a sin. As Christians, we are called to carry our crosses, not complain about them (Matt. 16:24; Mark 8:34; Luke 9:23). To be on the way to salvation means being on the path of sanctification, which is a path of increasing self-denial (taking up your cross) and increasing desire to do God's will more than your own. But that desire to do God's will means *you* don't get to decide what is and is not God's will. You don't get to exempt yourself by assuming that it

[26] It should go without saying that my definition of *complaint* does not include the legitimate confrontation of injustice or the violation of human rights, such as when people gather to pray at an abortion clinic to fight for the right to life for the preborn.

couldn't possibly be God's will for you to be inconvenienced or annoyed or even humiliated. Maybe it *is* God's will — if only for the purpose of building your patience. We will go into detail on the subject of the will of God in the next chapter, but for now — no excuses!

Remember that Jesus, in His parable of the Pharisee and the tax collector, criticized the Pharisee for making the prayer all about himself. And remember what the content of the prayer was. It could be summarized as *I'm better than that guy*. And isn't this exactly what we do when we make excuses for ourselves? We justify our faults by saying, *Well, at least I'm not as bad as those other people*, or *I'm not really that bad in the grand scheme of things*, or even *Compared with a lot of other people, I'm basically a good person*. St. John Chrysostom, in commenting on this parable, notes that this kind of "I'm not so bad" or "others are worse than me" justification is not only exactly what the Pharisee was doing in the parable, but it effectively negates a person's prayers. He says, "Prayer is only effective if prayed with humility."[27]

Humility means not making excuses for yourself or justifying yourself, *even* when you truly believe that this is justified. Even when falsely accused, wrongly criticized, or unjustly humiliated, the humble person does not complain.[28] This is not to say that you can never defend yourself, but it does rule out arguing, lashing out, and payback. You have nothing to prove, and you do not owe explanations to anyone who is not in authority over you.[29] It also rules out gossiping, and the kind of complaining that forces people not involved to listen to you vent about it. Especially in the case of loved ones, the humble person discerns the difference between mutual support and simply spreading the anxiety around. As many saints have pointed out, it *may*, in fact, be God's will for you to be humiliated. And in any case, the Christian response is meant to be patience and silence — imitating Jesus Himself (Matt. 26:63; 27:12–14; Mark 14:61; 15:5; Luke 23:9; John 19:9; Acts 8:32; Isa. 53:7). Silence in the face of frustration and even antagonism.[30]

[27] John Chrysostom, *Homilies on Hebrews* 27.

[28] De Caussade, *Letters on the Practice of Abandonment* 2.11, 3.1.

[29] De Caussade, *The Sacrament of the Present Moment*, 20.

[30] De Caussade, *Letters on the Practice of Abandonment* 6.21. According to de Caussade, silence sanctifies.

Silence when we are tempted talk, and especially if we are tempted to call attention to ourselves. Before anyone should send me an e-mail to *complain* about what I'm saying, this does not mean that a person cannot speak to HR about an uncomfortable work environment or take appropriate measures to end an ongoing abusive situation. But these things are to be done calmly, patiently, and without resorting to revenge or escalating the drama. Leave the other person's punishment to God.

Humility means being so willing to acknowledge your faults that you consider it a gift when anyone points them out to you. Humility admits faults in order to improve.[31] Even when the acknowledgment of a fault includes accusations or results in humiliation, the humble person does not let humiliation lead to sadness but, rather, lets it lead to renewed commitment to relying on God rather than on himself.[32] In fact, by letting go of the humiliation, rather than retaliating, the humble person finds peace and joy. Focusing on resentment steals joy. Humility means accepting past humiliations as part of being human, and not going over them in the mind, fantasizing about what one should have said or done to avoid the humiliation. It means rejecting a mindset of victimhood because that often leads people to feel entitled to commit immorality in order to make up for the loss of pride, as if the individual can inflict some kind of self-imposed justice on the world.

Thus, the humble person does not dwell on the past, especially on anger from the past (anger is another one of the deadly sins, after all). This is where humility overlaps with the other meta-virtue, forgiveness. We have already discussed how holding a grudge and refusing to forgive blocks grace and negates prayer and how forgiveness is a prerequisite for prayer. Yet too many people give themselves permission to hold on to past anger and resentment, as if they are entitled to that. This kind of entitlement is perhaps the most insidious because by it a person convinces him- or herself that he or she *deserves* to live without peace. Dwelling on the past robs us of peace. If we ever hope to live in peace — not only peace of mind, but peace with others — we have to let go of the lie that we will have peace when we've been vindicated. In other words, we have to let go of the past, not fix

[31] De Caussade, *Letters on the Practice of Abandonment* 3.15.

[32] De Caussade, *Letters on the Practice of Abandonment* 4.15.

it. Peace comes from having enough humility to be willing to let go of past hurts *without* being vindicated.

Perhaps dwelling on the past is a symptom of the fear that the annoyance or humiliation will happen again. This is understandable, but the truth is that we can't prevent these things from happening again, and the harder we try, the more we trade our peace in the present for a possible peace in the future that is not guaranteed. Obsession over the past is just as damaging to our spiritual lives as obsession over the future. It can become a form of idolatry, taking center stage in our lives, displacing God. Letting go of the past will require courage, but it is essential if we don't want our prayers to be dragged down by the weight of resentment.

You may have heard of the practice of "offering it up." Although a whole book could be written on the concept of redemptive suffering, to put it very simply, the best Christian response to inconveniences, annoyances, antagonisms — in short, some of the smaller crosses we may be called to bear in life — is to bring them into our prayers. Offering it up means, among other things, praying about it. Especially when something is frustrating and part of that frustration is the feeling of helplessness, that you can't *do* anything about it — offering it up in prayer is what you can do. But it requires *not* complaining about it. To complain is to immediately negate any benefit of offering it up. To offer it up means to take it to God, not as a complaint, but as a penance. It is a penance because in it, suffering is endured with patience, the endurance of it is motivated by a desire to submit to God's will, and it is endured without complaining. To "offer it up" means to absorb it and not to reflect it back to its source, echo it to others, or amplify it. It means *not* asking God to take it away; *not* asking God to change your circumstances, but, rather, asking God to change *you* in the circumstances, to use these crosses you bear as fertilizer, if you will, for your growth in the fruit of the Spirit, especially patience and peace.[33]

At this point, one might object, *I've read the Psalms, and the psalmists seem to do a lot of complaining.* This is true; there is a good bit of self-righteous complaining in the Psalms. But you need to keep in mind that the Psalms are not an instruction manual for prayer but, rather, the record of certain prayers of the Hebrew people before the coming of Christ. We are not necessarily

[33] De Caussade, *Letters on the Practice of Abandonment* 3.15.

supposed to pray exactly as they did, or to pray everything they did (sometimes they even prayed for revenge), though the Psalms do give us some measure of comfort that the people of Israel had those very real feelings. In any case, we should treat those parts of the Psalms as a record of very human emotions, not as guidelines on how we as Christians should pray.

What About When Prayers Are Not Answered?

We'll start with the cliché — though it is absolutely true: *God always answers prayer; sometimes the answer is no*. This is true, but it's a bit incomplete, since very often the answer to our prayers is actually "Not yet. Wait. Be patient."[34] And sometimes the worst part is that when we've prayed for something, and we haven't gotten it, we don't know whether the answer is "no" or "wait"; we don't know whether we will get what we've asked for at some point in the future. And I've been known to complain to God (yes, complain) that this makes it hard for me to plan the future, this not knowing. And it's taken me sixty years of life to figure out that often God doesn't *want* me to plan the future. He wants me to put my trust in Him, even when I don't know the future. Sometimes God wants me to focus on some other priority at the present time. Sometimes He wants me to grow in discipline, in accepting delayed gratification (obviously without complaining).

St. Ambrose, in his eulogy for his brother Satyrus, said that we shouldn't complain when our prayers are not answered in the way we want, since this would be a failure to trust in the will of God.[35] The assumption here is, of course, that God always answers prayers according to His will. God is never forced to act apart from His will, and so there is never a case when God answers a prayer in any way other than what is aligned with his will. In fact, we should not be surprised when our prayers are not always answered the way we wish, since if God always answered our prayers with a yes, He would be doing our will (and then He *would* be a vending machine). But we can never think of God in a way that would imply that He is forced to do anything He doesn't want to do. After all, if God answered every prayer with a yes, no one would ever die. The bottom line is that God's ultimate will is for the salvation of as many people as will accept it (1 Tim. 2:4), and

[34] John Chrysostom, *Homilies on Matthew* 10.

[35] Ambrose of Milan, *On the Death of Satyrus* 1.65.

so we must assume that all prayers are answered with that end in mind. We will return to this in our final chapter.

Remember that praying in humility means acknowledging that our minds are limited, we are not omniscient, and so our wants are short-sighted, and only God knows what's really best for everyone in the long run. How often do we pray for our comfort, not realizing we are praying against our sanctification? How often do we pray for something that is not good for us? As St. John Henry Newman wrote, "God knows what is my greatest happiness, but I do not.... Thus God leads us by strange ways.... We are blind; left to ourselves we should take the wrong way; we must leave it to him."[36]

So there's nothing inherently wrong with asking for whatever we want (James 4:2) — assuming what we want is not a sin, of course (see James 4:3). But it is wrong to demand to know why we don't get what we want — because, in fact, we already know why. If we don't get what we asked for, it was not what was best for us, or for someone else, or for the sanctification and the salvation of the most people possible. After all, even Jesus in the Garden of Gethsemane got a *no* answer to His prayer, and that was for our benefit.

St. Augustine wrote that even if you don't get what you asked for, your prayer is answered in your best interests, though you may never know it in this life.[37] He said in his *Confessions*, speaking to God, "Sometimes, for my own good, you did not grant my prayer."[38] His own mother, St. Monica, waited for her prayers to be answered, and at one point, she thought that God had answered with a no, when, in fact, He was doing exactly what was needed to answer with a yes. Augustine said that God answered her prayers by not answering them. In other words, God granted her deepest wish (for his conversion) by ignoring her advice on how to make that happen![39] In

[36] John Henry Newman, *Meditations on Christian Doctrine*, Meditation I, "Hope in God — Creator," quoted in Juan Vélez, *Holiness in a Secular Age: The Witness of Cardinal Newman* (New York: Scepter, 2017), 106–107.

[37] Augustine of Hippo, *Homilies on the Letter of I John* 6.8. See also John Chrysostom, *Homilies on Colossians* 10. See also de Caussade, *Letters on the Practice of Abandonment* 6.7.

[38] Augustine of Hippo, *Confessions* 1.9.

[39] Augustine of Hippo, *Confessions* 5.8.

fact, sometimes getting what we want is the cause of our suffering.[40] If all prayers were answered with a yes, some of them would turn out bad for us, and in any case, it would cause us to believe that it is our own will that matters.[41] So, once having prayed, our job is to wait in peace, with patience, and continue to pray.

Therefore, we should not try to figure out why God doesn't do what we want, because no matter how much we work at the problem, we won't get it right, and we run the risk of making assumptions about what God is doing and then operating on false assumptions from then on. Our perspective is so limited that if we try to figure out the answers to why God does or does not do what we wish, and if we come to incomplete or incorrect answers, or simply answers that we don't like, we may end up resenting God and moving further from Him, instead of doing what we should, which is to let disappointment drive us closer to Him. If we believe we need to have the answers before we trust God, then we have misunderstood the definition of *trust*. We need to trust God when we don't have the answers. That's faith. And just as there could be no courage if there was no danger, so there can be no faith if there is no mystery. And humble faith has to mean not needing to know why. In this life, we see everything as though through a dark glass (1 Cor. 13:12). We can't see all the variables, and to expect answers in this life is premature. Remember the words of Jesus: *What I am doing now, you do not understand. But you will understand later* (John 13:7).

Finally, we have to address the very painful reality of losing loved ones before what we perceive to be their time. We pray for healing, yet healing does not come. And it is difficult to imagine how their loss could be part of a larger plan that is oriented toward the good. As we wrap up this chapter, I will only say two things and leave the rest for the next chapter. First, when we lose loved ones, they are not lost. We say we lose them because they are taken from us, and we miss them — and this is not to minimize the pain — but it is *our* pain, not theirs. Second, even a life taken young is not being cheated. Only those left behind are left with the feeling of missing out on something. The one who dies in Christ is not dead but passes into

[40] De Caussade, *Letters on the Practice of Abandonment* 1.9, 1.10.

[41] De Caussade, *Letters on the Practice of Abandonment* 3.16.

life beyond life (see my book *What Really Happens After We Die?*). As we read in the book of Wisdom:

> But the righteous one, though he die early, shall be at rest.
> For the age that is honorable comes not with the passing of time,
> nor can it be measured in terms of years.
> Rather, understanding passes for gray hair,
> and an unsullied life is the attainment of old age.
> The one who pleased God was loved,
> living among sinners, was transported —
> Snatched away, lest wickedness pervert his mind
> or deceit beguile his soul. …
> Having become perfect in a short while,
> he reached the fullness of a long career;
> for his soul was pleasing to the Lord,
> therefore he sped him out of the midst of wickedness.
> But the people saw and did not understand. (4:7–14)

Therefore, to pray like the earliest Christians:

1. **Make humility your lifestyle, and your worldview.** In order for your prayer life to be fruitful and sanctifying, your whole life must become one that exhibits the meta-virtues of forgiveness, gratitude, and humility. If you feel as though your prayers are "bouncing off the ceiling," as we used to say, there is a good chance that you lack one or more of these meta-virtues. We have no merit to bring to our relationship with God, but the things we can bring are forgiveness, gratitude, and humility. When Manasseh prayed, in 2 Chronicles 33:12–13, we are told:

> In his distress, he began to appease the LORD, his God. He humbled himself abjectly before the God of his ancestors, and prayed to him. The LORD let himself be won over: he heard his prayer.

2. **Remember that less is more when it comes to prayer** — not less prayer, but fewer words and less talking about yourself. If you find that you spend a lot of time in prayer talking about yourself, it could be that your prayers lack humility. Say less in prayer, especially about yourself. If you feel as if your prayers are dry and heavy, maybe it's because you talk too much. Make

sure you're not making it all about you, and make sure you're not trying to give God advice about how to fix everything and everyone. Give yourself permission not to have to come up with the words all the time. Everything you struggle to find the words to express is already known intimately by God. Begin to think of growth in your prayer life in terms of subtraction rather than addition, in terms of streamlining and simplifying rather than getting more complicated.

3. **In prayer, let go of the past.** If necessary, pray for the grace to let it go. Remember that holding on to anger, resentment, and grudges will negate your prayers. If you feel as if God is refusing to hear your prayer, ask yourself if you are refusing to forgive someone.

4. **In prayer, do not be overly focused on the future, as a goal.** Avoid praying for something that will supposedly allow you to "achieve" peace or arrive at happiness. Avoid missing out on peace in the present because you're trading it for the illusion of peace in the future. Avoid trying to use prayer to control or guarantee some future. Leave the future to God's providence.

5. **Be grateful for the things God has *not* given you as well as for the things God has given you.** Thank God for the protection you don't even know about and for the ways God is taking care of you by not giving you the things you have asked for that would not be good for you.

6. **Don't let shame or embarrassment keep you from prayer.** First of all, not every kind of shame is shameful (Sir. 41:16). So it may be the case that you are feeling a healthy kind of shame that is telling you to get to Confession or humble yourself before God. But even if you have some big thing that you feel is coming between you and God, even if you find yourself in a place where you feel too ashamed to approach to God at all in prayer, or for any reason you feel you cannot talk to God, begin by asking Mary and the other saints to pray for you. Just do not stay away from prayer; ask for the grace to approach God, and ask for His mercy. Remember that no matter what you have done, no matter how distant from God you feel, God is not far from you; He wants you to pray, and He wants to give you what you need (even if that isn't always what you want).

To Go Deeper

Primary Sources

Benedict of Nursia, *The Rule of St. Benedict* (written in the sixth century).

Jean-Pierre de Caussade, *Letters on the Practice of Abandonment* (eighteenth century).

Secondary Sources

Michael Casey, *A Guide to Living in the Truth: Saint Benedict's Teaching on Humility* (Liguori, MO: Liguori Publications, 1999).

John Michael Talbot, *The Lessons of St. Francis: How to Bring Simplicity and Spirituality into Your Daily Life* (New York: Penguin/Plume, 1998).

James L. Papandrea, *What Really Happens After We Die?: There WILL Be Hugs in Heaven* (Manchester, NH: Sophia Institute Press, 2019).

Implied Insight 8

How to Be Certain You Are Praying according to the Will of God

---

Ask and you will receive; seek and you will find; knock and the door will be opened to you. For everyone who asks, receives; and the one who seeks, finds; and to the one who knocks, the door will be opened.

—Jesus, Luke 11:9–10; cf. Matthew 7:7–8

Whoever says to this mountain, "Be lifted up and thrown into the sea," and does not doubt in his heart but believes that what he says will happen, it shall be done for him. Therefore I tell you, all that you ask for in prayer, believe that you will receive it and it shall be yours.

—Jesus, Mark 11:23–24; cf. Matthew 21:21–22

Whatever you ask in my name, I will do, so that the Father may be glorified in the Son. If you ask anything of me in my name, I will do it.

—Jesus, John 14:13–14

We haven't yet dealt with the bold and surprising promises of Jesus in the passages above. And given what we know from our own experience, they are difficult to accept at face value. But if the apostles were embarrassed about them, or if they felt that they were at all questionable as to their truth, they easily could have left these promises out of the Gospels. And yet they didn't. There they are, staring us in the face — and for some of us who grieve and mourn, or who have had major disappointments in life, these passages in the Gospels seem almost insulting. If we're honest, at the very least they seem to question our faith, since either the promise is unfounded or the problem lies with us. How are we to read these passages in light of our experience in the Christian life, in which it is obvious that not all prayers are answered with a yes? Let's start by asking how the Church fathers interpreted these passages, and how the early Christians understood them.

First of all, the Church fathers did understand that *asking, seeking,* and *knocking* all refer to prayer.[1] But the first qualification is that these promises apply only to those who are baptized Christians, remaining in connection to Christ through regular reception of the Eucharist. In other words, one must be within the life of the Church and the sacraments in order to even read these passages as a promise to oneself, let alone ask how they are to be interpreted in the Christian life. As far as *receiving, finding,* and *opening,* these

1 A few, like St. Augustine, also saw *seeking* as seeking after knowledge and understanding, so that would include study of the Scriptures, though they did not see study and prayer as completely separate. As far as I know, none of the Church fathers argued that these promises were for the apostles only. They all believed that these passages are relevant for the prayers of all Christians, as long as they are interpreted correctly.

refer not to the obtaining of material goods or even God's intervention in life situations but, rather, to spiritual goods, such as the fruit of the Spirit, understanding, and other virtues, such as moral courage.[2]

St. John Chrysostom and other Church fathers specifically connected the concept of *seeking* to the passage "seek first the Kingdom of God" (Matt. 6:33; cf. Luke 12:31).[3] The point is that in His Sermon on the Mount, Jesus has said, "*Seek* first the Kingdom" just a few verses earlier, and now He uses the same word (in Greek) to say, "*Seek* and you will find." So the *seeking* refers to the spiritual life of sanctification, leading to eternal life. The promise, then, is this: if what you seek is the Kingdom (or at least if your priorities are right and you are seeking the Kingdom above all), then you will find the Kingdom. That's Jesus' promise: not that you will receive whatever you ask for but that you will receive salvation. Chrysostom also pointed out that Jesus did not promise that you would receive what you ask for *immediately*. It could take a very long time, he says, for the door (to the Kingdom) to be opened to you.

When it comes to the passage in Mark, it does seem as if Jesus is promising that we will receive whatever we ask for, provided that we ask with sufficient faith, and without doubt (cf. Matt. 17:20–21; Luke 17:6). However, the Church fathers knew that the confidence Jesus is speaking of is not confidence in our own faith or in our own prayers but confidence in God — that God has heard our prayers and that He has the power to do anything.[4] Jesus says, "It shall be done *for* him," not *by* him, and so it is not the prayer that would move the mountain but God, in answer to the prayer — but even then, only provided the person is sufficiently faithful, which Augustine equated with righteousness, and bearing fruit (unlike the barren fig tree in the context of the passage).[5] And we must notice that immediately after the words "it will be yours," Jesus reiterates the requirement of forgiving others (Mark 11:25). So the implication is that if any prayers are not answered, it is because the

[2] Augustine of Hippo, *Our Lord's Sermon on the Mount* 2.21.

[3] John Chrysostom, *Homilies on the Gospel of Matthew* 23.4.

[4] John Cassian, *Conferences* 1.9. It is possible that the reason the disciples could not cast out the demon was that they were trying to do it by their own power or with confidence in their own prayers.

[5] Augustine of Hippo, *On the Spirit and the Letter* 63, *Sermon* 89.3–6.

person praying is lacking in faithfulness or has failed to forgive someone or, as other Church fathers would point out, lacks humility.

In John, Jesus seems to promise that He will answer any prayer that is asked "in [his] name." In more recent times, this has led to the habit of ending prayers "in Jesus' name. Amen," as if these are the magic words to make the prayer work. But this is not at all how the early Christians read this. Ending a prayer with "in Jesus' name" does not automatically guarantee an affirmative answer. Keeping in mind that, in the context of this passage, Jesus has just been speaking of His relationship to the Father and to the Holy Spirit (the reason His followers would be able to do the things He does, and even greater things [v. 12]), the Church fathers point out that Jesus' reference to praying "in his name" means that He is to be called upon in prayer *along with the Father and the Holy Spirit*. Any prayer that is answered, and, in fact, anything God does, is not a work of one Person of the Trinity only but of all three Persons of the Trinity working together.[6] And so what Jesus is saying is that prayer should be made *also* in His name, but not in His name only. This is why the early Christians made the Sign of the Cross: in the name of the Father, and of the Son, and of the Holy Spirit.

Still, this passage is perhaps the most straightforward in terms of apparently promising a blank check in prayer. St. Augustine addressed this directly.[7] If Jesus promised to do anything we ask, why do believers often ask and yet not receive? St. Augustine listed the following reasons why prayers are not answered in the affirmative, in spite of the apparent carte blanche promises of Jesus.[8] Prayers may not be answered with a yes when a person is asking for something that would be used for a bad purpose or if

6 This doctrine is called *inseparable operation*: all three Persons of the Trinity are at work in all divine activity.

7 Augustine of Hippo, *Tractates on the Gospel of John* 73.1–4.

8 It is worth noting that there are promises made in Scripture that are not made to us or meant for us. This is especially true in the Old Testament. There is a tradition among some Protestant groups of "claiming the promises" of Scripture, as though any promise of God is applicable to us. However, this is an erroneous way of reading the Bible, and one must be careful not to assume that promises made to other people in the context of a biblical narrative are necessarily also for us as Christians. It may also be the case

a person is asking for something that would be bad for him or her. In fact, God is being merciful by not granting these requests. Augustine says that (regardless of how we end our prayers) whenever we ask for something that would hinder our sanctification and block our way into the Kingdom, we are *not* asking "in Jesus' name" because Jesus is our Savior, and it's not consistent with His "name" as Savior if we ask for something that will work against our salvation. If a sick person goes to the doctor and asks for the wrong medicine, a good doctor will give the medicine that the patient *needs*, not the medicine that the patient *wants* — even if the best medicine is the one that tastes the worst. As Augustine said, God "prescribes bitter medicine to retrieve us from the noxious pleasures which cause us to desert [Him]."[9] The same goes for when we pray for something that may be granted eventually but the timing is not yet right. In those cases, the answer is to wait.

When we put all of this together, we can see how the Church fathers understood these promises of Jesus and how they taught the early Christians to understand them. God wants to answer our prayers but only with what is best for us and specifically with what will bring us into the Kingdom. Whenever we ask for anything that brings us closer to that goal, our prayers will be answered in the affirmative, at least eventually. As we have already discovered, the goal of prayer is not our comfort but our sanctification and salvation, so it should not surprise us that Jesus was not really promising us the power of magic spells to enact our own wills and have whatever we want. He was, in effect, saying that every prayer that is prayed *in alignment with the divine will* is going to be answered. None of this should surprise anyone who has gotten this far in reading this book. You probably already knew, if only in your gut, that the reason some of our prayers are not answered is that, for whatever reason, we are not praying "according to God's will." So how can we make sure that we are praying according to God's will?

---

that certain things Jesus said were for the apostles only, such as granting the authority to forgive sins ("bind" and "loose").

9 Augustine of Hippo, *Confessions* 1.14.

The Will of God

There are two aspects to the will of God: what we will call God's *absolute* will and God's *permissive* will.[10] God's absolute will includes the salvation of all (1 Tim. 2:3–4), and, of course, God wills that no one should sin. However, to enforce God's absolute will would require that people do not have free will. But God is love, and love is never coerced, always voluntary. If we are to return God's love, it must be by our own choice, which means we must have free will. And free will requires the option to reject God, or it isn't truly free. So, from a strictly logical point of view, it is impossible to have love without free will, and it is impossible to have free will without the possibility of sin.[11] Therefore, there is another aspect to God's will that we call God's permissive will. God wills to permit sin for the sake of free will — even sin that causes people pain, since God values human freedom (to love Him voluntarily) over and above human comfort.

What this means is that there are things God allows but does not cause. Even things He wishes would not happen he sometimes lets happen. This is not because He is incapable of preventing those things but because He has chosen to allow them for a greater purpose — a purpose that we may never

[10] In this section, I am relying on not only the Church fathers but also the work of later interpreters, including Luis de Molina (1535–1600) and Jean-Pierre de Caussade (1675–1751), with a bit of St. Thomas Aquinas and St. Bonaventure for balance. Both de Molina and de Caussade wrote brilliantly on the will and providence of God, yet both of them have some weaknesses in their teachings. Nevertheless, when used together, they balance each other out nicely. Luis de Molina is a kind of Catholic middle way between John Calvin and Jacob Arminius, preserving both the sovereignty of God (yet without drifting into predestination) and also real free will (without placing any necessity on God to respond to temporal events). Thus, God's freedom is also preserved because God is never forced to respond to anything, and when He does respond, His response is proactively built into creation by foreknowledge.

[11] This is precisely the point that atheists do not understand. They argue that if God exists, He should have created a perfect world, one in which there is no suffering, and since there is suffering, they conclude that God must not exist. However, they miss the point that it is logically impossible to have a world without suffering but with free will, since the only way God could prevent suffering would be to prevent sin.

see or understand, at least not in this life. Tertullian wrote, "Although some things have the semblance of the will of God, seeing that they are allowed by him, it does not immediately follow that everything which is permitted proceeds out of the pure and absolute will of the One who permits."[12] Tertullian specifically cited the persecution of the Church as something that God allowed but had not caused.[13]

We ended the last chapter with the question of why God allows suffering. We can now make the clarification that although God does allow suffering, He is not the cause of it. God's absolute will is that no one should suffer. And yet God allows suffering for certain reasons, including that God values free will more than comfort and that sometimes suffering sanctifies (we will return to that thought below). So not everything that happens is God's will, in the sense of His absolute will.

But everything that happens in the world is at least allowed by God. He either causes or allows everything.[14] There is no third category of events that God does not permit but happen anyway, as if He were powerless to stop them, since that would contradict His omnipotence. Things that God does not permit simply do not happen. So, in that sense, there is nothing that happens that is not God's will, at least His permissive will. There are some who believe that God allows suffering because He can't help it — He's doing his best, but He can't prevent all the bad things — or because He is figuring things out along the way, as we are. But this is heresy. We don't know why God allows specific events that entail suffering, but it is not because He is unable to prevent them. Everything that happens is something God has chosen to allow.

We do know that God is able to turn everything that He allows to the benefit of those who are in relationship with Him. When St. Paul wrote, "All things work for good for those who love God, who are called according

[12] Tertullian, *On Exhortation to Chastity* 3. Tertullian also talks about degrees of God's will, in the sense that God wills some things more than others and is willing to accept some things that He wills less than others, but that does not mean that those things that He wills less than other things are completely outside of His will.

[13] Tertullian, *On Fleeing in Persecution* 10.

[14] Augustine of Hippo, *Confessions* 11.3. Augustine says to God, "No moment of time passes except by your will."

to his purpose," he meant that God will not allow anything to happen that He cannot use for our sanctification and salvation (Rom. 8:28).[15] What's more, He allows us to participate in the turning of things to the good for those who love Him. Sometimes, His reason for allowing something might be exactly for that purpose — so that we might cooperate with Him in bringing good out of it. The point is that nothing happens without God's permission, and whatever He permits He *will* turn to the good, which is "according to his purpose."[16] And part of trusting in God at this point means truly believing that even when sinners reject His absolute will and cause suffering, God's permissive will can make a way for it still to turn out "according to his purpose" — that is, according to His will. To accept St. Paul's promise in Romans 8:28 is to truly believe not only that God *can* work everything together for our good but that He *always does*.[17] But if we are to believe that this promise applies to us, we must be in submission to the will of God, submitting our will to His in complete trust (we'll have more to say about this below); this is a big part of what it means to be among "those who love God."[18]

Therefore, from our perspective, we have to treat everything that happens as God's will. God's permissive will is still His will, after all. As Jean-Pierre de Caussade wrote, "We ought to say to ourselves: God wills it by permitting it."[19] God does not have two wills — in fact, there is just one divine will in the Trinity, not three — and while we may think of God's will in its two aspects, absolute and permissive, this is really only a distinction

[15] Cf. Augustine of Hippo, *Confessions* 13.17. Here Augustine says that sometimes God does limit the free will of people with evil desires in order to prevent something from happening that would have no redeeming value. He says to God, "You keep even the wicked desires of men's souls within bounds."

[16] The verse should not be read as though it is saying that all things work for the good of those who are "called according to his purpose," since that would result in the illogical implication that it would be possible to be called but not according to His purpose. Instead, the verse should be read to say that, for those who love Him and who, in loving Him, are called, "all things work for good according to his purpose" — that is, according to His will.

[17] De Caussade, *Letters on the Practice of Abandonment* 1.3, 4.3, 4.14.

[18] De Caussade, *Letters on the Practice of Abandonment* 3.3, 4.14.

[19] De Caussade, *Letters on the Practice of Abandonment* 1.9.

meant to help us understand that God is not the cause of evil and that He would rather have a world without it but that He allows some things that He does not cause. God is morally responsible only for what He causes, not for what He allows, since what He allows is often the sin of people who are misusing their free will. So the moral responsibility for sin is on the humans who commit it, not on God. And yet if sin happens at all, it means that God has allowed it for some specific purpose. Even seemingly random events of natural disasters or chance tragedies are things that God allows, not because He wills suffering but because they are part of the world as He has created it.

Some people prefer to use the phrase God's *contingent will,* rather than *permissive will,* in order to focus not on what God allows but on what He will *do* with it to turn it to good. But we have to keep in mind that God is not surprised by anything, including human sin, and so He never has to say, "I didn't see that coming," and He never has to come up with a plan B. Because God is both omnipresent and omniscient, He knew before the creation of the world every choice that every human would ever make. He is never forced to respond to human choices because He sees every choice coming, so if we want to speak of God's *contingent* will, we would have to understand it more as proactive than reactionary. In any case, in some mysterious way, God is able to turn everything — even the rejection of His absolute will — back to His will in the end, at least in the big picture of eternity, if not in the details.

Having said all that, we only talk about the distinction between God's absolute will and His permissive will so that we don't blame God for our suffering; but the truth is that we cannot ever really know if something that happens was God's absolute will or His permissive will. We can make some assumptions; for example, when someone clearly violates the expectations God has set for us in divine revelation, we can say with some confidence that this was not God's absolute will. But to begin to speculate about other people's behavior will quickly take us down the path of judgmentalism, so it is to be avoided. We cannot presume to know whether something was God's absolute will, and we cannot expect God to explain it to us when we ask why something happened.

So then, how does this way of thinking of God's will help us in our prayer lives? For one thing, we have to understand that even when we know for certain that something is according to God's absolute will, God values human free will to the extent that He usually will not take away someone's free will, even if we pray for Him to do just that. So, for example, you may know that a loved one is engaging in self-destructive behavior, and you may pray for the person to stop that behavior, knowing with certainty that you are praying according to God's absolute will. And you pray hard, wishing God would work so powerfully in the person's life that he or she cannot help but be converted. However, the "cannot help but" part of the equation is the problem. We're asking God to force someone against his or her will. But in the end, He does not take away that person's free will. God will allow that person to continue down a path that leads him or her away from Him and away from salvation, if that is the person's choice. We all know from experience that sometimes, no matter how much we pray, God will not necessarily stop someone from doing what that person is determined to do.

God will not even take away *your* free will — even if you ask Him to. If I ask God to prevent me from eating unhealthy snacks after 10:00 p.m. and when 10:30 rolls around, I'm looking through the pantry, God does not take way my free will in that moment, even though I asked Him to in prayer earlier that day! This means that another reason our prayers may not be answered in the way we hope is that what we are really asking God to do is to take away someone's free will, and God will not normally do that. Yes, He is in control, but He chooses not to control everything.

So in the paradox that is our Christian faith, both of these statements are true:

- Not everything that happens is God's will (that is, caused by God).
- Everything that happens is God's will (that is, permitted by God).

This Is the Best Possible Universe

So then, what does it mean to pray for God's intervention in a person's life — or in the world, for that matter? Are we always asking for a miracle? And if so, is that too much to ask? Remember that God cannot be surprised by anything, and He cannot be forced to respond to anything. This is because He is eternal, omnipresent (present in all places and times), omniscient (all-knowing), and immutable (unchanging). God is not limited by the flow of time, as we are, and so, for Him, there is no past, present, or future.[20] All is present in the mind of God, and the mind of God is eternal.

[20] Augustine of Hippo, *Confessions* 11.11, 11:13–14, 11: 23, 13.29.

This means that God's will is also eternal, not only in the sense that it will never change or go away, but also in the sense that it takes into account everything throughout all of human time. St. Augustine wrote:

> Since the Creator is truly eternal, his substance is utterly unchanged in time and his will is not something separate from his substance.... It follows that he does not will first one thing and then another, but that he wills all that he wills simultaneously, in one act, and eternally. He does not repeat his act of will over and over again or will different things at different times, and he neither starts to will what he did not previously, nor ceases to will what he willed before. A will which acts in this way is mutable, and nothing that is mutable is eternal. But our God is eternal.[21]

God doesn't have to come up with a plan B for anything because His will has always taken into account all future contingencies. We call it "foreknowledge" — knowing ahead of time — but, for God, there is no "ahead of time" because He exists outside of time and rules over time. So, for Him, it's just "knowledge." It's just what God knows, and what He knows is everything. His knowledge includes every possible circumstance, with all possible contingencies; He knows every possible decision faced by every possible person, and the consequences of every possible choice, including the ones nobody chooses (cf. Matt 11:23). And He knew all of this before He ever created the universe. In fact, the universe we live in, the one that actually exists, was created with all events of all time in God's mind and was created to be the best possible universe, so that all things would work together for the good of those who love God.

But wait! It seems as if we could come up with a long list of things that are wrong with the world — ranging from the existence of evil to the existence of mosquitos. How could this be the best possible universe? In fact, as you may know, this is the whole basis for much of what passes for "evidence" in atheist arguments against the existence of God. The reality of evil is said to be evidence that God does not exist, since if there was a God (they

[21] Augustine of Hippo, *Confessions* 12.15, cf. 12.28. Translation by R.S. Pine-Coffin (New York: Penguin, 1961), 290.

say), at least one who was both all-powerful and loving, then surely such a God could (and would) create a world without evil. This argument is not new — St. Augustine himself had, early in his life, fallen for it. He writes, "My own specious reasoning induced me to give in to the sly arguments of fools who asked me what was the origin of evil."[22]

We have already hinted at the primary flaw in this argument, in that it doesn't understand that you can't have a universe that has free will and yet is also free of sin. We can now point out another flaw in the argument. To say that God should create a world without suffering is to presume to know that God's top priority must be the elimination of pain and suffering in the world, but, in fact, that is not the case. When we say that God has created the best possible universe, *best* is not defined as the most comfortable. Rather, *best* is defined according to God's true number-one priority, which is the goal of human redemption. Therefore, the best possible universe is the one in which the most people possible end up in the Kingdom of God.

We know that God's absolute will is for everyone to be saved (1 Tim. 2:3–4). And yet we are also told in Scripture that not everyone will be saved in the end. So it's not enough to say that God wills everyone to be saved. The answer to why all are not saved is that God wills all to be saved *by love*, which requires free will, and so those who are not willing to be saved, because they have rejected God's love, will not be saved in the end. If a world of universal salvation were feasible, God would have created it, but it is not, because the only way to have that would be to force salvation on people against their will, by some form of coercion.[23] In the same way, a world without evil is not feasible because evil could not be eliminated without also eliminating free will, which would eliminate love.

Therefore, in the end, we must trust that God has, in fact, created the best of all possible worlds. To speculate about a better universe than the one God created is to invite the question why God did not create a better

[22] Augustine of Hippo, *Confessions* 3.7.

[23] Some atheists will ask why God requires faith at all: Why not just reveal Himself to everyone and prove His existence? But this would be another form of coercion, since by revealing Himself in such a way that no one could deny His existence, He would, in fact, be leaving them without the free choice to reject Him.

one, and this is above our pay grade, so to speak. Understanding the why of this would require a mind equal to God's, so it is probably the case that there are some things we will never understand, not even in eternity, when we see God "face to face" (1 Cor. 13:12). Incidentally, too many contemporary theologians have erred by trying to answer the atheists' question with a conception of God that is good, but not that great. They argue that God can't really help it but is doing His best. But they have given up too much by accepting the assumption (not unlike the early Marcionites and gnostics) that God has somehow created a flawed world and by presuming to know that they can envision a better one according to their own sensibilities. It is not creation that is flawed. It is not that God wanted to create a better world but couldn't. It is also not that God could have created a better world but chose not to. It is that God did create the best possible world.[24] To believe otherwise is to put oneself in a position to judge the creative work of God, which is an act of pride. The very presence of suffering does not rule this out as the best possible world, since God values free will over comfort and even safety; free will necessarily allows for sin, and sin always leads to suffering. But nothing that God permits to happen negates this as the best possible universe, since everything still works together for the (eternal) good of those who love God.

With this in mind, we can see that there is actually no such thing as divine intervention, if we define that as though God is responding to human events as they happen. Since God, in His (fore)knowledge, created the best possible universe, He has already taken all human choices and actions, and all events — both planned and chance — into account at the creation of the world, and has already factored all of that into the order of the universe. In fact, divine omniscience is more than just the sum of God's eternality and omnipresence because, in addition to knowing everything that *will* happen, He also knows everything that *won't* happen. As Judith says of God:

> It is you who were the author of those events and of what preceded and followed them. The present and the future you have also planned. Whatever you devise comes into being. The things you decide come

[24] Augustine of Hippo, *Confessions* 7.13.

forward and say, "Here we are!" All your ways are in readiness, and your judgment is made with foreknowledge. (9:5–6)[25]

So then, what is the point of prayer? If God has already taken everything into account and factored it all into the creation of the universe at the beginning, and if God's will is unchanging, why pray? Why pray if we can't get God to respond to a situation? Why pray if we can't get God to possibly change His mind about something? The answer is that when we pray, although we pray within the stream of time at a certain point in our lives, God has known from before the creation of the universe that we *would* pray and what we would pray for. And so when we pray, it is true that God hears our prayers, but it is also true that He has already heard our prayers, long before we were even born, in eternity before creation, and He has taken our prayers into account at the creation of this best possible universe. God doesn't have to wait for you to pray — He already knew that you would pray — but *you do still need to pray,* or He would have already known that you didn't.

At this point, we have to be careful that we don't turn God into the cosmic clockmaker of the Deists, a distant, impersonal god who created the universe, wound it up, and walked away. God is love, and that means He is eternally and immutably loving and cares for each of us. He is always right there with you. But because God is immutable, He does not actually work one day and rest the next (Genesis 2:2–3 notwithstanding); He is eternally at work and eternally at rest.[26] God doesn't even really do one thing one day and something else the next. In reality, He is always doing everything; He is eternally active and eternally creative. God's work of creating is never done and it is not really a separate thing from His work of sustaining creation or revealing Himself within it. So although God is never forced to react to any event in time, He *does* hear and respond to our prayer. It's just that His hearing and His response are not bound by time.

For example, let's say there is a mother who has a daughter living in a foreign country. And the mother hears on the news that there was an earthquake in the place where her daughter lives — but the phones aren't working so she can't reach her daughter. The mother might pray for God to

[25] Note also Tobit 6:18: "For she was set apart for you before the world existed."

[26] Augustine of Hippo, *Confessions* 12.27, 13.37.

protect her daughter, to keep her safe and away from harm. Now someone might object and say that since the earthquake was already over before the mother even heard about it, whatever was going to happen to the daughter has happened. She is already either safe or not — it's done. What's the point of praying about it? In reality, though, God has heard the mother's prayer outside of time and knew about it from before the foundation of the world, and He had already taken that prayer to heart when He created the universe. The decision as to how to answer that prayer may be a mystery to us, but God did not have to wait until after the earthquake to hear the prayer. He may, in fact, answer the mother's prayer with the protection of her daughter because, long before the earthquake happened, He knew that she would pray for it. This is how God's knowledge of our prayers works. Our prayers are effective *because of* God's foreknowledge; God never has to play catch-up. If you pray for something today, or tomorrow, for that matter, God knew before the creation of the universe that you would, and so He has already factored your future prayers into the creation of this best of all possible worlds.[27]

God's will does not depend on human actions in any kind of cause-and-effect chronology that would require God to act in any particular way or at any particular time — and certainly not in any way that would require Him to act "in a hurry." He is never taken by surprise and never limited by a deadline. And God's sovereignty and human freedom are not a zero-sum game, or in some kind of inversely proportional relationship, as if the more sovereign God is, the less free we are, or vice versa.[28] God is fully sovereign, and yet humans do have real free will (albeit limited by Original Sin). God's sovereignty is not threatened by human freedom or even by random chance because He has already taken everything into account in organizing the universe. The point is that we, as humans, are not in competition with

[27] See Kirk R. MacGregor, *Luis de Molina: The Life and Theology of the Founder of Middle Knowledge* (Grand Rapids: Zondervan, 2015), 121–130.

[28] This is, in fact, what St. Augustine struggled with and what led him to certain teachings on free will and predestination that the Church would reject but that John Calvin would later pick up and make the core of his whole theological system. With regard to free will, we must maintain that the human will, though limited by Original Sin, is still free enough to be morally accountable for a person's actions.

God. We may misuse our free will by making choices that cause suffering or drive us away from God, or both, and yet God can and does take (and already has taken) all of this into account, to orchestrate everything together toward the goal of our sanctification and salvation — as long as we don't persist in rejecting Him. At some point, if we continue in mortal sin — God in His foreknowledge already knowing when that point comes — we are abandoned to our will. If we insist on going our own way, away from God, God will grant our wish. But for those who wish to do God's will — that is, for those who love Him, all things will work together for their ultimate good, which is their salvation (Rom. 8:28).

It should be clarified that free will does not mean absolute freedom. Another tactic of atheists is to argue that if a person does not have absolute freedom, then we really don't have free will. However, the fact that I cannot choose to fly like Superman does not negate my free will. Free will means being able to choose to love God or not; to respond in faith to God's invitation to forgiveness or not; to forgive others or not; and free will means that when we do choose, we are held accountable for our choices (see Sir. 15:11–12).

But this leads us to the point that sometimes our choices are limited by circumstances. Yet the fact that our circumstances, and events outside of our control, limit our choices is not a negation of free will. In fact, it might be part of God's plan of working all things together for good; it might be that the limitation of our choices by circumstances is a form of divine guidance. God can, and does, orchestrate events in our lives to guide us, to protect us, and to help us avoid temptation. So we need to see the limitation of choices as a gift and as a form of God's guidance. This is the way God works in the world — not watching and waiting for the right moment to "jump in" but, rather, having worked it all out ahead of time.

So we should not hesitate to pray, even if we are tempted to think something is a done deal. We should not hesitate even to ask for a miracle because, within the context of creation, nothing is really any more or less miraculous for God. Or maybe it's better just to say that everything is a miracle from our perspective, and nothing is a miracle from God's perspective. What we see as a miracle is business as usual for God. In any case, we, as Christians, *do* believe in miracles, so we're being a bit hypocritical if we refrain from praying for them because we don't think they will happen. It's probably true that most people pray for a miracle only when they're desperate. Don't wait until you're desperate to pray for a miracle; instead, remember that everything is a miracle, but nothing is difficult for God. When we pray for a miracle, we are not asking God to go against Himself, or change the laws of physics for us, nor are we inconveniencing Him. Every prayer, prayed in humility, is taken into consideration as much as any other. Then, having prayed, faith guides us to accept whatever answer is given as part of the bigger picture of God's best possible universe, and all things working together for the most good, for the sanctification and salvation of the most people possible.

So in the paradox that is our Christian faith, both of these statements are true:

- God's will is eternal and unchanging (God doesn't "change His mind").
- God does hear our prayers and respond to them (prayer is effective).

You Can't Fix the Future

We already know that you can't change the past, yet many of us fall into the habit of trying to *fix* the past. Often we don't even know we're doing it. We go over in our minds a conversation we wish had gone differently. We ask ourselves why we weren't wiser in making a particular decision. We wonder if doing something differently would have avoided a tragedy.[29] And sometimes we try to heal past suffering by holding on to anger and resentment in the present. We ask, "Why me?" and we complain. And when we do these things in our prayer time, we are not praying at all; we're daydreaming or nursing

[29] Given what we have clarified about the will of God, the fact that he has created the best possible universe, and the fact that God does work all things together for the good of those who love Him, anyone who has suffered a tragedy should know that it is possible to see all events as being within the will of God, who has permitted even such tragedy for an eternal purpose. My hope for those who grieve a tragedy is that you will take to heart the truth that *it was not your fault, and you could not have prevented it.* This assumes, of course, that the cause was not intentional, but it may be helpful to remember that the conditions of mortal sin require that it be committed deliberately and with full understanding. If you have committed a sin, the solution is the Sacrament of Confession and Reconciliation. If not, God does not want you to be mired in questions of "What if . . . ?"

grudges.[30] It's an act of selfishness — making it all about us — and an act of pride; it's not prayer.

Having said that, there are healthy ways to make sense of the past and heal from past pain, but that is done in therapy, and you need another person who is trained to walk with you through that process; you can't do it alone. But even with therapy, there is no way to erase past embarrassment, pain, or regret. Those unfinished or awkward conversations, hurtful comments, and poor choices will always be a part of your story. The only way to heal those things is by letting them go and replacing them with something: replace embarrassment with humility, acknowledging and accepting your personal weaknesses, and accepting God's forgiveness of you, especially through the Sacrament of Confession. Replace regret with lessons learned, and by learning to trust that God really is working everything toward the good. Replace resentment with reconciliation, by forgiving others and rebuilding relationships. These are just some ways to let go of the past, but let it go we must. To dwell on the past is to waste the present — we all know this intellectually — and yet we still do it. We still let the past make us miss opportunities in the present that would give us a more peaceful and joyful future.

Now, just as the past has its regrets, the future has its worries. And just as the past is a mystery (we have no idea how God's plan was active in any given moment, and we have no idea how many things God protected us from that we will never know about), the future is even more of a mystery. And so it turns out that just as we need to let go of the past, *we also need to let go of the future.*[31] Perhaps one of the most ignored teachings of Jesus is His advice to live one day at a time and not to worry. He said, "Do not worry about tomorrow; tomorrow will take care of itself. Sufficient for a day is its own evil" (Matt. 6:34). Another translation says, "Do not worry about tomorrow, for tomorrow will bring worries of its own. Today's trouble is enough for today" (NRSVCE). The Greek text says something like this: "Tomorrow

[30] Gregory of Nyssa, *Sermons on the Lord's Prayer,* Sermon 1.

[31] Augustine of Hippo, *Confessions* 11.29. Note that St. Paul's advice to let go of the past, "straining forward to what lies ahead" (Phil. 3:13), is not about focusing on one's earthly future but about sanctification and salvation (Phil. 2:12).

will worry about itself." And yet we worry about tomorrow — so much so, in fact, that we can waste the present trying to fix the future.

What do I mean by "trying to *fix* the future?" Just as it is impossible to do anything in the present that will change the past, it is impossible to do anything in the present that will guarantee a particular future. And yet, depending on our individual personality types, we may plan the future down to the last detail, or we may go over in our minds scenarios we wish to prevent, or we may take measures to protect what we have or to get what we want. Or perhaps we don't plan, but the lack of planning makes us worry even more. Don't get me wrong, I'm not saying that we should not plan for the future. We have to be responsible with our money and provide for our families into the future. And for some of us, the planning is the way we mitigate the anxiety about the future. But it must be pointed out that St. (Mother) Teresa of Calcutta *did* say that we should not plan for the future. She saw planning as limiting God's providence and preferred not to plan anything. She found the lack of planning ultimately very liberating and believed that she was being proactive by not shutting God out of the equation ahead of time. So, often — even though she was responsible for her community — she just refused to make plans, saying, "If I need something later on, God will help me then."[32]

Clearly, there is a balance to be found between irresponsibility of resources and overplanning. And in finding that balance, I think Mother Teresa would say that we have to be careful that our planning for the future does not limit God. We also have to be careful that our efforts to plan for the future are not based on fear because this is, in its essence, a lack of faith in God's providence. As St. Augustine pointed out, all sin comes from fear — either the fear that we will lose something we have (and so we sin to protect it) or the fear that we will never get something that we want (and so we sin to get it). And so often we let planning morph into scheming, or we obsess over our fears for the future and call it being responsible. But when we do this, we forget something very important: we are wasting the present by focusing on a future that we cannot control.

[32] Leo Maasburg, *Mother Teresa of Calcutta: A Personal Portrait* (San Francisco: Ignatius Press, 2011), 58.

The truth is, it is better to lose some possession in the future than to lose peace in the present. Or, it is better never to get what we want in the future than never to live with peace in the present. In terms of the things that often give us anxiety — money, possessions, and so on — peace is more valuable than the things we worry about, and to trade peace in the present for the illusion of controlling the future is a poor trade indeed. Remember that peace is not something we "achieve" or arrive at, and yet how often do we let the attempt at guaranteeing peace in the future rob us of peace in the present? But peace is more valuable than money, possessions, even time, since by worrying over the shortness of time, we waste more time and fail to make the most of the time we have.

Jesus said not to worry about tomorrow, because He knew that worrying about tomorrow will get in the way of your sanctification today. Living by faith means not being so attached to anything that the fear of losing it (or never getting it) prevents us from trusting God completely. And as we have already noted, living by faith means rejecting the attempt to be self-sufficient, and acknowledging our dependence on God for everything. In the big picture, we do not actually provide for ourselves; we can't, because tomorrow will come with problems we cannot anticipate. As St. James wrote, "You have no idea what your life will be like tomorrow" (4:14). But God knows, and it is God who provides for us.[33]

What does all of this have to do with prayer? Well, if you're reading this book, you probably already have a strong desire to make the most of your time in life, to live in peace, and to make your life count by doing God's will. The dilemma, though, is that we usually don't know what God's will is, not in the details anyway. How can we pray according to God's will, if we don't know what His will is? And so we do the obvious thing: we pray for God to tell us what His will is. We think that part of planning the future is discerning God's will for us in the future. But this is where we get off track. Don't get me wrong, I'm not saying that we should not pray for discernment

[33] See de Caussade, *Letters on the Practice of Abandonment* 5.4, 5.8, 6.10. De Caussade uses the account of the gift of manna (Exod. 16) as an example of concern only for the present day. The Israelites were not allowed to save any of the heavenly bread from one day to the next so they would learn to rely on God rather than on their own resources.

when we have decisions to make — the Church fathers modeled this kind of prayer. But in general, praying according to the will of God does *not* mean figuring out what God's will is and then praying for that. It doesn't even mean praying to know God's will and then doing that. If we pray as though the goal includes knowing God's will, we will always be frustrated. And frustration is the opposite of peace. The goal of prayer is not to know God's will but to be receptive to it when it comes to us.

Notice that the only place in the Bible where this idea of "praying according to the will of God" is expressly mentioned is in Romans 8. Immediately before the verse about all things working together for the good of those who love God (v. 28), St. Paul says, "the Spirit too comes to the aid of our weakness; for we do not know how to pray as we ought, but the Spirit himself intercedes with inexpressible groanings. And the one who searches hearts knows what is the intention of the Spirit, because he intercedes for the holy ones according to God's will" (vv. 26–27). So the idea of praying according to the will of God is mentioned here in the context of the Holy Spirit's praying for us, *when we don't know what to pray for*! Praying according to the will of God means *praying in such a way that we are ready to submit to God's will, whatever that turns out to be, and even if we will never know or understand it.*

Praying according to the will of God, therefore, means being humble enough in the present to acknowledge that we are not self-sufficient and that it is God who provides for us. It means being thankful enough in the present to let go of the future, in faith, since the same God who has provided for us in the past will continue to provide for us in the future.[34] In fact, trying to fix the future by overplanning or obsessing about it is a form of discontent, since it implies that God has not sufficiently provided for us so far, that we should have to worry about the future.

But what about when something has gone wrong in the past, and we are praying to prevent that from happening again? This is a natural desire, to try to fix the future by preventing something from happening again. But it remains impossible to guarantee any future, and often by trying too hard to do that, we can actually bring about suffering in the future. In this kind of situation, you still do not really know what God's will for you is in the

[34] This is the theme of many of the psalms.

future; you may think you do, at least in that there is something you want to avoid, but you really don't. You do, however, know what God's will for you is in the present, which is to be faithful, to resist temptation, and to produce the fruit of the Spirit. And by focusing on the present, and on being faithful in the present, we are being faithful to the future as well, since we don't limit God's work in our lives in the future. So rather than trying to fix the future, in prayer at least we need to let go of the future and ask ourselves what God's will for us is *in the present*. No doubt it will be whatever leads us to embody the character traits that are the fruit of the Spirit — that is, to be loving, joyful, peaceful, patient, kind, generous, faithful, and gentle (Gal. 5:22–23).[35] To be like that is what it means to act according to the will of God, and to pray for the grace to be like that is one way you can be absolutely sure you are praying according to the will of God.

It is in prayer that we really learn to live one day at a time. If we can't do it in prayer, we won't be able to do it in life; but if we can do it in prayer, then from our prayer we can go out into the world and live by Jesus' advice in our daily lives. In prayer, we let go of the past, *and we let go of the future.* This doesn't mean we can't pray for the future, but our prayers for the future are not meant to be prayers for God to reveal His plan, solve our problems, or promise to give us what we want. Our prayers for the future are meant to be prayers for God's help to be receptive to His will, whatever that is, and as for the rest, to lay all our anxieties at the foot of the Cross, as St. Peter wrote, "Cast all your worries upon him because he cares for you" (1 Pet. 5:7). Beyond that, focusing on the future only gets in the way of being faithful in the present. This is what Jean-Pierre de Caussade called "obedience to the present moment."[36] We might call it "being present in the moment." The point is that you have to pray in the moment, in the present, if you want to follow Jesus' advice to live one day at a time.

[35] On the last in the list, self-control, see the section on discipline, below.

[36] De Caussade, *The Sacrament of the Present Moment*, 11. This concept was an important part of the teaching of the Desert Fathers: attention to the present moment, along with detachment from one's own will and not trusting in one's own ability to control one's circumstances or even to resist temptation. For the early monastics, attention to the present moment also meant self-accusation, leading to repentance and confession.

No one is saying that this will be easy. For some of us, letting go of the overplanning for the future will be difficult. I am what we used to call a type A personality: hyperorganized, overplanning everything.[37] My way of dealing with stress used to be to plan even more. I figured that if I was still worried about something, it meant I hadn't planned it enough. However, I eventually realized that what I was really saying was that I wasn't *controlling* it enough. But the belief that you can control the future is an illusion. And it turns out that my personality — if I'm not careful — can actually be an obstacle to my own sanctification because it often does not allow me to do a very good job of letting go of the future and relying on God's providence in faith. Don't be like that. If that's your personality, too, give yourself permission to be more carefree; not careless — that would be going too far — but carefree, in the sense of giving up your cares to God.

To be guided by God requires *letting* ourselves be guided, which means giving up control and admitting that we are not the guides: God is the guide. Sometimes we look for God, and think He can't be found, but it's because we're running ahead of Him, trying to get Him to follow us. We are supposed to be following God, not leading Him. And to really put this into practice is liberating because we can relax with the knowledge that we are not responsible for the outcome. If things don't go as we hoped, that's not our fault. That's just the result of the simple fact that no one can see the future, let alone control it. Let God guide you on your journey, and give yourself permission to leave the destination up to God.

Therefore, we have to "place our confidence in God at the present moment" and leave the future up to divine providence, and as de Caussade says, "This protects me from a thousand useless thoughts and from all uneasy desires and anxieties about the future."[38] But this is good news for us, because it means it is not up to us to fix the future; the pressure is off us to even know what to do in the future, let alone do it. Yet if we try to control the future by controlling events in the present, or overplanning everything, we actually run the risk of limiting God and ruining our future. As Jeremiah said, "I know, Lord, that no one chooses their way, nor determines their course, nor directs their own step" (10:23).

[37] On the Myers-Briggs scale, INTJ.

[38] De Caussade, *Letters on the Practice of Abandonment* 2.29.

We do have an obligation to the future, but it is not to control it. We fulfill our obligation to the future by being willing to submit to the will of God (whatever that is) in the present, without hesitation or reservation based on fear for the future, and *that* is what sets us up to receive God's providence and follow His will in the future.[39] It is the right and proper use of the present that brings us to a good future. As de Caussade says, "We must therefore allow each moment to be the cause of the next; the reason for what precedes being revealed in what follows, so that everything is linked firmly and solidly together in a divine chain of events."[40] And so there is a cause and effect that we participate in, not by planning the future (which, at the end of the day, is just trying to enact *our* will in the future) but, rather, by our submission to God's will in the present. And we may not see the connections or the reasons for anything until later, if at all.

In St. Faustina's diary, she described one of her visions, in which Jesus explained what He meant by "childlike faith," saying to her, "A child does not worry about the past or the future, but makes use of the present moment."[41] The child trusts the parent for the future, and is humble enough to embrace that dependence. Just so, we trust our heavenly Father, making use of the present moment by letting go of the past and the future.

We often speak of this idea of making the most of the present, or making the most of our time in life, in terms of "living intentionally." We all want to live intentionally because we don't want to get to the end of our lives and feel as if we wasted our time on this earth. Some, of course, are so focused on making the most of their time that they foolishly think that prayer itself is not worth their time. But I'm guessing that's not you, if you're reading this book. But the mistake that even the very spiritually minded among us often make is to think that living intentionally means controlling everything. Living intentionally does not mean fixing the future; it means living in the moment with your eyes open to the reality that God has provided for you thus far and will continue to do so. It means living with intentional *gratitude* and *contentment*. Living intentionally is not controlling your destiny; it's counting your blessings. Being proactive is not planning everything,

39 De Caussade, *The Sacrament of the Present Moment*, 16, 86.

40 De Caussade, *The Sacrament of the Present Moment*, 21.

41 Kowalska, *Divine Mercy in My Soul*, 150–151.

thinking through every contingency and working it out (since only God can actually do that); rather, being proactive is about not ruining the future by misusing the present, not creating regrets for the future by wasting the present. Faithfulness in the present is more important than planning the future.

So if you're tempted to think that praying in accordance with God's will means that God will reveal His will to you and tell you what to do, remember these two points:

- You won't know God's will for your future until after the fact, if at all.
- You already know God's will for you in the present moment: faithfulness.

Pruning and Chiseling

Jesus said that if we hope to bear fruit, we have to remain connected to Him, as a branch remains connected to the vine (John 15). But, He said, even the branches that do bear fruit are to be pruned, so that they will bear more fruit. Then He said that His disciples were already pruned. What does He mean by this pruning? One way to interpret this is that the pruning refers to letting go of attachments, either material attachments or other obsessions that get in the way of our sanctification. Some of the Church fathers believed that persecution was a pruning agent, since the persecution of the Church forced Christians to prioritize what was really important, and not focus on the things that weren't.[42] Over the centuries, many of the saints have said that trials, hardship, and suffering help us to streamline our lives down to the essentials and refocus on God.[43] So pruning is a purification; that is to say, it is part of the process of sanctification (see Deut. 4:24; Heb. 12:29).[44]

[42] For example, see Justin Martyr, *Dialogue with Trypho* 110; John Chrysostom, *Homilies on the Gospel of John* 76.1.

[43] Though he is not a saint, see de Caussade, *Letters on the Practice of Abandonment* 2.22. It is a tragedy that so many people choose to be driven away from God by suffering, rather than driven to Him.

[44] Cf. *Odes of Solomon* 11.1. Another analogy for purification is the refining fire, in which precious metals are purified, though, in this analogy, what is removed are impurities, more likely to represent sins. The concept of detachment is broader than that, since God may ask us to detach from things that are not sinful in themselves and may not even be encumbrances for another person.

Another analogy for this purification is a sculptor's chiseling away at a piece of stone to make a statue. The sculptor begins with more stone than is needed for the masterpiece, and the way he creates is not by adding anything but by taking something away. The unneeded stone is chiseled away to reveal the statue. This is another way of thinking of the detachment that is part of our process of sanctification. It is what I call *growth through subtraction.* We mature spiritually, not by addition but by subtraction, by getting rid of whatever holds us back (Heb. 12:1). And since prayer is an important part of our sanctification, this applies to prayer as well. In prayer, we learn detachment from the things of the world, but also, when it comes to our prayer itself, we have discovered that less is more, and progress in prayer means that our prayers become simplified over time, not more complicated.

We've already touched on the necessity of letting go of any disproportionate concern for money and material things — that is, to detach from anything that comes between us and our sanctification and salvation. Detachment doesn't necessarily mean getting rid of possessions altogether, though, of course, for some, a religious vocation might require a vow of poverty. But for most of us, detachment means caring less about these things, so that we are free to live in the present without the fear of losing them. It may also mean getting rid of *some* of our things. In addition to the material things, we might also have to detach from some of our relationships that have become unhealthy attachments. And this detachment includes not inserting ourselves into controversies that don't concern us.[45] Too many people today mistake drama for entertainment. But getting involved in arguments and controversies only robs us of peace. Detachment means staying out of the drama, refusing to become argumentative, and even refraining from defending yourself if what's at stake is only your pride. Remember that it is humility, not vindication, that leads to peace.[46]

So in spite of the fact that the word *growth* implies increase, spiritual growth happens through pruning and chiseling — that is, by taking something away to make more room for grace to produce the fruit, which is the

[45] See St. Paul's advice in Galatians 5:15, 26; Ephesians 4:3; 5:6; 1 Timothy 6:3–10; 2 Timothy 2:14–26. See also de Caussade, *Letters on the Practice of Abandonment* 2.28, 6.19.

[46] De Caussade, *Letters on the Practice of Abandonment* 6.20.

fruit of the Spirit. Growth and the production of fruit happen by purification, not by amalgamation; by reduction not augmentation; by pruning and pulling weeds, not more planting. But so many people live their whole lives as though what they need is more of something, when what they really need is less. What they really need is to be pruned, chiseled, purified. What we all need is to have the rough edges chiseled off. Jesus is our sculptor, and we are His blocks of stone. What we need is to detach — to let go of the attachments that slow our growth and block our sanctification.

As I write this, this week's Gospel reading is the parables of the hidden treasure and the pearl of great price (Matt. 13:44–46). The point of these parables is that in order to have the most valuable thing (that is, the Kingdom of God, and making it a priority, seeking it first), one may have to give up other things of less value. The characters in the parables sold everything to buy the field and the pearl. And although we may not all be called to sell everything and take a vow of poverty, it does sometimes mean that we will need to "buy" the Kingdom by letting go of things that are otherwise good in themselves but are getting in the way of our sanctification.

Attachments are like wearing a tie to a fight. It gives the enemy something to grab onto. Attachments are temptations that lead us to sin, either because the fear of losing these things makes us try too hard to control everything or because we tell ourselves that if we can just get that one thing that we think we need, then we will have "arrived" and we can really start living. Those who have gotten that one special thing will tell you that there's always another thing out there that they think they need in order to be content. But contentment does not come from getting what you don't have; it comes from being grateful for what you do have and even getting rid of the things that don't matter to appreciate the important things more. The goal is to detach from anything that calls attention to itself in our lives because, by drawing our attention, it eclipses our relationship with God and causes us to focus on the fear and anxiety associated with the thing itself, rather than trusting in God for the future. In other words, anything that pulls your mind toward worrying about the future is an attachment. Even concern over loved ones can be an attachment if it causes us to try to control the future rather than trust God and live in the present.

This practice of letting go of the future and detaching from the things that cause us to fail to trust God out of fear is called *abandonment to divine providence* or *total submission to the divine will*. It means absolute trust in the providence of God and truly believing that God's will for our future is better than ours. This is, in fact, the whole secret to life[47] — knowing that God's will for us is better even than our own fantasies. In our wildest dreams, we cannot imagine what God may have in store for us in a year or five years from now. And if we can't know it, we certainly can't plan it or control it. But faith means really believing that what God has in mind for us — if we remain open to it — is better than anything we could come up with or hope for. This is the hard truth: there is no reason to believe that our plan is any better than no plan at all because having no plan leaves room for God's plan. As Jean-Pierre de Caussade wrote, "Can I mark out a path for myself? And if I could, would it not be like the path of a blind man, leading to destruction?"[48]

In the end, submission through detachment is a decision we make because we have come to believe that it is the right thing to do. It is not a matter of *feeling* submissive to God or even of being *ready* to give something up, but rather, it is an act of our will to submit to the will of God. We choose to submit to God by detaching from the things that get between us and God, including our own will.[49] Yes, you must detach even from your own will.[50] It's one thing to talk about detachment from things, and even the self-denial involved in fasting and almsgiving, but the hardest detachment, the most difficult self denial, is the denial of our own ideas, fantasies, plans, judgment, and will. But this is the path to peace, joy, and salvation.[51] To insist on our own will is a form of pride and a lack of faith in God. Detachment means letting go of our own will, to be truly ready for whatever God might have in mind for us, as de Caussade prayed: "Grant me the grace never to have my own will, which is always blind, and often dangerous."[52]

Detachment from the world and attachment to God are in an inverse relationship, meaning that the more you want to be attached to God, the

[47] De Caussade, *Letters on the Practice of Abandonment* 1.8.

[48] De Caussade, *Letters on the Practice of Abandonment* 4.14.

[49] De Caussade, *Letters on the Practice of Abandonment* 4.16.

[50] De Caussade, *Letters on the Practice of Abandonment* 4.7.

[51] De Caussade, *Letters on the Practice of Abandonment* 2.13, 3.12.

[52] De Caussade, *Letters on the Practice of Abandonment* 5.18.

more you must detach from the things of the world (be pruned and chiseled). And the more you want to be in union with God, the more you must detach from your own will — in a sense, stepping back from yourself in humility and patience, trusting God enough to wait for God's will and God's timing. And one way to know how you're doing in this is to check your patience. Patience is itself a sign of trust in God, and if you find yourself lacking in patience, it might be because underneath you are lacking in trust of God.

Total Submission to God's Will Requires Self-Distrust

Paradoxically, submission to the will of God requires this one act of our own will: to choose to surrender that self-will. As we have noted, this requires truly believing — and living as if we believe — that God's will is better than our own. I love how de Caussade says so matter-of-factly that God "knows, too, that you don't know what is for your good, and makes it his business to provide it, little caring whether you like it or not."[53] Of course, he's exaggerating. God does care about how you feel, and He does have compassion for you when you are disappointed, but He will usually answer your prayers based more on what you need than on what you want; this is an indication that His will is better for us than our own. Certainly, we can all admit that this is true, but do we really practice the kind of trust in the will of God that causes us to distrust our own wills? Often we do not. Often we are willing to give implicit lip service to the fact that God's will is better than ours, but before we are willing to live that way, we act as though God first has to tell us His will, so we can approve it.

The problem is, it doesn't work that way. If God's will were a GPS, we would get only the turn-by-turn directions, never the overview of the whole route. God is usually not going to give you the opportunity to know what His will is first, before you choose whether to approve it and submit to it. The whole point of submitting to the will of God is that we have to submit to it without knowing what it is — that's what it means to trust God. That "peace that surpasses understanding" (Phil. 4:7) is actually a peace that doesn't require understanding. But usually, in the absence of knowing what God's will for us is going to be, we just do our own thing, choosing our own known will over the unknown will of God. But submission to the will of

[53] De Caussade, *The Sacrament of the Present Moment*, 34.

God means submitting even to the *unknown* will of God, not just impatiently pushing ahead with our own will.

Remember that God has, from before creation, orchestrated everything to work together for the greatest good, for the greatest number of people who respond in love and gratitude to His invitation to forgiveness and the Kingdom of God. Therefore, God will sometimes use circumstances to give us that turn-by-turn direction. Even annoying or frustrating circumstances may very well be God's way of getting you to course-correct. And when we sin and get off the path, God recalculates (or rather he has already taken the recalculation into account, in His permissive will) and gets us back on a path to the goal of sanctification and salvation.

To be clear, Romans 8:28 does not say that all things work together for good, for *everyone*. It says that all things work together for good for *those who love God*. However, to love God is to trust God, and if we don't trust God completely, then we don't love Him completely (John 14:15, 23; cf. Matt. 12:50). If we want things to work together for our good, then we have to follow God's will, not try to get Him to follow our will, for if we misuse our free will, He is ready to let us go so far off track that we fall out of relationship with Him and risk losing our salvation. The Church fathers all believed that even after Baptism one could lose one's salvation through habitual sin and by making the rejection of God's will a lifestyle. Faith is not simply belief. It is belief plus trust. It's one thing to believe in God (the demons believe, says James 2:19), but it's another thing to trust God, and it is the trusting that gets us to the place where we really love God. Submission to the will of God requires really believing, and trusting, that nothing happens that God does not at least permit, and nothing is permitted that cannot be turned to good, if we love God.[54]

All of this is to say that we should default to distrusting our own will and our ability to discern. St. Augustine said, "When my mind speculates upon its own capabilities, it realizes that it cannot safely trust its own judgment."[55] Even when this distrust leaves us with no direction at all, the thing to do is patiently to wait for God's will to be revealed in our lives. Sometimes that means doing nothing other than waiting. Jean-Pierre de Caussade wrote

[54] De Caussade, *Letters on the Practice of Abandonment* 1.9, 2.12, 3.5, 5.2–3, 7.9.

[55] Augustine of Hippo, *Confessions* 10.32; cf. 10.38.

that "the giving up of our own will is a necessary and important condition of our sanctification," but that this means being "prepared to do anything, or nothing."[56] He went on to say that true submission to the will of God is a "complete self-distrust," and that just like attachment and detachment, distrust and trust are also in an inverse relationship — the more we trust ourselves, the less we are trusting God, and the more we distrust ourselves, the more we are free to trust God.[57] The more we focus on ourselves, the less we are focused on God, and the more our thoughts are weighed down with anxieties, fears, doubts, and uncertainty, all of which is not conducive to peace or joy, and, in fact, can lead to depression.

So the more self-confident we are, the less confidence we have in God, and vice versa.[58] As we noted above, however, this is not to promote a low self-esteem. This is simply to acknowledge the reality that we cannot see the future. It's just honest humility. But we go through life as though self-confidence leads to peace. It doesn't.

Often we think that all we need is encouragement. We say to ourselves (or others say to us), "You got this." But the truth is, you don't "got this." Not on your own, anyway, and the "I got this" attitude is getting in the way of many people's spiritual growth, because it's a form of pride. Humility means saying to God, "I *don't* have this; I need *You* to have this." In Psalm 51, the sacrifice that the psalmist offers God is a humble heart. To be humble of heart is to be humble of will, since, in the worldview of the Scriptures, the heart is where the will resides. To offer God a humble heart is to have broken the hold of pride, to be ready to admit that we don't have it all under control, and to be ready to submit control to God. Humility in action is the total submission of the human will to the divine will.

Sirach 2:13 says, "Woe to the faint of heart! For they do not trust." To trust God takes guts. It takes courage and discipline. But too often we don't trust God because we're afraid to. We're afraid of the unknown, and we're afraid that it might be worse than whatever we would come up with. Of course, we know that's not true, but it's the fear that we act on. We fear that there's too much to be lost in detachment from the things of the world. We

[56] De Caussade, *The Sacrament of the Present Moment*, 10.

[57] De Caussade, *Letters on the Practice of Abandonment* 2.16, 3.1, 3.4.

[58] De Caussade, *Letters on the Practice of Abandonment* 4.17.

fear that God will ask us to give up something we love (and He might). We fear that self-distrust and total submission to the will of God will somehow lead to our annihilation — but those who have been to the bottom of the humility well will tell you that it leads to liberation and eternal life.[59] What we should fear is the very real possibility that our own will is going to lead us astray. But there is a sense in which we are constantly having to die to ourselves in order to live for God, and one of the hardest parts of this is that living for God means not knowing what tomorrow will bring.[60] Never mind the fact that you still don't know what tomorrow will bring, even if you do try to control the future. But again, all of this is good news for us because we can let go of the need to plan the future in a way that would guarantee a certain outcome. We can truly leave it to God.

Discipline: Not Willpower but Will-Surrender

In St. Paul's list of the fruit of the Spirit, the last one he mentions is self-control (Gal. 5:23). The problem, though, is that when we hear *self-control,* we immediately think of willpower. But even Paul himself realized from personal experience how unreliable willpower is. He said:

> What I do, I do not understand. For I do not do what I want, but I do what I hate. Now if I do what I do not want, I concur that the law is good. So now it is no longer I who do it, but sin that dwells in me. For I know that good does not dwell in me, that is, in my flesh. The willing is ready at hand, but doing the good is not. For I do not do the good I want, but I do the evil I do not want. Now if [I] do what I do not want, it is no longer I who do it, but sin that dwells in me. So, then, I discover the principle that when I want to do right, evil is at hand. For I take delight in the law of God, in my inner self, but I see in my members another principle at war with the law of my mind, taking me captive to the law of sin that dwells in my members. (Rom. 7:15–23)

If St. Paul had trouble exercising willpower, what hope do the rest of us have? St. Augustine said, "The will and the power to act are not the same."[61]

[59] De Caussade, *Letters on the Practice of Abandonment* 1.8, 4.3.

[60] De Caussade, *Letters on the Practice of Abandonment* 4.16, 6.23.

[61] Augustine of Hippo, *Confessions* 8.8.

And what gets in between wanting to do the right thing and actually doing it is habit.[62] What this means is that if we want to be faithful and obedient to God in our lives, we need to replace the habits that follow our own will with habits that submit to the will of God. We cannot hope to resist temptation in any given moment simply on willpower. What we really need is discipline, and that requires training. It's not for nothing that Paul refers to the Christian life as a kind of training (1 Cor. 9:24–27; 2 Tim. 4:7; cf. Heb. 12:1).

So self-control is not a matter of willpower, but a matter of *discipline*. Perhaps that would be a better translation of the Greek word, to avoid confusion.[63] It does not mean that *I control myself* as much as *I surrender myself to God's control*. This discipline, however, has to be a lifestyle, and it has to be supported by a prayer life that is in submission to the will of God.[64] The rhythm of life in which the early Christians "prayed without ceasing" contributes to this lifestyle of discipline. And, in turn, the lifestyle of discipline contributes to a prayer life in which one is praying according to the will of God because, before one ever prays, he or she is already used to being in an attitude of humility and surrender to the will of God. So when we put it all together, prayer is not separate from life. How you pray and how you live are part of the same discipline.

Therefore, to pray (and live) according to the will of God:

In Prayer

1. **Never hesitate to pray, even if you think it's too late.** Remember that even prayers after the fact are not too late to God, since He exists outside of time. Every prayer you will pray, regardless of where it comes in the chronology of events, was already taken into account at creation. And in any case, creation

[62] Augustine of Hippo, *Confessions* 8.9.

[63] The Greek word translated "self-control" seems to be most often used in Greek culture to refer to sexual continence. It could legitimately be translated *chastity,* meaning faithfulness in marriage and celibacy outside of marriage. But in a broader definition, we usually associate it with resisting temptation, and there the point would be that whatever it is, it is a lifestyle.

[64] Gregory of Nyssa, *Sermons on the Lord's Prayer,* Sermons 1, 3.

is not just a past event — God is eternally creative.[65] Never think that prayer won't do any good. God does hear and respond to prayer, just not in linear time because He is not limited by time. To be clear, it's not that God does not work within time; it's just that He is not bound by time. So you may be called to pray in a particular moment when something is happening — and many people, myself included, have felt a call from God to pray for someone "right now" even though we never find out why. That is God letting you cooperate with Him in that moment — not because He needs you to pray before He can work, but because He is asking you to participate in what He is doing in that moment. Think of it this way: when we pray, we are actually participating in the creative work of God, contributing to creation itself, as God takes our prayers into account in His foreknowledge, to create the best possible world. We are also participating in the way God is at work in other people's lives. You never know; your prayer may be the answer to someone else's prayer.

This also goes for people who have already died. God may not bring them back, but they can still benefit from your prayers. It is never too late to pray. Also, don't assume that there is no need to pray, thinking, "God's gonna do what God's gonna do." The fact that God already has a plan does *not* mean that we don't need to pray, because God's plan includes our prayers. It is God's will that we pray — Jesus told us to — so we don't want to go to the absurd extreme of thinking that not praying at all is some kind of act of trust in God. That would be to miss the point. St. Augustine said that God wants us to pray, in part because, through prayer, we become more invested in what is truly important. He reasoned that if we were just given everything without prayer, we would consider the gifts from God to be cheap, since they were easily gotten.[66] More important, though, is the fact that even though God doesn't technically need us to pray, we need to pray, because the very act of prayer contributes to our sanctification and empowers the fruit of the Spirit in our lives. Praying according to the will of God is really about finding the balance between the extremes of not praying at all and babbling on like the pagans.

[65] Augustine of Hippo, *Confessions* 11.7, 12.11, 13.29.

[66] Augustine of Hippo, *On the Lord's Prayer* 6.4.

2. **Let go of the past.** Spending your prayer time going over past events, rehearsing what you wish you would have said, complaining about being mistreated — none of this is prayer. It's daydreaming. Do not waste your prayer time daydreaming. It is especially a waste of time to worry about lost things or time or money that's already gone. Remember that to waste more time obsessing over lost time is to make things worse. As far as money goes, consider all money lost to be a form of almsgiving and let it go. If there is a true injustice that needs to be righted, or a true sin that needs to be forgiven, or a true estrangement that needs to be reconciled — take care of that first. You can pray for the grace or the strength or the courage to do it, but then go out and do it. Make amends, forgive the person who wronged you, reconcile. *Then* pray. And pray for your enemies before you pray for yourself.

This also means that you do not have to keep feeling guilty about old sins (assuming you are not committing them again). The point is that when it comes to things you have done in the past, you can leave that to God's mercy. Once a sin is confessed (venial sins, by bringing them to mind in Mass; mortal sins in the Sacrament of Confession and Reconciliation) — and yes, even the really bad ones that horrify you to think of them — let them go. It is a temptation, and exactly what the evil one wants, for you to waste your prayer time fussing over the sins you've already confessed.[67] And it is a lack of trust in God, who has promised to forgive them. If St. Peter, who denied Jesus, and St. Paul, who persecuted the first Christians, can be reconciled to Jesus, so can you. Jesus said, don't put your hand to the plow and look back (Luke 9:62). No need to look back at your (confessed) sins. As St. Paul advised, leave the past behind and move on (Phil. 3:13–14; cf. Heb. 12:1–2).

I used to think the expression "Let go, let God" was trite and superficial. But now that I'm older, I see the wisdom in it. If life feels like a tug-of-war, the solution is not to pull harder. The solution is to let go — not to let go of life, obviously, but to let go of the past, and opt out of the drama. Sometimes the only way to win the game is to refuse to play it.

3. **Don't ask for anything for yourself but the fruit of the Spirit.** Remember that less is more in prayer. Don't go on and on about yourself, don't complain

[67] De Caussade, *Letters on the Practice of Abandonment* 7.2.

about your situation, and especially don't give God advice on how to fix your problems. Don't ask for material things, apart from your daily bread.[68] As Gregory of Nyssa wrote, "It would be a very silly thing indeed, to approach God in order to seek temporal things from the eternal, earthly goods from the heavenly goodness."[69]

Don't ask God to change your situation; ask Him to change you. Pray for the pruning and chiseling that you need to detach from the things of the world and rely more on God. In fact, prayer itself can sometimes be the pruning shears or the chisel that God uses to purify us. But remember that He can also use annoyances, inconveniences, and even suffering, so to pray for Him to remove these things may be the equivalent of asking Him *not* to purify you. Remember that you are the patient who does not know what medicine is needed. God is the physician. He knows what medicine you need. Don't be that patient who thinks he knows more than the doctor.

You can certainly ask for wisdom and discernment in decision-making and for the grace to resist temptation, but in general, you already know what is God's will for you in the present moment — that is, to be loving, joyful, peaceful, patient, kind, generous, faithful, gentle, and disciplined. So if you're wondering what to *do*, do whatever allows you to be more like that — and sometimes that means doing *nothing* (and *saying* nothing). Remember that praying according to the will of God does not mean first figuring out the will of God and then praying for that. It means submitting to the will of God, whatever that turns out to be, "desiring nothing and being prepared for everything."[70]

What about when there is something really big, even potentially life-changing, that is causing great anxiety? How do you pray about that without giving God advice? What about when it seems as though you just can't pray enough for this concern? And you want to know *how* to pray, what words to say? Remember that less is more, and God already knows. The good news is that you don't need to find the words. All that is necessary is to call your

[68] Gregory of Nyssa, *Sermons on the Lord's Prayer,* Sermon 1.

[69] Gregory of Nyssa, *Sermons on the Lord's Prayer,* Sermon 1. Translation in the Ancient Christian Writers Series, vol. 18, trans. Hilda C. Graef (Mahwah, NJ: Paulist Press, 1954), 25.

[70] De Caussade, *Letters on the Practice of Abandonment* 2.13.

concern to mind while you pray, even while you pray the Our Father, the Rosary, or other repeated prayers. Or use the prayers in Scripture to speak for you. Find fitting psalms in the companion volume to this book, *Praying the Psalms*, and pray the relevant psalms, making them your own. Then call your concern to mind while praying a prayer of submission to the will of God (see below for examples), and give it over to God. Finally, remember that prayers for things that cause anxiety are prayers for the future. Try to focus on what you know God has called you to do in the present, and leave the future to God's providence.

4. **Don't ask God for any particular future.** God's will is the eternal order which has resulted in the best possible universe. Our will is short-sighted, piecemeal, disconnected, and not part of the eternal order. So the more we insist on our own will, the less we participate in the eternal order.[71] Do not trust your own instincts about what the future should look like.[72] You cannot fix any future, and even if you could, you would get it wrong. Keep in the front of your mind that you cannot see the future and that, even if you were being completely selfish, it would still be in your own best interests to trust every moment of the future to the One who can see the future and wants what's best for you.[73] In prayer, try not to focus on the future at all; instead, ask God for the grace to submit to His will in the present, so you will be ready for the future He has in mind for you.

In trying to fix the future, you may, in fact, be trying to prevent God from helping you grow and from sanctifying you. Let's face it: most of our prayers for the future come from anxiety and are prayers to avoid loss and suffering. But maybe the loss (detachment) or suffering (purification) is exactly what you need.[74]

I used to be skeptical of the adage "Live in the moment." I thought it was hedonistic, as though it advocated living irresponsibly in the present at the expense of the future. But now that I'm older, I see that this is, in some ways, a key to happiness. It's what Jesus meant by saying we should not worry

[71] De Caussade, *The Sacrament of the Present Moment*, 46.

[72] De Caussade, *Letters on the Practice of Abandonment* 6.23.

[73] De Caussade, *Letters on the Practice of Abandonment* 2.26.

[74] De Caussade, *Letters on the Practice of Abandonment* 5.18, 6.24, 7.12.

about tomorrow. Pray in the moment; live in the moment. Don't spend the present on a future you'll never get. To do that is to put your money in a bag full of holes (Hag. 1:6).

5. **Don't ask God to limit someone else's free will.** Chances are He won't do it anyway, but in any case, prayers to limit another person's free will usually tend to be selfish prayers. If you need to pray for someone who is willfully engaging in self-destructive behavior or is in some way clearly operating outside the will of God, simply remember that person in prayer, and ask for God's mercy.

6. **When it comes to intercession, don't tell God what to do for another person.** Just as you can't see the future, and you don't know what's best even for yourself, you certainly don't know what's best for another person. Even when a person is sick or needs healing, God knows what that person needs better than you do. You can't even really assume that living longer is what's best for that person. Having a loved one live longer may be better for you, but it may mean more suffering for that loved one; you don't know, and God doesn't need you to give Him suggestions. If you want to beg God for a loved one's life, then do that, but don't call it intercession — that's a prayer for you.

Also, do not think that more prayer — especially if that means more words — automatically increases the chances of your prayer being answered in the affirmative. That is simply not how it works. In fact, St, Augustine said that it is our ignorance that causes us to multiply words.[75] You may remember James 5:16, which is sometimes translated, "the fervent prayer of a righteous person is very powerful." But this translation is misleading because the word *fervent* is not in the Greek text. It should be translated as the NRSVCE has it: "the prayer of the righteous is powerful and effective." The point is that what makes the prayer powerful and effective is the *righteousness* of the person praying, not how "fervently" he or she prays. You will not increase the chances of getting the answer you want by praying more "fervently." This doesn't mean that we shouldn't pray as much as possible — we should — but you should never think that more words equals a better outcome. The urgency of your prayers reflects your personal involvement in the situation and your perception of the risk level if the prayer is not answered in the affirmative, but these are not things that compel God to

[75] Augustine of Hippo, *Confessions* 12.1.

answer the prayer with a yes. All of this is good news, though, since it also means that you never have to feel guilty for not praying "enough" if things don't turn out the way you had hoped.

Remember that all that is really needed is to remember a person in prayer. Think of that person in prayer. You don't even need to tell God what's wrong with him or her. God knows. Just ask Him to have mercy on that person and grant His grace. Ask for healing, but don't be too specific. And definitely pray for the person's salvation. Anything more than that is trying to impose your will on God. Trust God for the outcome. It may be hard to leave this much to God, but the best thing you can do for your loved ones is to hand them over to His care.[76] Leave them on the doorstep of God's mercy. And do it with a spirit of gratitude for them, rather than out of fear of losing them.

7. **When it comes to suffering, offer it up.** Remember that one reason God allows suffering is to get us to let go of our attachments. Suffering is pruning, chiseling, purification. And remember that the more purification from our attachments we endure in this life, the less will be required in Purgatory.[77] Jean-Pierre de Caussade spoke for the marble under the sculptor's chisel when he wrote the following:

> The cruel chisel destroys a stone with each cut. But what the stone suffers by repeated blows is no less than the shape the mason is making of it. And should a poor stone be asked, "What is happening to you?" it might reply, "Don't ask me. All I know is that for my part there is nothing for me to know or do, only to remain steady under the hand of my master and to love him and suffer him to work out my destiny. It is for him to know how to achieve this. I know neither what he is doing nor why. I only know that he is doing what is best and most perfect, and I suffer each cut of the chisel as though it were the best thing for me, even though, to tell the truth, each one is my idea of ruin, destruction and defacement. But, ignoring all this, I rest contented with the present moment. Thinking only of my duty

[76] De Caussade, *Letters on the Practice of Abandonment* 3.5.

[77] See Papandrea, *What Really Happens After We Die?*, 78.

> to it, I submit to the work of this skillful master without caring to know what it is.[78]

Offering up suffering means taking it into prayer, without complaining, in submission to the will of God. You may want to pray this prayer, given by the Blessed Virgin Mary to the visionaries at Fátima. Here is the traditional version:

> O Jesus, I offer this for love of Thee, for the conversion of sinners, and in reparation for sins committed against the Immaculate Heart of Mary.

And here is my translation, a bit more modern:

> Jesus, I offer this up out of love for you, for the conversion of sinners, and as penance for sins committed against the Immaculate Heart of Mary.

Finally, you might want to find one or more saints who could sympathize with your particular suffering. Saints who have some affinity with your situation become your patron saints. Ask them for their intercession.

8. **Don't ask why**. God's will is given out on a need-to-know basis, and it seems that He thinks it's usually better if we don't know. Accepting this fact is a big part of trusting God.[79] In any case, asking for answers will leave you disappointed. Sometimes answers come, but we don't like the answers we get. Other times answers come in less than concrete ways, and we can't know for sure if that voice in our head is our own mind engaging in some wishful thinking or the voice of the Holy Spirit forming our conscience. Usually answers come only after the fact. No matter how the answers may come (if they come), it is not the getting of the answers that leads to peace. What leads to peace is growing in our confidence in God's mercy and our trust in His will. And just as it is an act of trust in God not to tell Him how to answer our prayers, so also it is an act of trust in God not to require Him to explain Himself. Fortunately, trust is like a muscle. It grows with exercise. So if you

[78] De Caussade, *The Sacrament of the Present Moment*, 56.

[79] Augustine of Hippo, *Confessions* 7.6.

find your trust isn't where it should be yet, try to be patient, and trust God a little more every day.

The point is that we cannot presume to act as though we need God's explanation for His will before we will agree to it. We are not in a relationship of equals with God, in which we get to read the fine print in the contract before we sign it. We are being asked to submit to God's will without knowing what we're signing up for. But after all, if we had all the answers, there would be no need for faith. The Christian faith is not something you agree to; it's something you submit to. It is not a project to be managed but a gift to be accepted. To ask why is to fail to trust God.

9. **Say *fiat*.** John Cassian advised that we should always end our prayers with the words of Jesus: "Nevertheless, not as I will, but as you will" (see Matt. 26:39, 42; Mark 14:36; Luke 22:42).[80] This is a good practice, though it's not really a requirement, and it's not as important as ending your prayers with the Sign of the Cross and the name of the Trinity. The point is what it represents, which is an attitude of submission to the will of God that covers all of our prayers.

In Daily Life

1. **Treat everything that happens as the will of God.** Sirach 2:4–5 says, "Accept whatever happens to you; in periods of humiliation be patient, for in fire gold is tested, and the chosen, in the crucible of humiliation." In real life in the world, it doesn't matter whether something that happens is the result of God's absolute will or His permissive will. If He has allowed it (and obviously He has, or it wouldn't have happened), then, as far as we may be concerned, it is God's will.[81] Everything that happens is either caused by God, or allowed by Him and will fit into His plan to bring about good for those who love Him, so from the human perspective, it's all God's will. And to live a life of gratitude means being thankful for what God *doesn't* give you as much as for what He does give you. Jean-Pierre de Caussade wrote that a truly grateful soul is one who can see God at work in everything, including

[80] John Cassian, *Conferences* 9.34.

[81] De Caussade, *Letters on the Practice of Abandonment* 1.9.

the little things, and even in suffering.[82] This means that we have to see the hand of God even in the things we didn't want to happen.

St. (Mother) Teresa of Calcutta wrote, in a letter to a bishop, "I accept whatever he gives, and I give whatever he takes."[83] This is such a beautiful example of total submission to the will of God, and it makes a nice breathing prayer as well (I've included a version of her quote in the examples below).

Never assume that you deserve anything better than what you have been given in the present. Train yourself to refuse to complain. The only difference between the "Good Thief" on the cross next to Jesus and the other criminal had nothing to do with their lives up until that moment. One went to Paradise, and one went to Hell, only because the former humbled himself in submission to Jesus, and the latter complained and gave Jesus attitude and assumed He was entitled to His own version of right and wrong.[84]

2. **Treat frustrations as course corrections.** Sometimes the future we think we are entitled to is only a few minutes from now. We get stuck in traffic and can't get where we were going as fast as we want to. There's an accident or construction on the highway, and we're forced to take a detour. An unexpected task requires our immediate attention and diverts us from another project or from something fun. A customer-service experience requires us to waste time on the phone on hold or deal with an undertrained employee. These, and other scenarios like them, are small things that can cause great frustration. But trying to insist on a particular future — whether that's a few minutes from now or a few years from now — will always lead to frustration. The only way to avoid that frustration is to detach from the expectations and the entitlement. In spite of what you might think, you do not *deserve* to have your detailed plan for the day work out perfectly. You are not entitled to convenience or to freedom from all disappointment. We have to be ready at all times to surrender expectations like these and to detach from the entitlement to even momentary expectations. This detachment makes room for

[82] De Caussade, *The Sacrament of the Present Moment*, 63. Cf. Rom. 5:3–4; 2 Cor. 12:9–10.

[83] Teresa of Calcutta, *Letter to Bishop Picachy*, September 21, 1962, quoted in Paul Murray, *I Loved Jesus in the Night: Teresa of Calcutta, a Secret Revealed* (Brewster, MA: Paraclete Press, 2008), 50.

[84] De Caussade, *The Sacrament of the Present Moment*, 61.

God to work His will in both the present and the future. To remain attached to these expectations is to invite frustration, which quickly turns to anger and resentment. And then nobody wants to be around you. Above all, avoid complaining. Say *fiat* when you want to say the other F-word.

So when the annoyances and inconveniences come up, treat them as course corrections from the divine GPS. Take the turn that circumstances are forcing you to take, with the realization that the circumstances might just be God's way of guiding you. Treat the delay or detail as though it's protecting you from something. Treat that customer-service agent's failure to serve you as an opportunity, realizing that it might just be God's way of training you in patience and kindness. The very circumstances that you think are unexpected and unwanted may be part of the divine plan that God orchestrated from the beginning of creation. So don't fight it — embrace it. If you fight it, you may be fighting against the will of God.

If you can do this, seeing frustration as guidance (and this is one of the hardest things for me), with practice you will free yourself from anxiety about the future. And that will lead to more peace and joy in your life, and then people will want to be around you. Believe it or not, God gives us only the turn-by-turn because He doesn't want us to worry about the destination.[85] If He gave us more information along the way, it would just be more for us to worry about. It is interesting to think that God's will may include inconvenience, humiliation, and even suffering — that is, God may actually *want* us to experience these things because of the opportunities they afford for sanctification (if we experience them, it is because He has allowed it). But God *doesn't* want us to be afraid or anxious (Matt. 6:34). Wasn't Jesus always saying, *Peace be with you* and *Do not fear*? So it is possible to have peace, avoid stress, and live in confidence of God's love, even through the trials. It's not freedom from these things that gives us peace; it is complete trust in God in spite of them.[86]

I used to scoff at the old saying "When God closes a door, He opens another." But now that I'm older, I've found that sometimes the path of least resistance is God's guidance, and forcing my own way is just choosing a harder path. How often have I forced open a door only to find that I didn't

[85] De Caussade, *The Sacrament of the Present Moment* 34.

[86] De Caussade, *Letters on the Practice of Abandonment* 1.2, 1.9, 2.28.

like what was on the other side! Sometimes the best things come from accepting what God is bringing me, rather than struggling for something else. Sometimes all God wants me to do is slow down, get my head out of the map, and appreciate the scenery. You can try to force open the door that has closed, or you can look for the door that God has opened and walk through that. On the other hand, God's will is not always the easy path. Most likely, His will is whatever serves others rather than ourselves, so we can't always assume that the easiest path is the door that God has opened. But the point is that if the path to our own will is blocked, the thing to do is let that path go and look for another.

3. **Avoid overplanning for the future.** If you're like me, you're tempted to try to mitigate anxiety with planning. For personalities like mine, it sometimes seems that having a decision made is more important than what the decision is. But this is a trap because we come to value the plan as though it is the reality, and then, if the plan has to change, we think of it as a loss, as much as losing something real, because it feels like a threat to our future. Another way to say this is that, if you overplan and treat the plan as if it's not flexible, you place more value in the roadmap than in the journey and the destination. The older I get, the more I realize the wisdom in waiting, and the more I come to believe that patience is in our own best interests. Waiting to make a decision often brings to light new information, or the situation changes anyway, with new or different options to take into consideration. Not that I would want to go to the other extreme and procrastinate everything, but there is a certain sense in which waiting to make a decision does make room for God's course corrections or other guidance. I love this quote from St. John Henry Newman, so it's worth repeating it here:

> God knows what is my greatest happiness, but I do not....
> Thus God leads us by strange ways....
> We are blind, left to ourselves we should take the wrong way;
> we must leave it to Him.

4. **Incorporate fasting and almsgiving into your life.** God is not coerced or cajoled by how "fervent" your prayers are, but He does take note of how righteous you are, and if there is anything that divine revelation and early Christian tradition tell us enhances our prayers, it is fasting and almsgiving.

Don't let these things be neglected or inserted into your life randomly, as you feel obligated or guilty. Be intentional about a rhythm of life that incorporates regular fasting and almsgiving — fasting as an act of self-denial in humility, and almsgiving is an act of self-sacrifice in trust of God. Together they contribute to a lifestyle of gratitude, humility, and trust that become the foundation for your prayer life.

For that matter, think more broadly about the discipline of your life. Will you make time for more than a few short prayers each day? Will you carve out a prayer hour each day, or can you build your days around three or more prayer hours? How will you practice moderation in your consumption of things? These things, too, need to be part of a rhythm of life, and not just catch as catch can. Are you stuck in a repeating cycle of gaining and losing weight, or overindulging and abstaining? How could you create a life that would avoid the extreme ups and downs and facilitate more peace? Be intentional as you think about these things.

Increasing Your Chances of Getting a Yes

I know that it seems as though I am saying, *If you want to pray according to the will of God, don't ask for anything*. And there is some truth to that. After all, the Church fathers interpreted Jesus' promises to answer our prayers with the caveat that we must be praying for spiritual things, not earthly things, and for sanctification and salvation, not comfort. All bets are off if we are not praying in humility, within the context of a sacramental life of faithfulness and obedience and in which we are forgiving our enemies. However, we never want to give the impression that God answers only the prayers that are asking Him to do what He was already going to do anyway. St. Padre Pio of Pietrelcina said, "It is true that God's power triumphs over everything, but humble and suffering prayer prevails over God himself." So prayer does work; it is effective in influencing the direction of God's activity, and in participating in the ongoing creative work of God in the world. God is still, and always, creating order out of chaos!

The fact that God is immutable (unchanging) means that He is not more or less loving or more or less active from one day to the next. He is eternally at the maximum of loving, creative activity.[87] But our prayers can influence

[87] For a detailed treatment on the doctrine of the immutability of God, see Papandrea, *Reading the Church Fathers*, chapter 1. Cf. Augustine of Hippo,

the *direction* of that activity, the "target" of it, so to speak, and the ultimate recipients of God's mercy. God cannot be obligated to do anything; He is not like a genie in a lamp. But He does allow us to both influence and participate in what He is doing.

However, He is not cajoled into acquiescing; He is not like the unjust judge or the friend at midnight. He does not respond to babbling on and on, as if the quantity or the eloquence of the words matters. In fact, when we go on and on with our words, we risk doing two things: insulting God's omniscience, as if He doesn't already know everything, and making it all about us, like the Pharisee whom Jesus criticized in His parable.

This does not mean that we can't pour out our hearts to God. You can share your whole life with Him, even the uncomfortable stuff. God is not shocked by anything you can tell Him about yourself. And it's not a sin to pray in our own words or to share our thoughts with God. It's just that *the more specifically you pray, the more you run the risk of not praying according to God's will.* And sometimes, bringing our worries into prayer can morph into something that is not prayer, such as obsessing over anxieties or complaining. The point of bringing our concerns into prayer is to hand them over to God and then let them go, not go on and on about them. The goal is to entrust them to God, eventually trusting Him to such an extent that we cease to worry.

Praying according to God's will means, above all, to follow the example of Jesus ("not as I will, but as you will") and Mary ("may it be done to me according to your word"), and as Jesus taught in the Our Father ("thy will be done"), which is to say that praying according to the will of God means being receptive to God's will, living faithfully and patiently in the present without too much concern for the past or the future. As Jesus said, "What I am doing, you do not understand now, but you will understand later." (John 13:7).[88]

Confessions 2.2, 2.6, 5.2, 7.7. Augustine says of God, "You were always present, angry and merciful at once." The point is that God does not change from angry to merciful, or vice versa. It is we who change. To move away from God is to experience divine anger; to move toward Him is to experience divine mercy.

[88] See also Sir. 11:4 and cf. Eccles. 7:13; 8:17.

So let's be honest — when we wonder about how to pray according to the will of God, what we're really asking is how we can increase the chances of God's answering our prayers with a yes. Thankfully, we have been told how to do that. But it's not about quantity, as if more words are better. In reality, fewer words are better because we avoid babbling on, and it's better to repeat a prayer of a few words than pray long prayers that go on and on. On the other hand, it's also not about quality, as if eloquence mattered or as if there was some measurement of how "fervent," or even sincere our prayers are. It's not about quantity or quality, but about regularity — making prayer a part of a whole life rhythm of discipline. So here's what we know — what we can say for sure: based on the prayer of the early Church, the teachings of the Church fathers, and the interpretations of later saints, theologians, and spiritual directors, here are the things that enhance and augment our prayers:

- The three meta-virtues, or "root" virtues:
  - Forgiving others
  - Gratitude
  - Humility
- Righteousness (James 5:16), which for our purposes is defined as:
  - Regular attendance at Mass
  - Confession of mortal sins through the Sacrament of Confession
  - A life rhythm that includes fasting
  - Regular and intentional almsgiving
  - The fruit of the Spirit
- Submission to the will of God:
  - Trusting that God's will is better than our own
  - Letting go of the past
  - Letting go of the future

But let us not forget that there are things that block grace and inhibit prayer in our lives. As we've discovered, some of these things are:

- Failure to attend Mass (Heb. 10:25–26)
- Refusal to forgive others, holding a grudge, holding on to resentment
- Pride, entitlement, and complaining

To Go Deeper

Primary Sources

St. Augustine of Hippo, *Confessions* (written around the turn of the fifth century).

Jean-Pierre de Caussade, *Letters on the Practice of Abandonment* (eighteenth century).

Secondary Sources

Kirk R. MacGregor, *Luis de Molina: The Life and Theology of the Founder of Middle Knowledge* (Grand Rapids: Zondervan, 2015).

Appendix A

Summary and Suggested Devotional Agenda with Sample Prayers

Putting together everything we've discovered about the prayer lives of the early Christians, we can now create something like an agenda for our prayer hour, if we should desire to pray like the early Church. The following outline is my compilation of the contents of this book, in a way that will give you a road map to follow for your prayer time. But keep in mind this is only a suggestion; prayer is not about the structure, especially since the danger of structure is that it can multiply words and overcomplicate things. Simplicity is a virtue here. Certainly we should avoid spending our prayer time thinking *about prayer* and how we should pray. Needless to say, that's not prayer.

The expectation of the earliest Christians was to attend Mass — daily, wherever possible. Even when it became a weekly liturgy with emphasis on Sunday, it was considered more pious to go every day. Outside of Mass, Christians were expected to pray the Our Father three times each day and fast two days a week (Wednesdays and Fridays). Beyond that, the practice of private prayer and a personal devotional life developed from the expansion of prayer times, from the prayer times becoming prayer hours, and then into the Liturgy of the Hours, or the Divine Office. This was primarily for clergy and those in religious communities, but as the laity desired to imitate them (subject to limitations of time and money to afford books), we see the development of *Lectio Divina* and eventually (in the Middle Ages) the Rosary and the Stations of the Cross.

I've written the agenda on the assumption that most people will be able to set aside time to pray once a day for more than just a few minutes. We're aiming for an hour, but if you don't have that much time, or can't imagine what you would do with that much time in prayer, then start small and work up to it. And if you have more time for prayer than just one hour per day, taking it to the next level might mean praying the Liturgy of the Hours. So I encourage you to at least give that a try, if that is something that is a possibility for you.

Another option would be to split up the outline and spread out the different parts over more than one prayer time in a day; for example, Roman numerals II and III in the mornings, IV and V in the afternoons, and VI and VII in the evenings. That would give you three prayer "hours," and you could pray one Our Father at each time. But remember that the outline itself is not something that comes from the Church fathers; it's just my attempt at collating everything. So you can change the order of things to suit your personality, though it seems that humility would dictate praying for others before you pray for yourself (Phil. 2:3).

After the outline, I've included a selection of prayers from the early Church and from some of our later interpreters, in case they seem appropriate for you to include in your devotional time. When it comes to the breathing prayers, remember that breathing prayer was something that developed only at the end of the early Christian period, and it was never practiced by most Christians. Incorporate it if it works for you, but it is not required, and you are free not to use it. Or perhaps it's not for you now, but you may want to give it a try someday. That's fine. However, it is the next step on the way toward contemplative prayer. God willing, I will write another book on *Praying Like the Mystics,* in which we will go deeper into meditative and contemplative prayer. So, for now, breathing prayers may or may not be a part of your prayer life, and that's fine.

I also encourage you to get a book of traditional prayers that come from later in the life of the Church. Catholic prayers such as the Angelus maintain the spirit of early Christian prayer. Incidentally, I did not set out to write a book about Catholic prayer; I set out only to write a book about prayer in the early Church. But it should not be surprising that Catholic prayer developed in a way consistent with the early Church. If the prayer of some Christian communions looks radically different today, this would be the result of the Protestant Reformation and its attempt to distance the Reformation movements from prior Catholicism.

Prayer Agenda

I. Make the Sign of the Cross often. Begin and end every prayer with it. Instead of ending a prayer by saying "in Jesus' name," make the Sign of the Cross and pronounce the name of the Holy Trinity: "in the name of the Father, and of the Son, and of the Holy Spirit." Pray without ceasing by training yourself to make the Sign of the Cross at every opportunity, as a blessing and a prayer. Remember to say grace at mealtimes and make the Sign of the Cross over your meals. Even if you're out at a restaurant and you don't feel comfortable saying a whole prayer of thanksgiving at the beginning of your meal, you can at least express your gratitude to God by making the Sign of the Cross over your food before you eat.

II. Go to Mass — every day, if possible. If you had to choose between personal prayers without Mass or Mass without any more personal prayer, you would want to go to Mass. If it's not possible to go to Mass daily, at least go on Sundays or to a Saturday vigil. But remember, going to Mass is not going through the motions: you need to really listen to the prayers that the priest prays so that you can participate in them and then really mean it when you say *Amen*. Pay attention to the Creed as well. The Church fathers treated the Creed like a prayer, so pray it when you say it. (In case you don't know what some of it means, I explain it line by line in my book *Trinity 101*.) In the Mass, you will say the Our Father. Since the early Christians were expected to pray the Our Father three times a day, perhaps you can set aside two more times that day to stop a moment and pray an Our Father. If you can't spread it out over the whole day, maybe you can get into the habit of praying an Our Father when you first come into the church and get into your pew and then say another one before you leave. That gets you to three. To be sure, the goal is not some legalistic checking off of three prayers but, rather, a commitment to sanctifying the day by stopping to pray and reset your priorities.

A. Prepare for Mass by counting your blessings
   1. Pray a prayer expressing appreciation to God (see the Prayer of Thanksgiving from John Chrysostom, below).
   2. Pray a preparation prayer, such as Psalm 115/116 (see below).

B. Prepare for Mass by calling to mind your sins
   1. Is there anyone you are refusing to forgive? Pray for that person!

2. Are there any unconfessed mortal sins on your conscience? If so, go to Confession before you go to Mass.
3. What other sins do you hope to be forgiven for?
4. Do you have any attachments you need to let go of? Give them over to God.

C. Prepare for Mass by fasting. The current expectation is that we not take anything other than water for an hour before receiving the Eucharist, but the early Christians fasted for longer than that, and by the fourth century, it was expected that everyone fast for twenty-four hours before Mass. Perhaps a good compromise would be (assuming you attend Mass on Sunday morning) to have no breakfast that morning before receiving the Eucharist.

D. Prepare for Mass by thinking about who you know that needs prayer. Make a mental list, so you are ready to call them to mind during the intercessions.

III. Pray the Our Father three times each day. If you go to Mass only once a week, consider praying the Rosary on the other six days. That way, you'll have at least a significant time of prayer on the other days as well. It is true that the Rosary didn't exist yet in the early Church, but it does include a whole day's worth of Our Fathers (and then some), as well as a Creed and the Glory Be. It also incorporates Scripture and the ancient practice of asking the saints for their intercession. If you have a bit more time, try the Stations of the Cross Rosary described above. As an alternative, you can pray the Divine Mercy Chaplet, which includes the ancient prayer the *Trisagion*. When you pray the Divine Mercy Chaplet, you can insert two extra Our Fathers on the single beads right before and after the adapted *Trisagion*, in order to get in three Our Fathers for the day.

You could also combine the Rosary or the Divine Mercy Chaplet with your intercessions by calling to mind the people you care about while you are praying on the beads. I do this a lot, and I generally group everyone in my life into five circles, and then with each decade of the Rosary or Chaplet, I remember in prayer one of the five circles of people (for example, you might name the people in your immediate family; extended family; friends who are like family; other friends; and colleagues). Always remember that whenever you pray the Our Father (or any "we/us" prayer), you are also praying for your family, your friends — in short, your people. So there is intercession built right into the Our Father.

IV. Pray for others

A. Pray for your enemies.
B. Pray for anyone you care about.
C. Ask Mary and the other saints to pray with you for your loved ones.

V. Pray for yourself

A. Offer up any frustrations, inconveniences, and anxieties (no complaining).
B. Bring your cares before God, but don't tell Him what to do about them. Keep them focused on *today* as much as possible, leaving worries about tomorrow to God, and letting them go.
C. Ask Mary and the other saints to pray for you.
D. Pray other traditional prayers, such as the *Trisagion*, the *Sub Tuum Praesidium*, and anything you might find in a book of traditional prayers.
E. End your prayers with some version of the *fiat* of Jesus or Mary, submitting your will to God's will. Or pray a prayer of submission to the will of God (see below).

VI. Pray the Scriptures (Lectio Divina)

A. Read the Bible using the method of *Lectio Divina* (remember, this is not Bible study; this is reading short passages slowly to turn them into prayer).
B. Use the companion volume to this book, *Praying the Psalms*.
C. Pray parallel lines of Scripture as breathing prayers.

VII. Pray the Jesus Prayer and other breathing prayers

A. Repeat the Jesus Prayer.
B. If you so desire, pray the Jesus Prayer as a breathing prayer.
C. Let the Jesus Prayer lead you into praying other breathing prayers.

Appendix B

Suggested Prayers

A Prayer of Thanksgiving of "a certain holy man," quoted by John Chrysostom

We give You thanks for all Your benefits, granted to us, the unworthy, from the beginning until now, for what we know about and what we don't know about, for what we can see and what we can't see, for benefits of actions and benefits of words, those according to our wills and those against our wills.

We thank You for all that has been granted to us, the unworthy: the suffering and the relief, the moments of hell and the moments of heaven, the discipline and the foretaste of the Kingdom of Heaven.

We beg you to keep our souls holy and our consciences clear, so that we may end our lives in Your mercy. You loved us enough to give us your Only-Begotten Son; give us the grace to become more worthy of that love. Grant us wisdom through Your word, and in Your reverence.

Only-Begotten Christ, inspire the strength that comes from You. Father, who gave the Only-Begotten for us, and who sent Your Holy Spirit for the remission of our sins, if in any way we have willfully or unwillfully sinned, do not hold it against us. Remember all who call on Your name in truth. Remember all who wish us well, as well as those who do not, for we are all human.

From Psalm 115/116, Translation taken from *Praying the Psalms*

Lord, how could I ever repay You
For all that You have given me?
I will receive the chalice of salvation
And I will call on Your name, Lord
I will keep my promises to You, Lord
In the presence of all Your people

Father, I am truly Your servant
You have broken my chains
I will receive the host of Thanksgiving
And I will call on Your name, Father
I will fulfill my vows to You, Father
In the sight of all Your people[1]

Prayers for Calling to Mind Sins in Preparation for Mass

God, You know my anxious thoughts
Search my heart and examine me
Show me if there is any immorality in me
And lead me on the path toward eternal life
(Ps. 138/139)

God, You know my foolishness
My sins are not hidden from You
Do not let those who trust in You
Be scandalized because of me
(Ps. 68/69)

1 The psalms in this section are translated by James L. Papandrea in *Praying the Psalms.*

God, have mercy on me
In Your unfailing love
In Your abundant compassion
Wipe away my offenses
Wash me of my many acts of selfishness
And cleanse me of my sin

For I know I have offended You
I am continually confronted with my sin
I have sinned against You above all
And You have seen the evil I have done
Which shows that Your words are righteous
And You would be justified to condemn me

Surely, I was born with sin
Guilty from the moment of my conception
Yet I know You want the honest truth
Reveal Your wisdom to my heart
Purify me with hyssop
Wash me cleaner than snow

Let me hear the sounds of joy and happiness
Let these crushed bones rejoice
Look away from my sins
Wipe away all my selfish acts

God, purify my heart
Renew the strength of my spirit
Do not give up on me
Or take Your Holy Spirit from me

Restore to me the joy of Your salvation
And establish an obedient spirit within me
Then I will teach the immoral Your ways
And the unfaithful will turn back to You

God, release me from mortal sin
God of my salvation

And my tongue will sing of Your holiness
And my mouth will proclaim Your praise

I would try to atone with sacrifices
But that could never be enough to satisfy
So my sacrifice to You, God
Is my broken spirit
God, do not reject
My broken and humble heart (Ps. 50/51)

Prayers for Enemies

O Lord, set free those who have not yet called upon you
So that they may pray to you, and you may free them from this
foolishness[2]

Father of infinite goodness, have mercy on those who are sick, and who, in their delirium, turn against you, their Good Physician, and refuse the medicine which is intended to procure them health and life....

Lord, from the bottom of my heart, and for love of you, I forgive the people who cause my suffering, and I ask for them all sorts of graces and blessings, and every happiness.[3]

(See also the breathing prayers for forgiving enemies, below.)

Prayers of Intercession

Merciful Lord, may your will be done.
You wish that all come to the truth and be saved.
Have mercy and save your servant [*name of person*]
Receive this petition from me as a cry of love,
Which you have commanded.[4]

2 St. Augustine, *Confessions* 1.10.

3 Jean-Pierre de Caussade, *Letters on the Practice of Abandonment* 5.2, 5.9.

4 Anonymous monk, *The Way of the Pilgrim*, chap. 7.

Mother of God, Most Holy Mary, My Mother . . .
O Mary, my dearest Mother,
Guide my spiritual life
In such a way that it will please your Son.[5]

Mother Mary, Mother of God,
Mother of the Church, and Untier of Knots,
Pray with me for [*name of person or concern*].[6]

Prayers of Submission to the Will of God

I abandon myself to divine Providence, in all things and about all things.

When the [worse] comes to worst, I defy it, like Saint Paul, to separate me from [your] love, [Lord] Jesus. I know that without your grace I could do nothing, but I know also that with your grace I can do all things. I beg you, therefore, to keep me, in all my temptations, from all sin; from all that could displease you.

But as for the bitterness of soul, the interior crucifixion, the holy abjection, and even the confusion before others, I accept them with all their consequences for as long as it pleases you. I desire the accomplishment of your holy will and not my own in all things, and I beg you not to allow me either to say or to do anything that might place any obstacle to the least thing that you will. And if, through weakness, error, or malice, I should undertake anything of the kind, I beg you not to allow it to succeed.[7]

Father, I abandon myself into Your hands — do with me what You will; whatever You may do, I thank You — I am ready for all, I accept all; let only Your will be done in me , and in all Your creatures. I wish no more than this, O Lord.

5 St. Faustina, *Diary* 1.111 (240).

6 James L. Papandrea, based on Irenaeus of Lyons, *Against Heresies* 3.22.

7 Jean-Pierre de Caussade, *Letters on the Practice of Abandonment* 6.14.

Into your hands I commend my soul; I offer it to you with all the love of my heart, for I love You, Lord, and so need to give myself to surrender myself into Your hands without reserve, and with boundless confidence, for You are my Father.[8]

O Lord, I accept whatever You send me
O merciful God, I trust in You....
O Eternal Truth, help me and enlighten me
 along the roadways of life,
and grant that Your will be accomplished in me.[9]

The Breastplate of St. Patrick

I bind myself today to the strong name of the Trinity
Through belief in the threeness; through confession of the oneness
 of the Creator of creation....
Christ be with me; Christ go before me
Christ watch my back; Christ remain within me
Christ support me; Christ uplift me
Christ guide me on my right and on my left
Christ be with me when I work
Christ be with me when I rest
Christ be with me when I travel
Christ be in the heart of everyone who thinks of me
Christ be in the mouth of everyone who speaks of me
Christ be in every eye that sees me
Christ be in every ear that hears me
So that I may see Christ in others
And I may be Christ to others[10]

8 Charles de Foucauld.

9 St. Faustina Kowalska, *Diary* 2.76 (615).

10 St. Patrick (adapted and paraphrased, and the last two lines by James L. Papandrea).

Sample Breathing Prayers

(For more breathing prayers based on the Psalms, see *Praying the Psalms*)

For Thanksgiving

Breathe in: *You are my Creator*
Breathe out: *You are my hope*[11]

Breathe in: *Father, Son*
Breathe out: *Holy Spirit*

Breathe in: *My Lord*
Breathe out: *And my God*[12]

Breathe in: *My Lord, and my God*
Breathe out: *You know that I love you*[13]

Breathe in: *Jesus*
Breathe out: *How great is Your mercy*[14]

Breathe in: *Jesus, I thank You*
Breathe out: *Jesus, I trust in You*[15]

Breathe in: *My God*
Breathe out: *And my all*

Breathe in: *Lord, have mercy*
Breathe out: *Grant us peace*

For Forgiveness of Enemies

Breathe in: *Father, forgive them*
Breathe out: *They don't know what they're doing*[16]

[11] Ps. 38/39.
[12] St. Thomas, John 20:28.
[13] St. Thomas, John 20:28; St. Peter, John 21:15.
[14] St. Faustina.
[15] Divine Mercy.
[16] Luke 23:34.

Breathe in: *Lord, do not hold this sin against them*
Breathe out: *May it not be held against them*[17]

For Personal Concerns and Intercessions

Breathe in: *Father I trust in you*
Breathe out: *My times are in your hand*[18]

Breathe in: *Purify my heart*
Breathe out: *Renew my spirit*[19]

Breathe in: *My Lord, my strong deliverer*
Breathe out: *Shield my head in the day of battle*[20]

Breathe in: *Lord Jesus Christ, Son of God*
Breathe out: *Call down Your mercy on me and her/him*[21]

Breathe in: *Lord I believe*
Breathe out: *Help my unbelief*[22]

Breathe in: *Your grace is sufficient for me*
Breathe out: *Your power is perfected in my weakness*[23]

Breathe in: *I am weak*
Breathe out: *But Your grace is sufficient for me*

Breathe in: *Shepherd of my soul*
Breathe out: *Guard my soul*[24]

[17] Acts 7:59–60; 2 Tim. 4:16.
[18] Ps. 31.
[19] Ps. 51.
[20] Ps. 140.
[21] For spouse; Tob. 8:7.
[22] Mark 9:24.
[23] 2 Cor. 12:9–10.
[24] 1 Pet. 2.

Breathe in: *O God, come to my assistance*
Breathe out: *Lord, make haste to help me*[25]

Breathe in: *Have mercy on me, O God*
Breathe out: *Because my soul trusts in You*[26]

Breathe in: *Lord, You can do all things*
Breathe out: *Have mercy on me*[27]

Breathe in: *Lord, I have only You*
Breathe out: *But You are enough for me*[28]

Breathe in: *Jesus, I trust in You*
Breathe out: *I trust in the ocean of Your mercy*[29]

Breathe in: *Jesus, I trust in You*
Breathe out: *Keep my steps steady*[30]

Breathe in: *King of Mercy*
Breathe out: *Guide my soul*[31]

Breathe in: *Jesus in my heart*
Breathe out: *I believe in Your faithful love for me*[32]

Breathe in: *O Mary, conceived without sin*
Breathe out: *Pray for us, who have recourse to you*[33]

Breathe in: *Have mercy on me*
Breathe out: *For I am weak*

[25] John Cassian.

[26] St. Bonaventure, Ps. 57.

[27] De Caussade 3.1. Breathing prayers with de Caussade references are taken from his *Letters on the Practice of Abandonment.*

[28] De Caussade 5.11.

[29] St. Faustina.

[30] St. Faustina.

[31] St. Faustina.

[32] St. Mother Teresa.

[33] Miraculous Medal prayer.

Breathe in: *I am not worthy*
Breathe out: *Lord, have mercy*

Breathe in: *You are my God*
Breathe out: *I am Your servant*

Breathe in: *Jesus, I trust in You*
Breathe out: *Lord, grant Your peace*

Breathe in: *Jesus, I trust in You*
Breathe out: *Lord, have mercy*

Breathe in: *Guard me (and my household)*
Breathe out: *Guide me (and my household)*

For Submission to the Divine Will

Breathe in: *Let it be done to me*
Breathe out: *According to your word*[34]

Breathe in: *My God, You are my all*
Breathe out: *I desire nothing but what You give me*[35]

Breathe in: *My God, I want whatever You want*
Breathe out: *And for as long as it pleases You*[36]

Breathe in: *My God, I accept all without reservation*
Breathe out: *I submit to all for as long as You wish*[37]

Breathe in: *My God, I abandon myself to You*
Breathe out: *Grant that I may desire only You*[38]

[34] Mary's fiat.
[35] De Caussade 5.11.
[36] De Caussade 4.6.
[37] De Caussade 4.1.
[38] De Caussade 3.10.

Breathe in: *Blessed be God in all things and for all things*
Breathe out: *Lord, may Your holy will be done*[39]

Breathe in: *Lord, I want what You want*
Breathe out: *I resign myself entirely to Your will*[40]

Breathe in: *Jesus, arrange things in such a way*
Breathe out: *That Your will may be done*[41]

Breathe in: *Jesus, drive away from me*
Breathe out: *All thoughts not in accord with Your will*[42]

Breathe in: *I accept whatever You give me*
Breathe out: *I surrender whatever You take away*[43]

Breathe in: *Lord, have mercy on me*
Breathe out: *Help me do Your will in all things*

Breathe in: *Jesus I trust in You*
Breathe out: *I surrender [name, concern, or struggle] to Your will*

Breathe in: *May your will be done*
Breathe out: *Whatever that is*[44]

39 De Caussade 2.35.

40 De Caussade 2.13.

41 St. Faustina.

42 St. Faustina.

43 St. Mother Teresa.

44 1 Macc. 3:60.

Appendix C

Did the Early Church Have Charismatics?

The early Church did have a subgroup of people who could be called charismatics. But two things must be clear from the beginning. First, it is not the case that the *whole* early Church was what we would call charismatic. Like today, the charismatics in the early Church were a very small group within the mainstream Church.

Second, there is no evidence that anyone in the early Church ever practiced "speaking in tongues" as it is practiced today by Pentecostals and other charismatics. No one ever claimed to be able to pray in an angelic, nonhuman, or unknown language. New Testament references to speaking in tongues were all understood to mean the gift of speaking in a real human language that the person speaking had never learned; so it is a miraculous gift of the Spirit, but for the specific purpose of sharing the gospel with those who speak a different language.[1] The Church fathers all understood the "various kinds of tongues" in 1 Corinthians 12:10 to be actual human languages, as St. Paul himself says in 1 Corinthians 14:21–22:

> It is written in the law,
>
> "By people speaking strange tongues
> and by the lips of foreigners
> I will speak to this people,
> and even so, they will not listen to me,

[1] See, for example, Clement of Alexandria, *Miscellanies* 1.16; Augustine of Hippo, *Confessions* 13.21.

> says the Lord." Thus, tongues are a sign not for those who believe but for unbelievers.[2]

Some of the Church fathers said that God might give the gift of tongues just to amaze unbelievers even if they didn't understand, or for Christians to speak so that enemies of the Church could not understand, but they still assumed this meant actual languages, and there are hints that any real nonhuman utterance would be a sign of demonic possession.

Even the concept of "angelic tongues" (1 Cor. 13:1) was interpreted as human languages, based on Deuteronomy 32:8.[3] However, most of the Church fathers seem to have believed that whatever "angelic languages" are, they are not *spoken* languages but have something to do with mental prayer, such as the hermits practiced, speaking to God in the silence of their hearts when they are alone.[4]

For the Church fathers, whatever St. Paul is referring to with the word *tongues* in 1 Corinthians is the same miracle as that which took place in Acts 2:3–11. And notice that the gift of the Holy Spirit, which gave the apostles this ability, is described as *tongues* of fire — the same Greek word used for the gift of *tongues*. Therefore, we cannot project the modern Pentecostal or charismatic practice of "glossolalia" back into the early Church. It simply did not exist.

The real identifier for the charismatics in the early Church had nothing to do with speaking in tongues but, rather, with prophecy.[5] They believed

[2] The Old Testament text that St. Paul is quoting is from Isaiah 28:11–12. On the assumption that "tongues" refers to real human languages, see Augustine of Hippo, *Confessions* 13.21.

[3] This comes from Severian of Gabala, *Pauline Commentary from the Greek Church*. The assumption is that each nation or language group has its own guardian angel, so the different human cultural languages can be described as "the languages of the angels." The point is that the passage was being interpreted in a way that did not leave room for a nonhuman language.

[4] See, for example, Theodoret of Cyrus, *Commentary on the First Epistle to the Corinthians* 251. This would also be the assumption in St. Athanasius's *Life of Antony*.

[5] Some of the Church fathers seem to have simply conflated the idea of "speaking in tongues" with prophecy, so that speaking in a tongue meant speaking

that they (or at least their leaders) had the gift of speaking with the voice of the Holy Spirit and that their preaching might include new revelation from God. But for the rest of the Church, this presented a problem.

So who were the charismatics of the early Church? The only group we can identify as such is a group known as the Montanists. They called themselves *the New Prophecy*, but everyone else just called them Montanists, after the founder of the movement, a preacher named Montanus, who came from Phrygia in the East. Montanus and his two daughters traveled around the empire preaching, claiming to be prophets, and claiming to speak with the voice of the Holy Spirit. They gained a significant number of followers, and the movement spread.

It used to be that Church history texts treated Montanism as a schismatic faction on the fringes of the Church, but more recent scholarship treats it as something like an attempt at a charismatic renewal movement within the Church.[6] In any case, later Montanists eventually claimed that Montanus *was* the Holy Spirit, so the problem becomes obvious. If people claim to be able to speak for God, and yet they are not under the authority of the bishops, who are in the line of apostolic succession from the apostles, then they are accountable to no one, and there are no checks and balances to prevent them from slipping into heresy and preaching things that will lead the faithful astray.

And this is exactly what happened in some parts of the empire. Some Montanists (though not all) adopted a heresy called *modalism*, which blurs the distinction between the Persons of the Trinity to the point where they say that it's really all Jesus, or it's really all the Holy Spirit. The names for the Persons of the Trinity (so modalists believe) are only labels that describe what God is doing or when He is doing it. So a modalist would say: call God "the Father" when He is creating; call God "the Son" in His life and

---

prophetically, and interpreting the tongue meant interpreting the meaning of the prophecy. See, for example, Ambrose of Milan, *On the Holy Spirit* 2.13 (143), and Basil of Caesarea, *Letter 204: To the Neocaesareans* 5.

[6] For a more detailed treatment of Montanism in the context of the early Church, see Papandrea, *Reading the Church Fathers: A History of the Early Church and the Development of Doctrine* (Manchester, NH: Sophia Institute Press, 2022), 146–152. In the textbook, the gift of prophecy is referred to as "ecstatic speech."

ministry on earth; and call God "the Spirit" in the age of the Church.[7] But this effectively negates the Triune nature of God, reducing the three Persons to one. And by their conflating the Persons of the Trinity, what is lost is the real humanity of Jesus; if the Father *is* the Son and the Son *is* the Holy Spirit, then the Incarnation is diminished to become nothing more than an illusion, and Christ is therefore not really one of us. As St. Augustine said, "A mediator between God and [humanity] must have something in common with God and something in common with [humanity]."[8]

This has real implications for our salvation. If Jesus Christ is not really one of us, then the atonement can no longer be an atonement of *one of us who died for the rest of us*.[9] So in modalism, the salvation of humanity is reduced to a kind of gnostic enlightenment or mystical wisdom, which quickly becomes an elitist view of salvation, assuming that only the "insider," the charismatic, is a true Christian. And it is no coincidence that the same heresy into which some of the early Christian charismatics fell is the temptation of modern charismatics to this day, evidenced by the modalism inherent in such groups as Oneness Pentecostals.[10]

It seems that, to some extent, the Montanists did operate outside the hierarchy of the Church, and when it came to choosing their leaders, they seem to have made the perception of charismatic gifts in a person more important than the approval of the bishops or perhaps even the Sacrament of Ordination. This, along with the potential for a heretical preacher to create division in the Church, made the Montanists seem to be a real threat to the unity of the Church. In response to this, the bishops of the early Church brought the gift of prophecy under the umbrella of preaching, and so it came to be a prerogative of the clergy, under the authority of the hierarchy. This is why, although St. Paul sometimes speaks of prophecy as though it is one

[7] The practice, popular in some Protestant denominations, of calling the Trinity "Creator, Redeemer, Sustainer" is a form of the heresy of modalism. See James L. Papandrea, *Trinity 101* (Liguori, MO: Liguori, 2012).

[8] Augustine of Hippo, *Confessions* 10.42.

[9] For more on the atonement in the early and medieval Church, see Papandrea, *Reading the Church Fathers*, chap. 14.

[10] For a more detailed treatment of modalism in the early Church, see Papandrea, *Reading the Church Fathers*, 272–275, 282.

of the "forms of service" in the Body of Christ, there was no office or rank of "prophet" in the early Church (2 Cor. 12:4–11).

But what about the early Christian charismatics who didn't drift into heresy? We know something about them. These were the North African Montanists, and their most famous member was our old friend Tertullian, who is one of our important sources for understanding early Christian prayer. It is because of Tertullian that we know that these Montanists were not heretics, since Tertullian was a great Latin theologian and wrote against modalism. But when it comes to Tertullian's writings on prayer, it must be admitted that sometimes it's tricky to know whether he is talking about Christian prayer in general or the practices of the Montanists specifically. So far, everything I've included in this book from Tertullian seems to apply to the mainstream Church in general. But we can also see that there were some practices unique to the Montanists.[11]

For example, the Montanists were criticized by the other Christians for keeping their fasts longer. As I noted above, the early Christians fasted on Wednesdays and Fridays, and for most, the fasting day ended at the ninth hour (by 3:00 p.m.). But the Montanists fasted until sunset.[12] In fact, they were criticized for this — perhaps they were making everyone else look bad by keeping a stricter fast.

It also appears that the Montanists had a practice of holding non-Eucharist evening prayer meetings during the week, though this does not mean that the Montanists were the only Christians who held these.[13] We assume that many Christians continued the evening agape meal as a kind of potluck with evening prayer, even after the Eucharist was removed from the evening meal and made a morning liturgy.[14] However, in the Montanists'

[11] We can assume that the practices in question, outlined here, were unique to the Montanists because none of the other Church fathers mentions them.

[12] Tertullian, *On Fasting* 10; *On Prayer* 23, 25.

[13] Tertullian, *Apology* 39. As far as we know, evening prayer meetings (both Montanist and mainstream) began with a lamplighting ritual, to which the Montanists added a handwashing ritual, possibly patterned after Jewish handwashing.

[14] *Apostolic Tradition* 25. The *Apostolic Tradition* assumes that the bishop and deacon are in attendance at the evening prayer meetings, though this may not have been the case for the Montanists. It may also not have always

meetings, it appears that the Montanists encouraged more extemporaneous, improvisational prayer (and by the laity) than would be expected in most of the mainstream Church.[15] We are also told that every meeting had time for people to volunteer (apparently spontaneously) to share a song that they had composed. However, it is not clear whether this means that they had written the song at home and brought it to sing for the group, or whether a person was making up a song on the spot, though it may be the latter, since Tertullian seems to be arguing that the fact that they can make up a song is proof that they are not drunk![16] It may be that they considered spontaneous songwriting to be a charismatic gift (though we can see that this would quickly become just as much of a problem as spontaneous preaching, if the theology communicated in the lyrics was not orthodox). We also don't know whether this impromptu singing means that the person who brought the song was teaching it to the group for them to sing along.

These Montanist evening meetings were followed by some kind of prayer or liturgy throughout the night, which we know because Tertullian advises people not to eat too much at the agape meal, so that they are not too sleepy to worship during the night. It may be that the Montanists were ahead of the curve in the development of the canonical hours and that their laypeople were encouraged to pray the hours together as a group. Finally, it is also clear that, for the Montanists, the evening prayer meetings served to provide fellowship in a way that Mass did not. Tertullian tells the people that they may talk freely (we assume this was not the case at Mass), though they should monitor what they say, since, as he reminds them, God is always listening.

To summarize, the early Church did have its charismatics, though they were few, and were often suspected of heresy. They did not "speak in tongues," but they did believe in the ongoing possibility of new revelation through prophetic preaching (though to be fair, Tertullian clarified that

---

been the case for mainstream Christians who were having their evening prayer meetings in the cemeteries or at the catacombs. In any case, what is described in the *Apostolic Tradition* may be more the expressed ideal than the reality as it was practiced.

[15] Tertullian, *Apology* 39.

[16] Tertullian, *Apology* 39.

they did not believe prophecy would ever contradict Scripture, only that it would help interpret Scripture).

When it comes to prayer, the charismatics apparently encouraged more improvisational prayer (and singing) than the mainstream and possibly even let lay people lead group prayer extemporaneously. Also, the Montanists fasted more rigorously than their mainstream counterparts and may have been more rigorous in observing the developing prayer hours. They may have even anticipated the monks' later practice of praying the Liturgy of the Hours in groups.

In the end, though, the problems with operating outside the hierarchy and the possibility of heresy in the group meant that the movement would not survive, as a movement, and that the early Christian charismatics would be folded into the mainstream to the point where we don't know any more about them. In fact, it must be pointed out that we do not know to what extent Montanists (in their various places across the empire) ever worshipped in separate Montanist-only assemblies, or whether they were always subgroups within parishes made up of both Montanists and mainstream Catholics.

Appendix D

Timeline of Church Fathers, Mothers, and Others Cited

First Century

The *Didache*, author(s) unknown
Clement, bishop of Rome, pope from AD 88 to 97

Second Century

Ignatius, bishop of Antioch, martyred in about AD 110
Polycarp, bishop of Smyrna, martyred in about AD 156
Justin Martyr, apologist in Rome, martyred in about AD 165
Irenaeus, bishop of Lyons, writing at the end of the second century, died in AD 202
Clement of Alexandria, catechist writing at the end of the second century, died in AD 215

Third Century

Tertullian, writing in North Africa at the turn of the third century, died in the AD 220s
Perpetua, martyred in Carthage in AD 203
Cyprian, bishop of Carthage from AD 249 until martyred in AD 258

Fourth Century

Helena, mother of the emperor Constantine, died in AD 330
Jerome, writing in Bethlehem, died in AD 347

Macrina the Younger, sister of Basil and Gregory, died in AD 380
Basil, bishop of Caesarea in Cappadocia, died in AD 379
Gregory, bishop of Nyssa, died in AD 395
Gregory, bishop of Nazianzus and Constantinople, died in AD 390
Cyril, bishop of Jerusalem from AD 350 to 386
Egeria, pilgrim to the Holy Land from AD 381 to 384
Monica, mother of St. Augustine, died in AD 387
Ambrose, bishop of Milan from AD 374 to 397
John Chrysostom, priest in Antioch and bishop of Constantinople, died in AD 407

Fifth Century

Augustine, bishop of Hippo, died in 430 AD
John Cassian, monastic who influenced St. Benedict, died in AD 435

Sixth Century

Benedict of Nursia, founder of the Benedictine Order, died in AD 547

Middle Ages

Anselm, bishop of Canterbury, died in 1109
Thomas Aquinas, Dominican scholar, died in 1274
Bonaventure, Franciscan scholar, died in 1274

Renaissance and Modern Era

Luis de Molina, Jesuit priest and philosopher, died 1562
Francis de Sales, bishop of Geneva, died in 1622
Jean-Pierre de Caussade, eighteenth-century spiritual director, died in 1751
Maria Faustina Kowalska, visionary, died in 1938

About the Author

Dr. James L. Papandrea is an award-winning author and professor of Church history and historical theology. His many books have been translated into multiple languages, and he has a significant presence on YouTube, including his video series, *The Original Church* (www.youtube.com/@TheOriginalChurch). He is currently the host of the *Way of the Fathers* podcast.

A Catholic layperson and catechist, Jim has an M.Div. from Fuller Theological Seminary and a Ph.D. from Northwestern University in the history and theology of the early Christian Church, with secondary concentrations in New Testament interpretation and the history of the Roman Empire. He has also studied Roman history at the American Academy in Rome, Italy. He is currently on the faculty at Garrett-Evangelical Theological Seminary and is recognized for his ecumenical work on behalf of the whole Body of Christ. He is a senior fellow of the St. Paul Center for Biblical Theology and was recently named a "Springtime Ambassador" by the Springtime of Faith Foundation, which is an organization facilitating ecumenical dialogue and Christian cooperation.

Jim is a member of multiple professional organizations, including the Academy of Catholic Theology, the North American Patristics Society, and the Society of Biblical Literature. More information can be found via Jim's website, www.JimPapandrea.com, and his Amazon author page, www.DoctorJimsBooks.com.

Other Books by James L. Papandrea

The Companion Volume

As a companion volume to this book, especially for the practice of *Lectio Divina*, see:

Praying the Psalms: The Divine Gateway to Lectio Divina *and Contemplative Prayer*

More Books on Related Topics from Sophia Institute Press

Reading the Church Fathers: A History of the Early Church and the Development of Doctrine

Reading Scripture Like the Early Church: Seven Insights from the Church Fathers to Help You Understand the Bible

What Really Happens After We Die?: There WILL Be Hugs in Heaven

From Star Wars to Superman: Christ Figures in Science Fiction and Superhero Films

How Christianity Saved Civilization … And Must Do So Again (with Mike Aquilina)

Other Books on Related Topics

Handed Down: The Catholic Faith of the Early Christians

The Early Church (33–131): St. Peter, the Apostles, and Martyrs

The Earliest Christologies: Five Images of Christ in the Post-Apostolic Age

Trinity 101: Father, Son, Holy Spirit

Praying a Christ-Centered Rosary: Meditations on the Mysteries

Novatian of Rome and the Culmination of Pre-Nicene Orthodoxy

Historical Fiction

A Week in the Life of Rome

The Squire's Journey

Sophia Institute

Sophia Institute is a nonprofit institution that seeks to nurture the spiritual, moral, and cultural life of souls and to spread the Gospel of Christ in conformity with the authentic teachings of the Roman Catholic Church.

Sophia Institute Press fulfills this mission by offering translations, reprints, and new publications that afford readers a rich source of the enduring wisdom of mankind.

Sophia Institute also operates the popular online resource CatholicExchange.com. *Catholic Exchange* provides world news from a Catholic perspective as well as daily devotionals and articles that will help readers to grow in holiness and live a life consistent with the teachings of the Church.

In 2013, Sophia Institute launched Sophia Institute for Teachers to renew and rebuild Catholic culture through service to Catholic education. With the goal of nurturing the spiritual, moral, and cultural life of souls, and an abiding respect for the role and work of teachers, we strive to provide materials and programs that are at once enlightening to the mind and ennobling to the heart; faithful and complete, as well as useful and practical.

Sophia Institute gratefully recognizes the Solidarity Association for preserving and encouraging the growth of our apostolate over the course of many years. Without their generous and timely support, this book would not be in your hands.

www.SophiaInstitute.com
www.CatholicExchange.com
www.SophiaInstituteforTeachers.org

Sophia Institute Press® is a registered trademark of Sophia Institute.
Sophia Institute is a tax-exempt institution as defined by the Internal Revenue Code, Section 501(c)(3). Tax ID 22-2548708.